PRACTICAL EQUALITY

PRACTICAL
EQUALITY

Forging Justice in a Divided Nation

ROBERT L. TSAI

W. W. Norton & Company
Independent Publishers Since 1923
New York • London

For information about permission to reproduce selections from this book, write to
Permissions, W. W. Norton & Company, Inc., 500 Fifth Avenue, New York, NY 10110

For information about special discounts for bulk purchases, please contact
W. W. Norton Special Sales at specialsales@wwnorton.com or 800-233-4830

Manufacturing by Worzalla
Book design by Patrice Sheridan
Production manager: Julia Druskin

Library of Congress Cataloging-in-Publication Data

Names: Tsai, Robert L., 1971– author.
Title: Practical equality : forging justice in a divided nation / Robert L. Tsai.
Description: New York : W. W. Norton & Company, 2019. | Includes
bibliographical references and index.
Identifiers: LCCN 2018037970 | ISBN 9780393652024 (hardcover)
Subjects: LCSH: Equality before the law—United States—History. |
Equality—United States—History. | Freedom of speech—United
States—History. | Justice, Administration of—United States—History. |
Equality before the law—United States.
Classification: LCC KF4764 .T73 2019 | DDC 342.7308/5—dc23
LC record available at https://lccn.loc.gov/2018037970

W. W. Norton & Company, Inc., 500 Fifth Avenue, New York, N.Y. 10110
www.wwnorton.com

W. W. Norton & Company Ltd., 15 Carlisle Street, London W1D 3BS

1 2 3 4 5 6 7 8 9 0

For the misfits and the losers

We have called by different names
brethren of the same principle.

—THOMAS JEFFERSON, 1801

CONTENTS

PRACTICAL EQUALITY

INTRODUCTION

On Friday afternoon, January 27, 2017, the news broke that President Donald Trump had signed an executive order that prohibited travelers from seven Muslim countries from entering the United States and suspended the refugee admission program for 120 days. President Trump found the admission of Syrian refugees "detrimental to the interests of the United States" and paused that program until further notice. Whether or not they agreed with the policy, most people took these actions for the fulfillment of his campaign pledge: "a total and complete shutdown of Muslims entering the United States."

Chaos reigned, as the changes were implemented in a hurry over the weekend. Travelers had no clue that they were now barred from the country until they landed at an American airport. A toddler who suffered severe burns in a refugee camp was prevented from making the trip to a U.S. hospital for surgery. A sixty-nine-year-old Iraqi man on his way to visit his son in Los Angeles had his passport seized in Qatar, so he missed a connecting flight. The president's order also prevented an Iranian baby with a heart defect from uniting with family in Portland, Oregon, and receiving urgent care.[1]

White House staff bickered publicly with Homeland Security over whether the ban included people who already had green cards. Customs and Border Patrol agents hid from inquiring reporters and distraught family members, uncertain what to say or do.

Eager to help, lawyers and activists descended on airport terminals all over the United States, while protests against these measures broke out in major cities: San Francisco, Los Angeles, Washington, D.C., New York, Chicago. Governors and mayors soon got into the act, vowing to help overturn the administration's "misguided" and "un-American" policy. In many ways, the spontaneous actions by ordinary citizens and professionals represented the best of our constitutional tradition, recalling other popular efforts to defend the principle of equality on behalf of an embattled minority. A few states led the way in the courts, with the states of Washington, Hawaii, Minnesota, and New York filing lawsuits against the administration.

Now, imagine, for a moment, you are an advocate involved in one of these disputes. In preparing your presentation, you have to anticipate your audience. You might dream of standing before a judge who is already sympathetic to your cause, but the reality is that most jurists are not crusaders but rather technicians. And you have to keep in mind not merely one person in power, but all of the others who might later weigh in on the matter, because democratic justice is ultimately a collaborative enterprise over time. A trial judge's decision can be reviewed by an appeals court. Every appeals court will have at least three decision makers with varying perspectives, and victory in the U.S. Supreme Court requires getting to five votes. Whatever the courts ultimately decide, the president, his advisors, and even Congress will always have another crack at the issue.[2]

This point can be generalized: To some degree, politics is always involved with questions of constitutional law. Especially in controversies that implicate national security and political identity, as this one does, the audience also consists of regular citizens not directly involved in protests or lawsuits. After all, judges typically only trim the edges of a national policy rather than lash themselves to a program so as to bring it to a screeching halt. It's important to reach activists and voters who might feel a kinship toward strangers affected by a policy, public officials who can influence the making of policy, and employees of bureaucracies charged with implementing it.

Concerned citizens face merely a slightly different version of the same situation faced by lawyers. The question for everyone is: What is to be done to confront injustice when the timing doesn't seem right or the odds appear stacked against you?

The most promising argument is that the government has denied the travelers equal treatment under the law, a principle guaranteed by the Constitution's Religion Clauses and the Fourteenth Amendment's Equal Protection Clause. As a candidate, Trump had repeatedly vowed to stop Muslim migration to the United States. He and his surrogates drew on the worst possible stereotypes of Muslims, broadly blaming them for terrorism, murder, and other unsavory acts. Stoking fear and suspicion of Muslims, they had advocated sweeping measures that would adversely affect this group of worshippers regardless of individual culpability. Characterizing plentiful evidence of ethnonationalism as a form of religious bigotry, a group of law professors argued in a friend-of-the-court brief that the president's order was infected with "anti-Islamic prejudice," and that such an illiberal sentiment "ultimately corrupts and distorts any motive it touches."[3]

As a partisan, it's easy to become enamored with one's own argument and overly secure in its correctness. But that's a mistake. For the federal government responded that it had legitimate national security reasons for issuing a policy that treated visitors from these countries differently from other travelers: the seven countries were experiencing some level of unrest and their security measures couldn't be trusted.

By the way, government lawyers pointed out, the executive order didn't exclude all Muslims in the world so it wasn't a total shutdown. Trump's casual and undisciplined statements aside, the policy did not amount to an act of religious animus.

Beyond these formal objections, what if more subtle considerations played a role in how judges saw the case? What if someone hesitated to declare the president a religious bigot so early in his tenure because that might cast moral aspersions on Americans who voted for him, many of whom backed his candidacy precisely because they shared his view of Islam as a threat to American democracy? Someone might also worry that an equality violation could hamstring a president's later policy decisions in the fight against terrorism. Others might fret that deciding the dispute on equality grounds would alter the social good at stake—admission into the United States—by making it available to foreigners in novel and troubling ways.

Faced with similarly controversial matters in the past, decision makers have sometimes recoiled from vindicating the ideal of equality. Instead, under stress, they have resorted to one of two options. One answer is to delay a final decision for as long as possible by manipulating technical legal rules, such as those governing access to the courts. The idea behind delay, or what we might call the strategy of *deferral*, is to give time for politics or cultural attitudes to catch up, so judges follow popular sentiment rather than try to lead it. That way, legal rulings seem more democratic and are less likely to be openly defied.

This is precisely what the Supreme Court did in ducking the issue of interracial marriage in the decades before the civil rights movement roused ordinary Americans to make racial equality a national priority. In the 1950s and early '60s, the Justices and their law clerks felt that voters were not ready to tackle such an explosive racial matter while dealing with segregated schools. So judicial officers manipulated legal rules to table the interracial marriage question indefinitely.

With the travel ban, the Justices could buy time by holding that some of the litigants, such as states, lacked proper standing to sue. That would deprive federal judges of the power to decide cases until more suitable plaintiffs could be found. Or they could make a drawn-out schedule for the filing of legal papers, hold a case over to the next term for reargument, or delay the release of a decision. Because the original executive order, and even the president's subsequent orders, contained specific time frames, some of the issues would eventually become moot—or no longer worth deciding—if judges sat on their hands long enough.

Proponents of deferral believe that once courts are taken out of the political firestorm, a highly charged issue might sort itself out in any number of ways. The administration could change its mind. Congress might be forced to stake out a position, by either repudiating the president's reading of immigration law or confirming the decision he made. Such a turn of events might then render judicial involvement unnecessary.

But the costs of deferral shouldn't be underestimated. Congress might do nothing. Delay breeds uncertainty and stress for travelers whose lives must be placed on hold and for government officials who must enforce the president's order. Haphazard decisions on visas and admissions to the country aren't good for anyone. In the meantime, families would be kept apart, and jobs, education, and other productive opportunities might be lost. One of the guiding convictions behind deferral is that it's better for political consensus to emerge before courts make decisive rulings, but what if no real consensus would ever arise for certain types of people seeking to vindicate certain kinds of rights? Refugees, by definition, are people without a home, displaced by war, natural disasters, or other forms of misery. If a majority of Americans never arose in support of refugees, would that mean it is right to table their claims indefinitely? Surely at some point, filibustering becomes its own kind of inequity.

Another option might be *appeasement*, or openly adopting the objections of your opponents as your own. The animating idea is that some recognition, however incremental, is better than none at all. In the past, advocates have sometimes settled for a more cramped version of equality than has been ideal. Gay rights activists had to decide whether to support civil unions or repudiate them as "separate but equal" to traditional marriage. Those who battled racial segregation decades earlier had to choose between equalization of resources and social integration.

As for President Trump's travel ban, one could cut refugees loose, on the view that their ties to the United States are more attenuated than those of people already on the path toward citizenship, and their claims are weaker under existing law. Another possibility might be to allow an emergency exception to equality, by saying that when national security is at stake, we should allow the state to treat worshippers of some religions differently from those of other religions.

But appeasing opponents of equality, too, has its drawbacks. We might be consigning vulnerable populations to legal purgatory or creating special exceptions at the very moment that someone desperately needs a robust theory of equality. By acceding to feeble slices of egalitarianism, we might then be colluding with oppressors to perpetuate injustice rather than committing to dismantle pervasive inequality. Once we draw legal lines, they can come to acquire a power of their own—to the point that boundaries are all we can see instead of the suffering they authorize.

■   ■   ■

THE CONCERNS I HAVE just described illustrate the perennial tussle between principle and realism, with these two possibilities—deferral or appeasement—seen as the best options if a constitutional ideal cannot be vindicated in a full-throated fashion. But neither option serves democratic justice or advances the principle of egalitarianism. Whereas the problem with deferral is that justice delayed may be justice denied, the flaw with appeasement is that justice in half measures could leave future generations worse off. Instead, we must strive to find a solution that neither abandons the project of equality when things get complicated nor drastically downscales what citizens deserve.

Practical Equality presents a way out of this dilemma. Where agreement cannot be reached on equality grounds, we must pursue alternatives that can plausibly serve the goals of egalitarianism. This involves taking a further step: being open to second-best solutions when we falter in doing the hard work of equality. It also means developing workable alternatives not merely because it's clever strategy, but because it's a matter of constitutional duty. This is a responsibility that falls on all of us: citizens, activists, elected officials, and judges.[4]

I call this approach *practical egalitarianism* because it entails creating a long-term backup plan to deal with recurring situations where we struggle to enforce equality's demands. Practical egalitarians take seriously the basic idea of civic equality for all. But they feel keenly the hardships when we dawdle in dealing with claims of injustice or openly settle for less than what people deserve. It's critical to win legal battles, but sometimes that means holding territory that has already been secured. Progress is wonderful, but to preserve gains it can be just as crucial to win skirmishes without draining resources or killing the spirit of supporters.

Whenever we struggle to agree about equality, we have an obligation to seek out alternative solutions. We do that by substituting the idea of equality with the next best thing. This way, we not only can break an ideological logjam and render justice in particular disputes, we also build a political culture that values respect, dignity, and the rule of law.

Next-best concepts that can do some of the work of equality include fair play, rationality, anti-cruelty, and free speech. These aren't the only useful tools for such purposes but they are excellent exemplars. Each of these legal ideas has, at one time or another, been valuable in promoting equality when people run into trouble reaching consensus. The norms are found in abundance in leading accounts of liberalism and codified throughout the U.S. Constitution, such as the Religion and Speech Clauses, the Fourth Amendment's search-and-seizure requirement, the twice-mentioned notion of Due Process, the Eighth Amendment's ban on cruel and unusual punishment, and the various guarantees of procedural fairness for criminal defendants. Our historical experiences confirm that these ideas are closely related to the principle of equality, and that we can choose to harness these connections for the ends of justice or to further oppression.

Each of these solutions can, in its own way, ameliorate some of the harms associated with inequity. As alternative reasons, they can also serve as common ground because they don't require a finding of malice, they are often less invasive in their reach, and they don't raise the same concerns about political backlash.

■   ■   ▦

EVERYONE ADORES EQUALITY IN the abstract, but we regularly have trouble agreeing to do something about inequality in practice. These difficulties are certain to continue. Let's start with a definition of equality that nearly all can embrace: individuals in similar circumstances ought to be treated the same. But consensus can begin to disintegrate once we move beyond the ideal citizen to other kinds of people who might be deserving of equal treatment: migrants, belligerents, criminals, social deviants, the disabled.

How we talk about equality can make things worse. The fact is that our lives are polarized by experience, politics, and values. Yet the very structure of equality discourse can exacerbate ideological differences because it is inherently judgmental and corrective. The whole point of equality law is to identify a major breach in society's organizing rules, to punish wrongdoers, and to restore a victim to her rightful place in civic society. To find an equality violation, a person must typically determine that someone else has acted out of malice. But an authority figure might resist reaching this conclusion because saying that someone has engaged in discrimination shames the wrongdoer publicly as a bigot or oppressor. It could also trigger anger and recrimination.

Because the social consequences that flow from a finding of discrimination are unpleasant, a person might be tempted to deny the very existence of inequality when he wants to avoid those consequences—even when the evidence of bias is plentiful. In fact, decision makers have sometimes engaged in outrageous contortions to avoid having to say that a fellow public official acted out of animosity. In the infamous *Plessy v. Ferguson*, Justice Henry Brown insisted that a law requiring black and white passengers on a train to sit in different cars treated everyone equally, and that any sense of racial hostility was "solely because the colored race chooses to put that construction upon it." In other words, a feeling of inequality should be dismissed as purely a figment of a complaining black person's imagination.

At other times, fear of too much equality can grip the imagination of people in charge. They might worry, as with claims that involve marriage or family or the military, that rendering justice will disfigure a cherished institution or way of life beyond recognition. This concern, too, is about the potential effects of equality—namely, what happens to a social good once the rules governing access to that good change.

Yet a third failure arises from uncertainty in the law. To some extent, the law is always in a state of becoming. It is incomplete. There might not be an exact precedent with identical facts or resolved by a person of the highest rank. Our legal texts promise equality but leave many things unsaid. When civic equality is at stake, the lack of clear guidance can cause people to reach for tried-and-true answers, even when those solutions reproduce injustice. That's why equality-friendly alternatives need to be already developed, so they can fill the gaps.

All of these regular obstacles to enforcing egalitarianism are utterly human and understandable. We cannot erase these instincts or concerns, any more than we can extirpate the root causes of inequality. What lies within our grasp is to come up with effective, everyday plans to overcome recurring impediments to democratic justice.

Although the ideal of equality can be difficult to enforce at times, we must protect the integrity of the concept. Egalitarianism is a moral principle that demands respect for others and rejects domination by one group over another. The principle works best when it is capable of expressing moral outrage and disrupting older social patterns that reinforce injustice. What makes equality so potent is also what makes it so hard to apply, but the solution is not to water down the idea. The answer is to come up with a backup plan.

None of the second-best solutions I discuss are ostensibly about equality, yet all of them can be used to produce effects that are a net positive, not only rendering justice in individual disputes but also helping to create a culture in which human beings are valued regardless of superficial differences. The idea of fair play, for example, can act as an effective substitute for equality when officials recoil from the prospect of enforcing egalitarianism. Fair play is closely associated with the text and history of the Due Process Clause, and encompasses the concepts of notice and a chance to be heard. When something important is at stake, these values of procedural regularity can help ameliorate problems of differential treatment.

Another basic concept—the rule of reason—can work wonders when people cannot agree about what equality requires. Every law must be justified and have an empirical basis. A law cannot be irrational, arbitrary, or based on unfounded fears of strangers. The Fourth Amendment essentially restates the rule of reason as a principle that governs everyday interactions between citizens and the police during searches or seizures. When implemented the right way, that approach can reduce reliance on outdated stereotypes and unfounded fears of others when the government uses force against human beings.

The prohibition on cruelty can also advance the cause of egalitarianism. It turns out that the most inhumane sanctions are usually inflicted on members of despised groups, such as the homeless, people with disabilities, and individuals convicted of serious crimes. Becoming more cognizant of atypical or harsh policies would help deter this kind of discriminatory treatment.

Finally, the closely related rights of free speech, petition, and assembly can serve as common ground to alleviate unfair burdens. At times, these ideas, which enjoy significant cultural support, can be used to do some of the unglamorous spadework of equality. Because Americans cherish freedom of thought above all other liberties, they are often more willing to deal with systematic inequities that raise First Amendment concerns.

If we use each of these techniques diligently, we can develop a body of justifications and practices that serve as second-best solutions when egalitarianism is unavailable as a consensus rationale. Doing so would best balance principle and realism. Once we get better at pursuing equality by other means, citizens and officials alike will be equipped to push for the ideal, maximize second-best solutions, and avoid worst-case scenarios.

In the spirit of the humanistic origins of American pragmatism, practical egalitarianism preserves equality as an effective civic ideal so we can express moral outrage when we are capable of doing so. This is critical to deterring misconduct by public officials, enabling the work of activists, and ensuring that remedies are available. It also prioritizes the immediate reduction of harms associated with inequality by vindicating rights straight away rather than allowing pernicious disparities to fester. And finding multiple ways to do justice reduces pressure on public officials to make bad law.

This last concern is a point of emphasis because some of the most dangerous things in the law are tragic precedents like *Plessy*, which spurred the creation of Jim Crow policies throughout the country, and *Korematsu v. United States*, which approved the wartime internment of Japanese Americans. Tragic precedents are incredibly hard to erase once created, and they can stoke further injustice and impede progress for generations. Practical egalitarians realize that it's essential to guard against the loss of morale and the formation of immovable obstacles to justice in the first place.

We can pursue equality by other means across a wide array of situations: the treatment of racial and sexual minorities; the plight of migrants; conditions of confinement, punishment, and release; felon disenfranchisement; and even routine encounters with the police. As we consider contemporary issues, we must draw lessons from past struggles so as to outflank enemies of equality and build alliances between devoted supporters and temporary associates.

There is reason to be optimistic because we already intuitively know that seeking justice requires commitment, ingenuity, and fore-sight. Historically, we have used all kinds of tools to advance the cause of equality indirectly when it seems impossible to do so directly. So pursuing equality by other means is not a matter of doing something entirely new. It's simply a matter of doing what we are already doing more systematically.

CHAPTER 1

PRACTICAL EQUALITY

I've been there so I know
They keep on saying "Go slow!"

—NINA SIMONE, *MISSISSIPPI GODDAM*, 1964

EQUALITY IS INHERENTLY, IRREPRESSIBLY righteous. At its best, it is unapologetically so. President John F. Kennedy said it best. "We are confronted primarily with a moral issue," he explained to the nation after federal authority was necessary to break Governor George Wallace's resistance to integrating the University of Alabama. "It is as old as the Scriptures and is as clear as the American Constitution." One's yearning to be treated as another's equal is "a matter which concerns this country and what it stands for."[1]

Beyond the irreducibly ethical nature of equality, Kennedy made two further points. First, the concept links free citizens to one another based on the belief that "all men are created equal" and that inequality suffered by some members of society creates a "moral crisis" for all. Second, while "law alone cannot make men see right," legal action nevertheless joins with "conscience" to create a transformative force capable of making "a great change," indeed, a "revolution" that is "peaceful and constructive for all." Because the "cruel disease of discrimination knows no sectional or state boundaries," he diagnosed, "[t]he continuing attack on this problem must be equally broad."

A society that aspires to justice identifies wrongdoers for having acted purposefully—and perhaps maliciously—to deprive someone of her basic rights. Because equality at its core is an ethical concept, those who act to ensure that people are treated the right way are worthy of praise, while those who obstruct the work of equality deserve condemnation. You can't stake out a vision of justice without taking sides.

Now, in a diverse democracy, people will disagree about what equality means. That's to be expected. But it doesn't alter the fact that a dispute over the allocation of precious resources or the role of prejudice in society is a moral disagreement. This is true whether you think that abortion treats the unborn differently by extinguishing potential life or you fervently believe that restrictions on a woman's decisions over childbirth are a form of sex-based discrimination. Either way, your arguments over equality are highly judgmental.

This is because the principle of egalitarianism doesn't seek the most efficient solution (an economic answer) or what would bring the most joy to the greatest number of people (the utilitarian approach). Rather, it calls on everyone to make arguments that presuppose a community based on mutual respect and to explain how a course of action will allow individuals to live a morally rewarding life.

Equality is a perpetual threat to the status quo. Traditions will be challenged, social patterns disrupted, policies reformed. Congressman John Bingham of Ohio, who helped write equality into the Constitution after the Civil War, emphasized that the Reconstruction Amendments "armed" Congress and the people "with power to enforce the Bill of Rights" against state and local authorities. The purpose was "to punish officials of States for violation of the oaths enjoined upon them by their Constitution." Public officials had to answer for any "violation of their oaths and of the rights of their fellow-men." Denying someone the rights of citizenship would now be treated as a crime against the political community itself. Ensuring equality would be "essential" to "unity of the government and unity of the people."[2]

Citizens who fail to act in the face of manifest injustice might be on the wrong side of history. In President Kennedy's words, "Those who do nothing are inviting shame, as well as violence. Those who act boldly are recognizing right, as well as reality." Moral outrage and historical perspective are necessary to convey the seriousness of the violation. They are also crucial to discouraging others from engaging in similar behavior.

Take the celebrated ruling *Brown v. Board of Education*, which struck down racially segregated public schools. "Separate educational facilities are inherently unequal," Chief Justice Earl Warren thundered on behalf of a unanimous Supreme Court. Public education didn't exist at America's founding, but it had steadily grown to become a social good crucial for civic education and upward mobility. Education had become so valuable to each person's ability to lead a morally rewarding life, the Justices explained, "In these days, it is doubtful that any child may reasonably be expected to succeed in life if he is denied the opportunity of an education."[3]

Denying black children the benefits of education was not merely debilitating for the children and their families. Segregation was also abhorrent because it damaged our expectations of how citizens ought to be treated in a modern democracy. Those involved in maintaining racial segregation had participated in "denoting the inferiority of the negro group" and creating a "sense of inferiority" in black children.

Fear of backlash against the controversial ruling prevented jurists from calling out the architects and perpetrators of racial apartheid in even stronger terms, but there should be no doubt that equality was a moral imperative in *Brown*. At times, a society's leaders go further by labeling someone's sentiments malicious through and through, something the Justices didn't quite come out and say in the school cases.

They did just that in *Yick Wo v. Hopkins*, a less well known controversy from the late nineteenth century. There, a Chinese immigrant named Lee Yick was convicted of violating a law that had suddenly changed the rules for running a laundry. Out of nowhere, the City of San Francisco barred all laundries from operating in wooden structures unless the board of supervisors issued a permit, but laundries in buildings made of other materials required no advance permission. Local officials claimed that wooden structures were more susceptible to fire, but it just so happened that the vast majority of Chinese-run laundries were located in wooden buildings. Most Americans living at this time would have found the changes in the law suspicious, given the sharp economic downturn in recent years that led to the scapegoating of migrants from China. Anti-immigrant activists in California blamed the Chinese for taking jobs, causing crime, and bringing disease to America.[4]

Writing for the Court, Justice Stanley Matthews explained that even a neutral law could still deny someone the right to equal treatment if it is administered "with an evil eye and an uneven hand." On paper, everyone had the same chance to seek a permit because the law did not mention race, but, in reality, city officials used the law to systematically shut down laundries operated by the Chinese. Every single Chinese applicant was refused a permit without explanation, while virtually every non-Chinese applicant received a permit. This stark disparity, which city officials could not explain and was too obvious to be the product of serendipity, proved their "hostility to the race and nationality to which the petitioners belong."[5]

Professor Deborah Hellman's definition of discrimination offers a useful description of animus: "To demean is to treat another as not fully human or not of equal moral worth." Similarly, Martin Luther King, Jr., described bias as behavior that "degrades human personality." The key is the social meaning of an act, not merely how the action is intended but also how it is likely to be received.[6]

Degradation of this sort violates our collective sense of who we want to be as a people, because it is deeply unfair to treat someone differently out of hatred or fear. In JFK's words, discrimination is an "arbitrary indignity." Traits like race, religion, or sex are things about us over which we have little control. They have a lot to do with the accident of birth, are shaped by cultural institutions in which we find ourselves, but they aren't reliable indicators of ability or a propensity for criminality. To indulge decisions that depend on these sentiments is to allow one group to dominate another based on social differences. We *should* be outraged when someone is mistreated in this way.[7]

Modern cases have fleshed out the precept that animosity or hatred on the part of the state can violate the principle of equality. In 2015, the U.S. Supreme Court ruled that laws preventing same-sex couples from getting married denied gay people the promise of equality. Although marriage had long been understood as an institution that brought together a man and a woman for the purpose of having children, no longer did states consistently promote such a narrow concept of marriage. Instead, states have tolerated a wide variety of family practices within marriage itself. What could still be said: "The nature of marriage is that, through its enduring bond, two persons together can find other freedoms, such as expression, intimacy, and spirituality." This meant that "[t]here is dignity in the bond between two men or two women who seek to marry."[8]

For states—even a majority of voters—to deny people the chance to marry simply because of their sexual orientation therefore "demeans or stigmatizes those whose own liberty is then denied." Those who treat gay unions differently than opposite-sex unions "disparage their choices and diminish their personhood." Their actions "harm and humiliate" the children raised by gay couples.[9]

The High Court expressed similar outrage against a Colorado state constitutional amendment that barred officials from considering sexual orientation. The passage of the referendum overturned state and local antidiscrimination laws and hampered the work of judges in interpreting the law. The Supreme Court's disapproval was swift and total. Invalidating the referendum, the Justices characterized it as an "unprecedented" effort to disadvantage gay people because of "animosity" toward homosexuals for who they are rather than what anyone has done. They stated, "A State cannot so deem a class of persons a stranger to its laws."[10]

So when we do the work of equality openly, our tone is necessarily judgmental. Those who violate the principle should expect to be excoriated. Publicly identifying injustices and making examples of wrongdoers are part of how a community makes good citizens "by habituating them to good works." As Thomas Aquinas pointed out, someone will follow the law out of virtue, "fear of punishment," or the "dictates of reason." Over the long haul, moral outrage harnesses social reputation to inculcate civic virtue. More immediately, however, it seeks compliance with the law by stoking a measure of fear of unwanted social effects and by appealing to everybody's rational self-interest to do the right thing.[11]

This is necessary because repairing one's damaged civic status is not just a matter of compensating someone for a tangible thing. It also involves symbolically reintegrating the victims of injustice into the political order, by calling out those who have wronged a fellow member of the community and by lifting up those who have been mistreated.

Public condemnation helps keep government officials in line by making routine but unjust actions more transparent. With transparency comes greater accountability. The judgmental nature of equality ensures there are social consequences for discriminatory behavior, irrational policies that stoke anger toward political minorities, or popular decisions that fall squarely on the backs of the least popular members of society.

Just as no political community can remain neutral as to the kinds of activities that are morally valuable, so the state may denounce sentiments that are destructive to basic notions of justice. Unreliable distinctions like ancestry, wealth, or religious affiliation are "odious to a free people whose institutions are founded upon the doctrine of equality." For equality to be promoted as one of society's dearest values, we can't be afraid of offending someone's sensibilities.[12]

WORRIES ABOUT DEGENERATION, STIGMA, BACKLASH

NOW FOR THE BAD news. It turns out the very things that make egalitarianism so vital to a harmonious political order are also what make the principle so challenging to enforce in real life. Some might not want to see a valuable social good altered or crucial relationships reconfigured. Others will worry about what happens to someone's reputation when he is labeled a bigot. Because equality disputes involve partisans who are emotionally and spiritually invested in their arguments, endorsing one side's vision of equality could anger the losing side, leading to resistance, outright defiance, or the dispersal of scarce resources.

Degeneration, stigma, backlash: These are all consequences that could flow from the enforcement of the ideal of equality. We shouldn't be surprised that some will wish to evade these effects. To avoid one or more of these effects, a person who worries about the consequences of equality will be tempted to avoid applying the principle in the first place. Alternatively, one might be willing to settle for far less than is deserved, simply to wring something, anything, out of the moment.

Each of these concerns works on us as human beings in advance of a decision about what to do about discrimination. Each can stifle our intellect and our imagination. They act on the intellect by causing us to play it safe, to stick with what we know, and to hew to legal lines that have already been drawn rather than discern what justice might require. Past outcomes are then treated as monuments to be rebuilt rather than useful guides for making good decisions.

Excessive anxiety about social consequences can also cause our imagination to fail. It can be so hard to envision how the world might look different, for the better, once social patterns are disrupted or an institution is reformed. If triggered, concerns of this sort can lead to a bunker-like mentality when one is confronted with other people's problems. What follows is a refusal to believe that change can do any good.

When a valuable social good is at stake, fear of its degeneration can also cause public officials to stumble. Consider the dispute over the Virginia Military Institute's males-only policy. For generations, the school prided itself on its mission "to produce educated and honorable men, prepared for the varied work of civil life" and "ready as citizen-soldiers to defend their country." The prospect of women in their midst spurred worries that the institution would be turned into "a pale shadow" of its former self and that the social good it offered—a distinctive military education—would be changed for the worse. Lawyers for the school decried "strict egalitarianism" out of fear "VMI could no longer offer the benefits of single-sex education or its particular methodology if it were to become coeducational."[13]

These concerns about degradation echoed earlier objections to the introduction of women into the military. "Admitting women into West Point would irrevocably change the Academy," the Secretary of the Army told Congress in 1975. The "Spartan atmosphere . . . would surely be diluted, and would in all probability disappear."

Key to the VMI experience was the "adversative method," a harsh leadership training technique where older students played a major role in breaking down younger students physically and emotionally through peer pressure. Because women were inherently unsuited for this approach, the school argued, their inclusion would strong-arm

VMI into radically altering or abandoning its unique educational technique. The admission of women might lead the school to create different fitness standards and other evaluation metrics for men and women. Allowing women to matriculate would actually disrupt the vision of male-only equality nurtured by the school: "VMI's egalitarianism, including its imposition of identical physical standards on all students, was an essential element of its program. . . . That egalitarian ethic would be severely undermined by abandonment of uniform physical standards, causing male and female students to 'perceive the treatment of them as unequal.' "

If applying the principle of equality to this situation augured such major changes, VMI's defenders insisted, then the right answer was to deny that any serious issue of equality was even involved. Or, alternatively, we could broaden how we think of equality: not so much as the right to access a particular institution but rather as the availability of comparable social goods throughout the entire state. So long as other public colleges were open to women, even if other schools didn't present VMI's identical experience, then the diversity of statewide offerings should be sufficient to meet equality's demands.

Ultimately, the Supreme Court rejected these appeals to keep the social good intact. If a VMI education was so valuable as a head start to a military career and high status in civil society, Justice Ginsburg asked, then how could we justify restricting the opportunity to half the population? Shouldn't the school at least try the adversative method at VMI in a coeducational setting before concluding that no women could possibly survive the program?[14]

In fact, angst that equality will destroy a valuable social good is a recurring feature of high-profile disputes. Opponents of same-sex marriage warned that allowing gay couples to wed would spur the decay of traditional marriage and, by extension, the nuclear family's role in a well-ordered society. "By suppressing and displacing the man-woman meaning [of marriage] in that way," the Coalition for

the Protection of Marriage predicted, "the law will cause the dimi-
nution over time and then the loss of the valuable social goods that
meaning now provides."

Similarly, public universities claimed that banning affirmative
action in the name of equality would devastate their mission to educate a diverse population in a rigorous academic environment by
"forc[ing] most of this Nation's finest institutions to choose between
dramatic resegregation and completely abandoning the demanding
standards that have made American higher education the envy of
the world."[15]

A second stumbling block to equality arises from trepidation about
branding someone as prejudiced. Justice Scalia, dissenting in the VMI
case, ridiculed Justice Ginsburg's opinion for "deprecating the closed-
mindedness of our forebears with regard to women's education, and
even with regard to the treatment of women in areas that have nothing to do with education. Closed-minded they were—as every age is,
including our own." Scalia's implication is that many judgments are
vulnerable to charges of discrimination.

He similarly criticized a proequality ruling for dropping "grim,
disapproving hints that Coloradans have been guilty of 'animus' or
'animosity' toward homosexuality, as though that has been established
as un-American." He even went so far as to imply that judicial efforts
to deal with prejudice against gay people were elitist, "high-handed"
projects to "stamp out" popular sentiment.[16]

Scalia's objection to the stigmatizing effects of equality reached a
crescendo when the Supreme Court invalidated the federal Defense
of Marriage Act in 2013. Dissenting once again, he denounced the
majority decision as an act of will "to impose change by adjudging
those who oppose it *hostes humani generis,* enemies of the human race."
This was quite a charge, for the opinion did no such thing. Justice
Kennedy's opinion in *United States v. Windsor* never equated supporters of traditional marriage with human rights violators such as pirates,

slavers, or terrorists. Nor had any of his colleagues ever suggested that anyone who found homosexually offensive should be silenced, as Communists were blackballed during the 1940s and '50s.

But Scalia's emotional reaction does reveal a reflexive desire to avoid the equality ruling's ethical message, namely, its disapproval of anti-gay sentiment. This is an entirely predictable human response. And if Justice Scalia reacted so angrily to the prospect of being tarred as illiberal, unsophisticated, or even retrograde, surely others share his reticence about the potent effects of equality. They might even feel silenced by the prospect of equality's stain, whether or not that is intended.

Scalia was both right and wrong. He was correct that the language of equality is opinionated and reformative. But he's wrong to imply that somehow it could be any other way. Equality is an inescapably moral concept. We can choose not to personalize a particular judgment, say, by not publicizing a violator's full name, or by stressing that a decision was made in the course of a person's difficult job (we often do this with police officers or national security experts), or by diffusing responsibility (acknowledging that it takes many actors to enact a law or create a pattern of wrongdoing).

Judges, politicians, employers—even friends—have done all of these things at one time or another to take some of the sting out of a finding that a person has discriminated against another. But these efforts to obscure or spread fault, or even to speed rehabilitation, can never obliterate the fact that a basic civic norm has been violated.

A third set of obstacles to equality comes from a fear of backlash. It arises once a person in power makes a prediction about how others will react to a finding that discrimination has occurred. Will they accept the outcome and work dutifully to implement the remedy? Or will they feel that someone has preached a false gospel, unfairly branded their heartfelt convictions, and then labor to undermine equality's ethical message? If backlash were to actually occur, spiraling acrimony can turn a win into a loss and unsettle social support for egalitarianism. For that reason, the prudent person thinks, it is better to bake into a decision the possibility of resistance—even if it means putting off that decision or offering less than what justice requires.

Blowback can come in many flavors. A civic leader could worry that his position on a controversial issue will cost him votes at the ballot box or political influence on a pivotal issue. A judge might fret that someone will openly defy a court order. An activist might be tormented by the thought that taking a stand on an equality dispute will fracture the social movement she has worked hard to build.

There was never any real risk that VMI would defy a court order. The issue didn't implicate questions of identity or livelihood beyond the handful of same-sex military schools and their alumni. If backlash operated as a constraint on decisions, it would have mostly impacted people closely associated with VMI. Some families might choose to send their children elsewhere or organize a donor rebellion, but nothing on a nationwide scale.

By contrast, the resistance to court-ordered racial integration anticipated by many leaders during the 1950s was both realistic and likely to be widespread. Even liberals who thought it might be the correct decision feared major blowback. Though he favored desegregation, Justice Hugo Black predicted "the end of Southern liberalism for the time being." Justice Tom Clark feared that ruling in favor of the black schoolchildren "would cause subversion or even defiance of our mandates in many communities. . . . Violence will follow in the South." Justice Robert Jackson worried that the public's "identification of left-wingers with this movement to end segregation" might give fascists in America an opening to exploit.[17]

Fear of resistance was paralyzing enough that the Justices initially split three ways when they first discussed the issue, with no clear path forward and a decent chance of a decision upholding segregation if they had pushed for a decision on the equality issue right then and there. Fortunately, they decided to keep talking.[18]

Backlash isn't a serious consideration in every dispute, but it often lurks as a possibility. That's because a change in expectations of right conduct naturally threatens all kinds of social patterns, opportunities, and even one's sense of identity. Injustice can become a lifestyle that won't be given up without a fight.

DODGING EQUALITY'S CONSEQUENCES

WHEN SOMEONE IS DISTRESSED about one or more of these things—degeneration of a social good, stigmatization, political blowback—it can become extremely difficult to reach agreement over how to do the work of equality. Egalitarianism itself no longer appears as a means of salvation but instead endangers a sense of well-being and way of life.

The temptation to escape the duty to confront injustice can be overpowering, even when a person comes forward with plentiful evidence of bias. In fact, that's when the pressure is greatest to bury one's head in the sand, make excuses, or run away. Let's take a deeper dive into *Plessy v. Ferguson*, the infamous 1896 ruling that hindered the Warren Court's efforts to deal with racial apartheid in America. Homer Plessy refused to obey a conductor's order to vacate a seat reserved for whites. With the aid of a police officer, the conductor forcibly ejected Plessy from his seat and had him thrown in the parish jail of New Orleans for his impertinence.[19]

Plessy challenged his conviction, arguing that the state law requiring racial segregation of trains violated the Equal Protection Clause. The Court disagreed and found the law to be an appropriate exercise of the state's police power. Why did the Justices have such difficulty seeing racial segregation as a form of injustice?

First, up until that point in time egalitarianism had mostly been vindicated when a dispute involved social goods like citizenship, voting, jury service, and property (like Lee Yick's business). How to deal with a state requirement of racial separation on private trains required innovative thinking. Instead of doing the intellectual work to fill that gap, Justice Henry Brown's opinion took what we already knew and made it a hard cap on the scope of equality: "[I]t could not have been intended to abolish distinctions based upon color, or to enforce social, as distinguished from political, equality."

Perhaps most alarming, the opinion cited the emerging, though still scattered, practice of racial apartheid in some states as a reason why segregating trains was permissible. No one on the Court had previously voiced any objection to bans on interracial marriage, segregated schools, or segregated theaters. How are trains any different? Easier to think of all of these measures as concerning nothing more than the "internal commerce of the State."

Second, jurists worried that ruling in Plessy's favor would have grave consequences, perhaps even creating a novel constitutional right to demand that someone of a different race socialize with you or, God forbid, pretend to like you. Justice Brown denounced efforts to enforce "a commingling of the two races upon terms unsatisfactory to either." A judicial remedy will not issue, he said, for "[i]f the two races are to meet upon terms of social equality, it must be the result of natural affinities, a mutual appreciation of each other's merits, and a voluntary consent of individuals."

Third, Justice Brown engaged in mental gymnastics to deny that ill will animated racial segregation. He said laws requiring racial separation "do not necessarily imply the inferiority of either race to the other." He called it a "fallacy" to assume that the law demeaned anyone that was affected. In one of the most insulting and clueless statements in all of American legal history, Justice Brown sniffed, should anyone take umbrage, "it is not by reason of anything found in the act, but solely because the colored race chooses to put that construction upon it."[20]

There are many excellent responses to the objections voiced by segregation's defenders. Social interaction on trains could be crucial to economic success and upward mobility. Privileging white people's comfort over black people's dignity and freedom reinforces white Americans' undeserved status and gives the state excessive control over black lives. Saying that the law can't impose racial segregation isn't the same as requiring people to interact with one another or express affection for them; it just means that we won't tolerate irrational obstacles to social discourse. Law can't solve every problem, but surely that doesn't mean you ought to throw up your hands at the first sign of trouble. At a minimum, justice requires us to act with a sense of humility and self-awareness, open to the possibility that if we belong to the majority that might impair our ability to appreciate the struggles of someone in the minority.

While all of these things could be said, the fact that they even needed to be said shows us the multiple pressures acting on public officials that can prevent them from seeing injustice, and if they do recognize inequality, to choose not to do anything about it.

These aspects of *Plessy*—a failure of intellect and imagination, the smug conclusion that there's nothing here to see, its fatalistic attitude that it wasn't worth getting involved because blacks and whites were too set in their ways—make it an infuriating decision. But the problems go deeper than that: generations of people would have been better off had the Court said nothing at all. The decision was unlike the thousands of others handed down across the country each year. What the Justices did was to establish a tragic precedent.

Tragic precedents, in law as in life, have four salient characteristics. First, they reject a person's grievance in extremely broad terms, often going out of their way to insulate a particular institution or practice. Second, they read like apologias for injustice because they fashion elaborate excuses for perpetrators or severely understate the harms to human beings. Third, they create significant obstacles to the pursuit of justice and stoke further violations of constitutional norms. Fourth, they are deeply demoralizing for those who love justice.

The *Dred Scott* decision of 1857, which invalidated the Missouri Compromise, represents a tragedy of epic proportions, a monument to terror and injustice. Chief Justice Roger Taney found that Congress had no power to ban slavery above the 36°30" parallel because it deprived slavers of their constitutional right to property. His ruling not only upended a carefully crafted, temporary settlement of the slavery issue, it did so on the broadest terms possible. The Court's reasoning not only denied constitutional status to freed slaves and their descendants, it also deprived black people of their basic humanity.

That's not all. Slaves could never be citizens, and could not become more than mere property, he also said, for at the country's founding they comprised "a subordinate and inferior class of beings, who had been subjugated by the dominant race." The "negro race," Taney wrote, "had been excluded from civilized Governments and the family of nations, and doomed to slavery." Treating them more like beasts than humans, the Justices then foreclosed the possibility of political agency for black people: they were not true Americans, and hence should never have a say in the country's future. As Taney put it: black people simply possessed "no rights which the white man was bound to respect."[21]

Many observers were "shocked at the violence and servility" of the ruling. "We are now told, in tones of lofty exultation, that the day is lost—all lost," observed Frederick Douglass. "[A]nd that we might as well give up the struggle." The *Chicago Tribune* lamented *Dred Scott*'s "inhuman dicta" and "the wicked consequences which may flow from it." By embracing white supremacy wholeheartedly and treating the slaver's rights as inviolate, the Justices guaranteed further social strife rather than support for its ruling. They decided the constitutional issue on such absolute terms that resistance to white supremacy would have to assume extralegal forms. In fact, armed settlers on both sides rushed to territories to fight out the slavery question mile by square mile. No matter how strongly some people felt about the dignity and equality of black Americans, there seemed nothing that could be done to make them citizens of any state or the United States, short of revolution.[22]

According to this criterion, *Plessy*, too, qualifies as a major tragedy. As a marker in the law, in politics, even in casual conversation, *Plessy* became a major obstacle to justice. It did so by making it exponentially harder to bring a grievance and closing off lines of possible argument. It was as if Justice Brown and his colleagues ran down a dimly lit hallway not just closing one door, but slamming shut several other doors along the way.

The power of white Americans over the social lives of black Americans grew dramatically, while the number of sympathetic partners for egalitarians dwindled. *Plessy* helped spread a noble lie that racial segregation was a harmless means of keeping the peace.

A tragic outcome like *Plessy* is profoundly demoralizing. It was disheartening because in deciding the equality question, the Court made it ethical to treat white people's comfort as more important than black Americans' freedom and sense of equal worth. And we knew that it was really about the comfort of white Americans, because local citizens and judges had no problem with black nannies and people of other races in the white car. On the day before state legislators enacted the law, the New Orleans *Times-Democrat* urged politicians to take the measure in order to prevent "indignity to the white women of Louisiana": "A man that would be horrified at the idea of his wife or daughter seated by the side of a burly negro in the parlor of a hotel or at a restaurant cannot see her occupying a crowded seat in a car next to a negro without the same feeling of disgust."[23]

If someone could not appreciate how petty, how humiliating the Louisiana law was, then how could he be counted upon as an ally to

deal honestly with more serious problems of racial injustice? *Plessy* cor-
roded belief in the law and politics on the part of racial minorities and
friends of equality, diminishing hope that racial indignities would be
addressed in the future.

At the same time, *Plessy* emboldened white supremacists and casual
segregationists alike. It confirmed their use of law to deal with their
racial anxiety and papered over racist policies with seemingly neutral excuses like "order," "custom," and "police power." Justice Harlan made this point in his dissent, predicting that the ruling would
"stimulate aggressions, more or less brutal and irritating, upon the
admitted rights of colored citizens" and "encourage the belief that it is
possible, by means of state enactments, to defeat the beneficent purposes" of the Fourteenth Amendment. After the Court handed down
Plessy, the *Times-Democrat* applauded the outcome and prayed that it
would "have some effect on the silly negroes" opposed to segregation.
Emboldened, the largest paper of record in the state expressed that
"what it would like to see, and what it hopes to see, is the extension of
this principle of keeping the races apart" throughout state law.[24]

Harlan turned out to be right: states and local jurisdictions fell over
one another to enact laws segregating eating establishments, pools,
neighborhoods, libraries, bathrooms—even schools for the blind. For
the next half century, defenders of racial apartheid in America could
simply point to the Supreme Court and say: if the smartest, most powerful judges in the land see no problem of injustice, then neither do
I. Not only does a tragic precedent fail to remedy existing injustice, it
becomes an instrument for worsening inequities.[25]

It took World War II, with a rising desire to distinguish America
from Europe's fascist nations, and advocates chipping away at segregation for decades, before *Plessy*'s pernicious effects could be undone.
Even then, the precedent nearly derailed the quest for justice in the
courts. When *Brown v. Board of Education* was initially argued in the
Supreme Court in 1952, several of the Justices, including the Chief

Justice, believed *Plessy* dictated that they must approve racially segregated schools. Justice Reed, for example, told his colleagues, "We must start with the idea that there is a large and reasonable body of opinion in various states that separation of the races is for the benefit of both." "On the basis of precedent," Justice Jackson similarly said, "I would have to say it *is* constitutional."[26]

Success on the equality claim came only after the case was held over to the next term for reargument, Chief Justice Vinson suddenly passed away, Felix Frankfurter and Robert Jackson discovered a rationale with which they felt comfortable, and Earl Warren helped forge a unanimous opinion as the new Chief.

So doing the work of equality is a delicate business. In the face of such difficulties, what's a practical egalitarian to do? We can't blithely enforce abstract principles without any regard for the consequences. Nor can we be so preoccupied with the possibility of imperfect outcomes that we shirk our responsibilities.

To dissolve the tension from recurring clashes between principle and realism, enlightened public officials have sometimes employed one of two strategies: deferring hard questions or appeasing opponents. The point of the first approach is to delay an answer until social conditions improve. It's better to say nothing now than to say something terrible. As for appeasement, the idea is to be willing to meet someone else halfway, so long as an equality-based judgment can be rendered immediately.

For an example of deferral, consider how leading statesmen handled the issue of interracial marriage in the mid-1950s, in the decade before the civil rights movement roused Americans to treat racial equality as a national priority. Rather than answer a couple's grievance, the Supreme Court sought to postpone the day of reckoning for as long as possible.

On June 26, 1952, Ham Say Naim, a Chinese sailor, and Ruby Elaine Lamberth, a white woman from Norfolk, Virginia, traveled to

North Carolina to be married and then returned to Norfolk. The problem was that Virginia's Racial Integrity Act of 1924 made it "unlawful for any white person in this State to marry any save a white person, or a person with no other admixture of blood than white and American Indian." Because their union violated the Commonwealth's public policy, it would be treated as "absolutely void." The couple had evaded the law and returned, so they could have been imprisoned for one to five years.[27]

Ham Say eventually returned to sea, and the distance proved too great a strain for their marriage. Ruby sought a divorce, which created an opportunity to challenge the constitutionality of the law. A trial judge granted an annulment and the husband then appealed to the Virginia Supreme Court of Appeals. By the time that *Naim v. Naim* reached the state's highest court in 1955, the U.S. Supreme Court had already handed down *Brown*, declaring that racial segregation "generates a feeling of inferiority as to their status in the community that may affect their hearts and minds in a way unlikely ever to be undone." Naim's case seemed to raise the exact same legal issue. Shouldn't the principle of racial egalitarianism apply with similar force to laws that barred interracial marriage? Didn't such laws, too, unfairly keep people apart on the basis of race and leave scars on "hearts and minds" in the community?

To Ham Say's dismay, the justices of the Virginia Supreme Court said no. They reasoned that Virginia's goal of preventing "miscegenetic marriages" constituted a valid exercise of the state's police power, and tried to distinguish it from the situation presented in *Brown*. It was one thing to make black and white children sit together in schools, they felt, but it would be quite another thing to render the state powerless to preserve the "racial integrity" of its people so that the community would be reduced to "a mongrel breed of citizens." In their view, the state's law helped "prevent the obliteration of racial pride" among whites, protected against "the corruption of blood," and ensured the "quality of its citizenship."

The Virginia Supreme Court extolled the virtues of racial separation as a social policy: "Both sacred and secular history teach that nations and races have better advanced in human progress when they cultivated their own distinctive characteristics and culture and developed their own peculiar genius." Virginians should defend that prerogative to their dying gasp, the Court urged, for it also implicated "that bastion of States' rights, somewhat battered perhaps but still a sturdy fortress in our fundamental law."[28]

Although Naim appealed the unfavorable ruling, the U.S. Supreme Court refused to hear the case. Behind the scenes, some of the Justices and their law clerks believed "it would be wise judicial policy to duck this question for a time." They manipulated procedural rules because they felt that Americans were not ready to handle such an explosive matter so soon on the heels of *Brown*. Judges had stepped well in front of public opinion on the issue of racial segregation and provoked an intense political backlash.

Fear of a public outcry had a multiplying effect on future decisions. The Justices worried that opening a new front on race matters would intensify that reaction, undermine school integration efforts, and damage the reputation of the Court for years to come. But in *Brown*, they had put off a decision for a year; now, they contemplated indefinite delay.

Justice Felix Frankfurter led the charge to table the matter. He argued that "as of today one can say without wrenching his conscience that the issue has not reached that compelling demand for consideration which precludes refusal to consider it." In other words, Frankfurter told his colleagues that delay served the institution's goals of enforcing the principle of equality in the school context, and, that, conversely, refusing a final resolution of the interracial marriage question did not offend the interests of justice, at least not yet. He left unanswered when justice delayed might become justice denied.[29]

The silent approach taken on interracial marriage until the late 1960s has been adopted in other times and places. This method of dealing with anticipated resistance conserves scarce resources and recognizes that every legal decision requires social support to be enforced. Deferral also has a certain intuitive charm, like a parent's advice: better to put off a life-altering decision until morning rather than do something rash while your judgment is gripped by doubt.[30]

Even so, there are undeniable costs to waiting until a consensus organically arises before entertaining a claim of injustice. How exactly does one determine when the time is right to resolve a controversial issue? After all, the same arguments for delaying justice in 1955 could be made every time the identical issue reappeared. What's more, deferral can turn into an abandonment of one's own responsibility. Justice Reed, who initially favored racially segregated schools, pleaded, "We must allow time." He argued that if judges did nothing about it, border states might start to get rid of segregation on their own in "fifteen or twenty years"—but how could he possibly know? And what about the Deep South states? Delay can simply be a form of polite surrender.

Perhaps it was only a matter of time before racial segregation provoked an uproar that could not be ignored. But for certain kinds of grievances brought by certain groups of people, no majority of Americans would ever be ready to accept the minority's perspective. Think of suspected murderers, sexual offenders, religious minorities, the homeless. It's difficult to imagine a social movement that could sweep the nation in a way that forced a public reckoning over their complaints. And if that outcry never came, does that mean government officials would be justified in never hearing their petitions?

Naim's lawyer expressed a sense of frustration that his client no doubt shared: the U.S. Solicitor General, who declined to support his appeal, and the members of the High Court too, all "want to have their cases without any complications." Martin Luther King, Jr., made this very point from a Birmingham jail when he confessed that he'd never been part of an effort to remedy injustice "that was 'well timed' in the view of those who have not suffered unduly."[31]

And what about the head-in-the-sand precedent that avoidance created: once it becomes acceptable to table this difficult question simply because it is politically fraught, doesn't that encourage efforts to duck other kinds of controversial subjects? Surely, at some point, filibustering turns into its own kind of inequity.

Another twelve years would pass before the Supreme Court confronted the issue of interracial marriage squarely in *Loving v. Virginia* and vindicated the idea of equality. In the meantime, interracial couples could get no relief from federal courts when states threatened them with jail time, fines, or banishment, or when public officials refused to recognize the validity of their unions. To preserve the usefulness of equality as a legal principle for some future point in time, the Justices sacrificed the happiness and welfare of the citizens before them.

If waiting for a "more convenient season" is one kind of response to the difficulties encountered in doing the hard work of equality, then appeasement represents another strategy. On the belief that some progress right away is better than none at all, proponents of compromise say that it is worth securing a measure of justice even if it means appeasing critics. For instance, this characterizes the position taken by some gay rights advocates who sought to persuade supporters to accept civil unions after Vermont became the first state to make it available.

Fear of anti-gay backlash certainly was not trivial at that point. Every time gay rights supporters won a case in court, it seemed that lawmakers or voters tried to take it away. After the Hawaii Supreme Court held that the exclusion of gay couples from marriage violated the principle of equality in 1993, voters there stormed the polls to enact a state constitutional amendment nullifying that ruling, 69 percent to 28 percent. A number of states, including California, subsequently passed laws to ban same-sex marriage, as did the federal government. Bill Clinton, a Democratic president, signed the Defense of Marriage Act in 1996.

In this climate, some gay rights activists found it tempting to settle for what civil unions promised when they became available: near-equal tangible rights, but a separate and different social status. Supporters of civil unions offered to acknowledge the other side's position as matters of religion and tradition. In turn, they hoped to continue to build momentum toward full marriage rights by showing skeptical voters that legal gay unions would not cause the downfall of Western civilization.[32]

Yale law professor William Eskridge, a prominent supporter of civil unions, embodied this uneasy position. He rejected comparisons of civil unions to racial segregation, though conceded that they entailed "a compromise of liberal principles, but a small and perhaps temporary one." Eskridge called it an exercise in "pragmatic liberalism" to accept an institution that represented an "accommodation of traditionalist anxieties for the time being" while continuing the fight for full marriage rights.[33]

Like deferral, appeasement has its fans. When the first-best solution is off the table, compromise can seem like a good outcome. A great deal of social progress does transpire slowly, so it makes sense to be open to incremental answers. To the hungry, half a loaf always looks better than none. Still, the problem with mollification is that it might crystallize the impression that half a loaf is all you deserve.

Moreover, what if those who are most hostile to gay rights did not see this as a cooperative exercise, but rather as the appropriate consignment of sexual minorities to inferior social status? What if opponents became emboldened by their success to try to roll back even that progress? Settling for less might dissipate the political energy necessary to achieve full civic equality. If that happened, conciliation would have served as the galvanizing moment to a reversal of fortune.

A cycle of appeasement, loss, and regret played out at the federal level in the '90s. President Clinton, in his own words, "long opposed governmental recognition of same-gender marriages." So when he signed the Defense of Marriage Act, he presented it as a compromise position on equality: gay people would have to accept they could not marry someone they love. But in exchange, he vowed to work hard to enact a federal antidiscrimination law to protect gays and lesbians in the workplace. Give up one valuable social good, President Clinton urged, in the hope of gaining another.

President Clinton believed this would be a grand bargain that all Americans could embrace. He turned out to be wrong. Signing the law didn't improve the odds of an antidiscrimination law passing. It never happened on his watch. Clinton gave up same-sex marriage without a fight, demoralized supporters, and, worst of all, pacification yielded nothing from Congress in return. Years later, he expressed regret for his role in endorsing discrimination during "a very different time."[34]

Although delay or capitulation can be attractive in the heat of the moment, neither removing the source of the stress nor giving in to it serves the goals of democratic justice. Doing justice isn't about turning a blind eye to glaring problems, or being quick to meet your opponent halfway. Instead, it requires being frank about one's objectives, committed to the project, and resourceful when encountering adversity.

EQUALITY BY OTHER MEANS

THERE'S ANOTHER PATH FORWARD through the usual tangle of lofty ideals and loss-cutting expediency. But we have to find our way to justice by keeping what has proved useful while shedding what doesn't work. To this end, we should adopt a form of pragmatism to protect our progress on equality and to find other ways of doing justice when we have trouble agreeing to do it explicitly.

This approach should come as second nature, because Americans have always been a practical people. It was Tocqueville who famously remarked on "the philosophical method of the American people," finding in them "a taste for the tangible and the real." No surprise, then, that the most distinctive approach to philosophy native to America has been pragmatism, an approach that can be traced back through John Dewey, and to Charles Sanders Peirce, William James, and Louis Brandeis. Mind you, not the modern form of legal pragmatism that has become a shell of its former self, highly clinical, neo-utilitarian, overly narrow in orientation. No, I am interested in recovering an older, holistic approach to politics and law that is at once clarifying, action-directed, and humanistic.[35]

William James, who presents the most compelling picture of pragmatism, harkened back to Socrates, Aristotle, Locke, and Hume to find elements of it in their thought. From his friend Peirce's work, James drew two ideas: pragmatism as a basis for action and as a theory for clarifying ideas. In particular, he proposed the pragmatic method as a way of cutting through intractable disputes, especially those that regularly descend into interminable arguments over abstractions.[36]

Equality is one of those subjects that has long been characterized by high-quality intellectual discussion but has produced few satisfying or permanent resolutions. In fact, intense battles over such abstractions have themselves sometimes become obstacles to meaningful reform.

Should we prefer formal equality or antisubordination, color blindness or race awareness? Is it better to police religious neutrality strictly or to permit more robust interactions between religious groups and the state? These are excellent questions but we can't possibly solve any real problems at that level of generality. And more energy expended on refining abstract concepts yields diminishing returns. It is ripe for a pragmatic turn—a new one.

The pragmatic method is no overarching theory and contains no fixed precepts. Instead, it is best described as a problem-solving method with some rules of thumb. First, the pragmatist possesses an "empiri-cist attitude," preferring facts to abstractions. Second, one must have a distinct preference for written solutions over verbal ones—because writing promotes clear and sober thinking rather than spontaneous, purely emotional reactions. Third, pragmatism shies away from fixed principles and closed systems. Instead, it turns "towards facts, towards action and towards power." Who holds power? How has it been used or abused? Who benefits, and who, if anyone, is harmed?

To address problems of inequality, a pragmatist should do three things. First, when ideological gridlock happens, turn your attention to the details, whose study can offer a path toward a workable solu-tion. Concepts matter, but not as much as the comparative effects of our actions on fellow human beings. Immersing oneself in what King called the "hard, brutal facts" of inequality helps us to appreciate the suffering of real people, as well as the varieties of wrongs that might be involved. It's the best way to get a fine-grained sense of what can be done and how to prioritize among harms faced by human beings trapped in the web of the law. If you can't see other people's pain, or if you refuse to prioritize among harms, you'll always be daunted by the sheer scale of injustice that exists in America.

Second, put aside the comforting illusion that there should only be one solution for every problem. That way lie stalemate and frustration—and quite possibly, tragedy. See pervasive inequality for what it truly is: a many-headed beast nourished by a multiplicity of beliefs, attitudes, traditions, institutions, and priorities. A dogmatic attitude about proper remedies can be just as dangerous as willful blindness to actual suffering while enforcing the rules. Strive instead to be nimble in selecting from among many possible tools for doing justice, and open to how nontraditional or eclectic solutions can actu-ally promote the values of equality. The rule of law is more than the law of rules. It is, rather, a set of legal practices with justice as its end.

Third, look for connections between egalitarianism and other bodies of knowledge. Don't treat equality as a hermetically sealed container of ideas. Be willing to borrow what has proven useful and discard what has outlived its usefulness and merely gives cover to injustice. If other ideas can do the job, if they fit well together, and if they are suitable for the problem, then don't adhere to past ways simply out of habit. Along the way, we must be attentive to imbalances of power and, above all, concerned with developing facility with a variety of problem-solving methods and a larger and more effective arsenal for doing justice. This is how we build a political culture that values equality and raise an army of citizens capable of great things.[37]

At its best, James explained, pragmatism "lies in the midst of our theories, like a corridor in a hotel." The metaphor is a useful one that underscores what is promising in the approach, but also what is risky about it. Pragmatism has a crucial role to play in matters of justice by helping to break an ideological stalemate and keeping one's eyes focused on human suffering, but it can't be allowed to drive the train. If we did, we might never know where we would end up. To avoid a situation where the ends always justify the means, pragmatism has to be pressed into the service of sound principles. If pragmatism is like a corridor, then the law of equality provides the overarching structure.[38]

Instead of a stand-alone approach, pragmatism works best as a supplemental one, an addendum to our regular operating procedures. It is a fail-safe, a backup plan, something every responsible citizen should help develop knowing what we know after more than two hundred years of experience in America: we face regular breakdowns in doing the work of equality.

Think of pragmatism's value on a sliding scale. Most of the time, we care about the consequences of our actions but we don't allow the ends to justify the means. The effects of our decisions are merely one among many things we take into account for getting things done. But where the democratic stakes are the highest, and the costs of failure most pernicious, it becomes more justifiable to tolerate a wider range of methods and to give greater weight to the consequences of our decisions.

Equality by other means isn't a clever strategy available only to the most gifted lawyers. Instead, it's a global approach to handling grievances that is accessible to everyone, whatever your role in these things. It means acquiring an informed and empathetic mindset for handling the competing pressures in disputes over equality, being committed to the work, and developing adaptive tools for breaking down inequities. In short, it involves cultivating good habits of justice. Each of us, whether we are an ordinary citizen or a high official, is capable of forming such routines.

Developing next-best solutions for inequality is something each of us can do, but it is also an obligation that each of must shoulder. That duty is implicit in the mutual condition of equality that we all enjoy, it is the price of having the rights of citizenship, it is a natural consequence of being "bound" to others. In fact, civic leaders regularly invoke the duty of all citizens to do the hard work of equality. The imperative to address inequality effectively, JFK reminded us, comes from the realization that "the rights of every man are diminished when the rights of one man are threatened." Or as King put it, "Injustice anywhere is a threat to justice everywhere." For public officials themselves, that special duty is underscored by the oath they take to "defend the Constitution" and to "bear true faith and allegiance" to its ideals.

Playing an active part in the search for second-best solutions is an excellent way to avoid being complicit in pervasive inequality. Complicity can be defined as helping perpetrators avoid responsibility either during the commission of a wrong or explaining away injustice after the fact. It can come from agreeing to pursue unjust goals, as the Justices did in *Dred Scott* when they approved a monstrous ideology that licensed profit in human flesh for the benefit of wealthy slavers and sought to establish a permanent black underclass.

But being responsible for injustice doesn't require a meeting of the minds about unjust goals or active participation in a wrongful act. A person can aid and abet wrongdoers later by refusing to interrogate the exercise of state violence against human beings, by willfully blinding oneself to the suffering that has been wrought, or by unthinkingly adopting a perpetrator's excuses as one's own. This account of complicity covers the actions of judges, elected officials, and bureaucrats who have the power to shape policies for the better, but fall down on the job. It also reaches each of us as citizens, who might be tempted to think it's someone else's responsibility to worry about injustice.

To be clear: I'm not making the case for lockstep answers. Instead, I am assailing a decision-making mindset and understanding of citizenship that lack habits of justice. The structural inequities that we now face could only have been created in the first place, and they are most easily maintained today, through the acquiescence of good-hearted people. So it's not enough to raise kind, hardworking children. They have to be equipped with the know-how to dismantle injustice they will confront one day.

How should a practical egalitarian handle a complaint about inequality? When someone comes forward with a grievance about inequality, the first order of business is always to try to resolve the dispute according to the methods created for such matters. Because someone has the courage to complain about being treated unfairly, we honor that request by considering it in good faith. But what if we quickly realize that consensus will be a tall order and pressing forward with that particular claim could do more harm than good?

If a grievance has revealed a serious injustice and we encounter difficulty resolving it, then the fail-safe must kick in: we must look for ways to do equality by other means. Our goal, as Bingham famously insisted, is to focus on reducing "unequal burdens," using whatever collection of methods can be most effective. While we need to honor someone's grievance, that doesn't entitle the person to a resolution on any particular ground, especially if doing so would worsen injustice for others. What matters, both legally and morally, is that justice is done. If backup solutions are available that would do nearly as well, then we have an obligation to pursue them.[39]

At this point, a pragmatist focuses on the potential consequences of alternatives lying before her, and if there is no difference among the options, then a dispute among those options is "idle." We might find that the practical differences between two or more ways of handling a problem of equality are minor. Substituting one solution for another would then be principled.

Would we lose anything by resolving a dispute some other way? We would certainly lose some of the special force associated with the rhetoric of equality. But if a second-best solution is nearly as effective, then principled substitution would still ensure that a person who violates another's rights is—in the words of Jefferson—"punished by the disesteem of his society." It wouldn't be exactly the same, but if we choose wisely among our options, we can still convey a sense of constitutional wrongfulness. And in many situations, it will be better to deal with suffering before it festers.[40]

For the average citizen, a useful historical analogue would be the Underground Railroad, which led to the liberation of thousands of slaves each year. Some enthusiastically described it as "practical abolition," which is another way of saying that it served as a second-best strategy for justice when legislative or judicial emancipation still lay beyond the realm of possibility for most slaves. Railroad activities were not random or sporadic acts of kindness, but rather part of an unconventional practice. For practical egalitarians of that era, railroad activities served as a partial solution to the problem of manifest injustice.

Social conditions determine the feasibility of ideas. Because a broad theory of equality had no real meaning for a major segment of the enslaved population, abolitionists turned to alternative concepts to justify helping fugitive slaves. Unable yet to achieve a national consensus that slavery deprived individuals of "equal protection of the laws," they created a counterculture by repurposing the common law notions of "assault," "battery," and "kidnapping," to describe the harms of slavery.

They also converted the ancient principle of self-defense into a term of popular resistance. Self-defense contained embedded ideas of equality: it established limits to the force that each human being could use against another, confirming each person's autonomy and bodily integrity. In the hands of abolitionists, self-defense was broadened to encompass the right of any friend of equality to rush to the aid of helpless runaway slaves and repel slave catchers, as if the slave were a friend or family member. Working from this view of self-defense, for example, the New York Committee of Vigilance established in 1835 vowed to "protect unoffending, defenseless, and endangered persons of color, by securing their rights as far as practicable."

There were downsides to aiding escaped slaves, for siphoning off so many of the oppressed from slaveholding states probably reduced the frequency of spontaneous revolts that might have brought the system of chattel slavery to a spectacular crash at an earlier point in history. Affording sanctuary to slaves was a grinding, arduous, and dangerous activity—one that entailed exposure to legal peril and, depending on a person's degree of participation, could even put him into physical conflict with slave catchers or law enforcement officers.[41]

On the other hand, it's not as if capitulating to calls for perfect law and order would have suddenly led Southern leaders and planta-tion owners to renounce a way of life in which they had become so deeply invested. What did resistance accomplish? Underground rail-road activities relieved the suffering of some slaves, while the regular drip, drip, drip of escapees eroded the outrageous myth of the con-tented slave perpetuated by those who benefited from human traf-ficking. Perhaps most important of all, because legal change depends on social transformation, the Underground Railroad ferried those in bondage to new places where they could access education, culture, and civic life so as to produce talented leaders—living, breathing proof that former slaves could become virtuous and patriotic members of society. Each of these incremental improvements, too, served as links on a chain toward a better theory of equality when the time came to atone for America's original sin.

Of course, the tactical choices facing an activist won't be identical to those encountered by a public official or judge. Those who hold positions of power must answer to other rules and constituencies, and differences in role can't be obliterated. But I wish to stress that the obligation to do equality by other means, in ways that are meaningful, transcend the roles we play in everyday society. It's never sufficient to cite one's position as a reason to shirk one's constitutional duty.

Now, let's bring *Plessy* back into the picture to see how equality by other means would work for someone in a position of authority. There are at least three other ways that jurists could have left some doors and windows open so the light of justice might shine through, without resulting in a tragic precedent. These solutions could have been pursued by anyone who might have faced segregationist demands: a local official trying to prevent a discriminatory law from being enacted in the first place, an advocate seeking to chip away at race-based laws that have already passed, or a jurist hoping to convince colleagues that such a law must fall.

One path not taken: saying that the law interfered with Congress's exclusive prerogative over interstate commerce. After all, trains don't just travel within one state, but often serve as the most efficient means of traveling between states—this was certainly true by the late nineteenth century. State and local laws that unjustifiably burden interstate commerce should be struck down because they impede the free flow of goods and services. And that solution would have made sense, too, since having to comply with a dizzying array of laws separating passengers on the basis of race or some other trait imposes enormous costs on businesses that operate in the national marketplace.

In fact, in 1877 the Justices struck down a Louisiana public accommodations law on this very ground, saying that "[i]f each State was at liberty to regulate the conduct of carriers while within its jurisdiction, the confusion likely to follow could not but be productive of great inconvenience and unnecessary hardship. . . . Commerce cannot flourish in the midst of such embarrassments."

The possible snag here is that Plessy rode on a line that began and ended within Louisiana's borders. But that seems to miss the forest for the trees. For the 1890 Louisiana law was written in broad strokes, requiring "all railway companies carrying passengers in their coaches in this State" to racially segregate the cars, excepting only street railroads. Because the law applied even to those railroad cars passing into Louisiana from another state or going elsewhere, the law burdened those companies doing business in, around, and through the state. If the Court had struck down the law on these grounds, there would have been no need to articulate a broad theory of equality.[42]

A second answer would have been to say that a different right was violated than the one Plessy had emphasized: the right to travel. At the end of their brief Plessy's lawyers suggested that the ancient concept, "Peace of the King's Highway," protected travelers from "molestation and annoyance." But they didn't develop this line of attack, and the Justices ignored it.[43]

Today, the right of travel is treated as a fundamental right under the U.S. Constitution because the choice-of-lifestyle benefits of federalism would be nonsensical without the ability to move freely around the country. In 1948, the Universal Declaration of Human Rights stated: "[E]veryone has the right to freedom of movement and residence within the borders of each State." This approach was viable in Plessy's time, even if it was not as developed then as it is now.

As early as 1867, the Supreme Court recognized the right of travel.

The case involved a Nevada law that required every person leaving the state by railroad, stagecoach, or other vehicle to pay a tax of one dollar. The challenger of the law hadn't even raised or briefed the issue, but the Justices found it to be so important that it had to be addressed. Striking down the law, the Court proclaimed that every citizen has "a right to free access to its sea-ports, through which all the operations of foreign trade and commerce are conducted, . . . and this right is in its nature independent of the will of any State over whose soil he must pass in the exercise of it." It then endorsed powerful language from an earlier controversy: "We are all citizens of the United States, and as members of the same community must have the right to pass and repass through every part of it without interruption, as freely as in our own States. . . . States [that pass laws inhibiting travel] produce nothing but discord and mutual irritation, and they very clearly do not possess it."[44]

The burdens on travel imposed by racial apartheid are obvious: black citizens would understandably avoid settling or working in places that exposed them regularly to the indignities of segregation. Frederick Douglass recounts how, on a trip to Nantucket, his steamer was detained at a wharf for two hours as the captain tried to "compel the colored passengers to separate from the white passengers . . . during this time, the most savage feelings were evinced towards every colored man who asserted his right to enjoy equal privileges with other passengers."[45]

Put to the test, Louisiana would have had difficulty rustling up a good reason for interfering with someone's right to travel. Because segregation was still relatively new to America, there wasn't an unbroken tradition of such practices reaching back to 1787 or even to Reconstruction. So it could hardly be said that they were authorized by the Constitution. To the contrary, this kind of law seemed to mark travelers in novel, awful ways to inhibit the choices of freed people as to where to live and work.

Racial segregation of railroad cars only began to appear in the late 1880s, in response to an increase in travel by middle-class African Americans and the passage of the federal Civil Rights Act of 1875. There were other laws of this genre that might also be said to violate the right to travel, such as Oregon's 1857 Constitution, which gave only "white foreigners who became residents" the same rights as the native-born and asserted that "no free negro or mulatto . . . shall ever come, reside, or be within this State."[46]

As a solution, the right to travel would have developed a constitutional right in a way that facilitated the Reconstruction goal of breaking down barriers for freed persons, but it wouldn't have required saying that every attempt to segregate people was morally or constitutionally problematic—leaving that question for another day. It would have advanced the notion that each citizen possessed a bundle of national rights of citizenship, something upon which the project of equality depends. A robust right to travel could have then served as a potent weapon against outlier states and local jurisdictions that used geographic and other spatial techniques to enforce white supremacy.

A third possibility is the simplest of all: concluding that the segregation law fails the rule of reason. This argument was presented in the case, but it was buried by equality as the lead argument, which attracted the most attention. It needn't have been that way. Imagine instead that Plessy had led with the reasonableness argument in a way that emphasized deficiencies in the record of the case. His attorney suggested that the segregation law couldn't be understood as a public health regulation by asking, "Does [black and white sitting side by side] contaminate public morals? If it does from whence comes the contamination?" This was a good start but they should have gone further by making the reasonableness question an empirical one.

The state of Louisiana claimed to be exercising its police power, but where, exactly, was the evidence of public disorder? What evidence, if any, could the state produce to suggest that disorder would likely erupt on railroads because black and white passengers couldn't keep their hands to themselves? Had there been past incidents or racial disruptions in this forum or was the law simply a solution in search of a problem? We can't just assume the state is correct or else we deprive citizens of their agency, treating them all as if they were young children who lacked impulse control.

Absent actual facts that would support a reasonable fear of a breach of the peace, no one should defer to blanket judgments that rest on conjecture or group stereotypes of criminality. Otherwise, as legal scholar Ernst Freund has pointed out, "the police power would be practically unrestricted." Surely securing the convenience of some citizens at the expense of others is not as urgent as that of health and safety.

If this had been the solution, it would have offered a temporary answer to the slippery slope problem. There would have been no need to make a global judgment just yet that separation was inherently and always racist—only that the state had to present actual facts showing that racial separation was truly necessary to keep the peace. One also would not have had to find something especially valuable about the social good involved. It only required saying that if a jurisdiction is going to allocate any resources or opportunities among citizens, it has to be grounded in a real problem. No new individual right need be created or extended.[47]

While this approach would have stopped short of a ringing denunciation of inequality, it still would have raised the costs of discrimination by making it harder to engage in hysterical, unscientific forms of segregation. Each state or city would have had to muster its own proof rather than rely on the experiences of others. This solution would also have sent an unmistakable signal that laws of this sort, with their totalizing effects, were dangerous to communal bonds. In the meantime, some measures of this sort could be stricken and help generate momentum against unjust policies.

Indeed, from the standpoint of egalitarianism, each of these outcomes is nearly as good as the rest once a vindication of equality seems out of reach. None provides a permanent answer to the problem of racial segregation, and each has its drawbacks, but all remedy tangible harms right away and give legislators a second chance to reflect soberly on their current path. Granted, none of these methods would have been a slam dunk in the late nineteenth century. But all of these arguments were available at the time. If only equality by other means had been practiced more systematically before that point, these arguments would have had a fighting chance.

And what justice demands is a multiprong strategy to neutralize the many-headed monster that is inequality in America. We must be passionate about equality as a moral idea and we have to be realistic about how to make progress on that front. And when we are prepared to make decisions we must act decisively, without making halfhearted statements or indulging backsliding. What remains now is to show how gridlock over equality can be broken through a variety of alternative concepts, rules, and rationales.

CHAPTER 2

FAIR PLAY

*All I ask is a square deal for every man. Give
him a fair chance. Do not let him wrong any
one, and do not let him be wronged.*

—THEODORE ROOSEVELT, MAY 6, 1903

ONE OF THE OLDEST legal principles is that of fair play, which runs
through various parts of the Constitution. It is codified in the Constitution's two Due Process Clauses, as well as in the many protections for people charged with crimes, such as the right to a speedy
and impartial jury trial, and the right to counsel. When we reach an
impasse over the meaning of equality, the idea that everyone deserves
a fair shake can serve as a productive substitute.[1]

Consider, for example, how judges dealt with a murder investigation that reeked of racial discrimination in the years before the civil
rights revolution. On the afternoon of March 30, 1934, a white planter
named Raymond Stuart was found clubbed to death in his home. Suspicion focused on three poor, black tenant farmers. The evening that
Stewart's body was discovered, a sheriff's deputy and a group of prominent men from the white community grabbed Arthur "Yank" Ellington, who lived on the land. When Ellington protested his innocence,
the mob hanged him by a rope from a tree. They took him down for a
spell, then simulated the lynching a second time. When that failed to

extract a confession, they tied him to the tree and whipped him. Eventually, after permanently damaging his spine, they let him go.

A day later, the same deputy visited Ellington's home, took him away to "make him belch up the truth," and administered more beatings until his spirit broke and he cried, "Tell me what you want me to say and I will say it."[2]

Meanwhile, two other black farmers, Ed Brown and Henry Shields, were arrested, taken to the county jail, and forced to strip. The deputy and his men laid the naked suspects over chairs and "their backs were cut to pieces with a leather strap with buckles on it." Law enforcement continued to beat these two men brutally until they not only confessed to the murder, but also did so to the exact detail demanded by the sheriff's deputy and his men. "He was whipping me so hard I had to say 'yes, sir,'" to his questions, Brown would later testify. The officers "tore me up," Shields said. "He whipped me so hard I had to tell him something."[3]

The next day, to stave off a growing mob, a grand jury indicted all three suspects. A trial was swiftly convened in a highly charged environment, with "deputies armed with machine guns, sawed-off shotguns and tear gas bombs following reports of mob threats." Asked about the severity of the beatings, the sheriff's deputy testified, "Not too much for a negro; not as much as I would have done if it were left to me." Within a week of the crime, an all-white jury had convicted the men based on their statements and a judge had sentenced them to death.[4]

The men appealed to the Mississippi Supreme Court, but that tribunal found no problems with what had taken place, emphasizing that all of the regular trial rules had been carefully observed and that the defendants' own lawyers failed to request that their confessions be excluded. Notably, Chief Justice Sydney Smith's majority opinion upholding the convictions made no detailed mention of the ferocious assaults against the defendants, adding only this obscure disclaimer to the end of his decision: "Nothing herein is intended to even remotely sanction the method by which these confessions were obtained."

Just as the county sheriff himself turned a blind eye to how his deputy procured evidence against the accused, so the justices of the highest state court ignored the barbaric and discriminatory actions of local officials by focusing only on the conduct of the trial. As far as they were concerned, the confessions were "competent" at the time they were admitted to the record, and that was all that mattered.[5]

The case became a national sensation, with many observers seeing it as the latest proof that the criminal justice system was racially biased. The NAACP and other activists rallied around these "friendless sharecroppers" and raised money for their appeals. Lawyers for Brown did gesture toward the idea of equality, pointing out the fact that "these appellants are negroes" and that they "stood before the trial court as helpless to defend themselves as sheep in a slaughter pen." But the state Supreme Court refused to even consider the fact that the defendants were black, poor, or uneducated. Treating everyone the same during trial would be enough. "All litigants, of every race or color, are equal at the bar of this court," Chief Justice Smith pronounced. He suggested that taking account of any differences in the condition of defendants would involve being "excepted" from the rules of procedure. But doing so would insult the integrity of justice itself. Speaking for his colleagues, he noted, "we would feel deeply humiliated" at such an outcome.[6]

This horrific case generated a powerful dissent from Justice Virgil A. Griffith, who painstakingly recounted the racially tinged investigatory tactics of the sheriff's office. He decried the convening of a "lynching party" and the use of "torture" to obtain evidence. Quoting the deputy's own testimony, he left little doubt that these techniques appeared to be standard practice for black suspects but not for white suspects. Justice Griffith called it a "solemn farce" that the Sheriff of Kemper County, who did not himself participate in the beatings but plainly saw the rope burns on Ellington's neck and injuries on all three suspects, calmly appeared in the light of day to listen to their "free and voluntary" confessions so he could serve as a witness in court. The sheriff even invited lawmen from other counties and a minister to listen to the incriminating statements by the suspects.

Characterizing the entire proceeding as a charade from beginning to end, Justice Griffith urged that "no court shall by adoption give legitimacy to any of the works of the mob." What occurred was "a pretended legal trial" that merely ratified "the product of the mob." He spared no words in excoriating his own colleagues, who "by closing the eyes to actualities, complacently adjudicate that the law of the land has been observed and preserved."[7]

When Brown's case reached the U.S. Supreme Court, the Justices ordered a new trial. Writing for a unanimous court, Chief Justice Hughes adopted Justice Griffith's lengthy factual dissent verbatim. This unusual move further publicized an already detailed and brave piece of writing, giving the strong impression that racial discrimination had infected the investigation and subsequent trial.[8]

Nevertheless, the Justices did not find a violation of the principle of egalitarianism. Instead, they held in *Brown v. Mississippi* that the state denied all three defendants the right of due process by contriving a conviction "resting solely upon confessions obtained by violence." What the state had done was to "substitute trial by ordeal" for a jury trial, rendering that proceeding "a mere pretense."

In other words, trials are run like a rule-based game with winners and losers, but the state had broken the rules by trying to cheat even before the game had officially commenced. Mississippi had swapped out "the witness chair" for the extralegal "rack and torture chamber." In doing so, government officials had subverted the entire point of the exercise. Chief Justice Charles Evans Hughes declared, "[T]he whole proceeding is but a mask" for "mob domination." The methods used by Mississippi to extract incriminating statements were truly "revolting to the sense of justice."[9]

But if the evidence of racial discrimination seemed so compelling, why not rule on equality grounds? For one thing, the criminal process has long been treated as a complicated phenomenon, one marked by significant discretion for prosecutors, judges, and jurors. Constitutional rules that imposed new obligations might interfere with how investigations are conducted, impairing the ability of authorities to solve crimes.

For another thing, judicial precedent at that point did not impose strong limits on criminal investigation. Public safety had traditionally been considered the responsibility of state and local authorities, governed according to their policies, customs, and priorities. The rule of federalism—or a fundamental division of power between states and federal governments—barred federal judges from later upsetting criminal convictions reached in state courts, except in rare circumstances. The federal government possessed no general power to prescribe ordinary rules or policies in matters of criminal law and punishment.

A landmark precedent from 1880 called *Strauder v. West Virginia* marked the first time the Supreme Court relied on the Fourteenth Amendment's Equal Protection Clause to overturn a conviction reached under state law. A black man was tried before an all-white jury because West Virginia permitted only white males to serve on juries. According to the Justices, that law amounted to "a brand" on African Americans "affixed by the law, an assertion of their inferiority," and operated as "a stimulant" to race prejudice. Though seemingly helpful, the decision had dealt only with the composition of juries, rather than the conduct of local lawmen or prosecutors. Using equality to resolve Brown's case required a major expansion of *Strauder*.[10]

And even if people could agree that egalitarianism should be the ground for a decision, many held sharply divergent ideas of what equality required. The vigorous dispute among the Mississippi judges over whether justice was done encapsulated the intractable nature of debates over equality. On the one hand, the jurists in the majority insisted that any recognition of a defendant's race or impoverished condition would be tantamount to unequal justice. On the other hand, Justice Griffith's dissent insisted that we should care about more than observing certain formalities—we should also worry about a miscarriage of justice.

All of these factors tended to push lawyers and jurists away from employing the principle of egalitarianism, even when faced with an egregious case of racial discrimination. That's the bad news. The good news is that the *Brown* decision by the U.S. Supreme Court offered a tantalizing roadmap of how to pursue equality by other means.

Taking practical justice seriously entails accomplishing three objectives. First, an official must find a way to address the harms of inequality suffered by a complainant without unreasonable delay. Second, where egalitarianism is not available as the justification for a decision, officials must fulfill their duty by using a next-best rationale. Third, one must strive to avoid creating a tragic precedent that serves as a significant new obstacle to grappling effectively with pervasive inequality.

By these lights, *Brown* accomplished these goals admirably, even if it did not vindicate the ideal of equality openly. To begin, the ruling offered tangible relief from the criminal convictions, and lifted the sentences of death. No delay of justice occurred simply because of a dispute over legal abstractions. Justice Hughes's opinion stressed how these "revolting" methods were employed against "three ignorant, Kemper county Negroes."

Judging by reactions to the ruling, the public saw that justice was served. "Negro Convictions Vacated by Court," the *New York Times* declared after the decision was handed down. "Justice Hughes Likens Mississippi Case to 'Rack and Torture' to Get Confessions." The

Washington Post applauded the Court's "rebuke" of the state's methods as a vindication of "the ideal of 'equal justice under law.' "[11]

Moreover, the Supreme Court's conclusion that the state had violated a basic notion of fair play not only offered a way of solving a discrete problem of "compulsion by torture," but also helped to foster a culture of equal respect. The ruling warned everyone who plays a role in the administration of the justice system—police, prosecutors, judges—they may neither participate in the denial of one's rights nor turn a blind eye to obvious evidence that manifest injustice has occurred. "In the instant case, the trial court was fully advised by the undisputed evidence of the way in which the confessions had been procured," Chief Justice Hughes diagnosed. "Yet it proceeded to permit conviction and to pronounce sentence."

Standing by stoically in this situation, as the trial judge had done, did not serve justice but instead thwarted justice. The introduction of tainted confessions required someone to "supply corrective process." If local officials did not provide that corrective, federal judges would have to intervene and ensure that a trial complied with basic notions of fairness.

In promoting equality through alternative means, the case could have a ripple effect. Prosecutors like to keep track of their cases in terms of wins and losses. So do ambitious judges. Since few prosecutors and judges enjoy being second-guessed by higher-ranking counterparts and having wins later turned into losses, they might think twice about introducing tainted evidence, and perhaps even monitor how suspects are questioned.

The use of the fair play principle in the criminal context paved the way for the creation of obligatory national legal norms over time. It did so by encouraging others to critique and expose state and local criminal practices for their unsporting nature. Even though *Brown* could not technically be called an equality-based decision, the Justices nevertheless exposed the inherent inequality of the lawmen's practice, in so many words. By using fair play as the rationale for a unanimous opinion, the Court showed that moral outrage at grossly unfair state actions could do nearly as much good as moral outrage that singled out perpetrators as bigots.

Finally, if *Brown* produced beneficial effects for equality, the flip side was also true: the Supreme Court avoided authoring an opinion that might have created a ruinous precedent. Imagine if the Justices had decisively rejected a racial discrimination claim, or followed the Mississippi court's example by completely ignoring how evidence was procured. Such a decision would have created perverse incentives for law enforcement. Like *Plessy v. Ferguson*, such an outcome would have given the green light to all kinds of oppressive and racially discriminatory methods—this time by entrenching them more deeply in the criminal justice system. So long as a judge and prosecutor later conducted the public trial strictly by the book, a conviction based on ill-gotten evidence would be unimpeachable. The disastrous message would have been unmistakable: the ends justify the means.

In a sense, the Justices of the U.S. Supreme Court faced a double responsibility by the time *Brown* landed on their desks: they had to do something about the tragic precedent created by the state court and they had to find a rationale that would not legitimize what occurred below or foster other forms of racial discrimination.

The ideal of fair play presumes that every participant in an important activity should be treated with a measure of respect, and that a departure from this norm of fairness casts the legitimacy of outcomes in doubt. This logic makes the concept of fair play a powerful tool because it forces law enforcement officers to think several steps ahead about the consequences of their actions. As Justice Hughes explained, practices that are "revolting" to our collective sense of fair play could throw the entire legal process into doubt down the road. This is no small thing: in criminal cases, it usually means a new trial or resentencing. Years later, the state may run into trouble locating witnesses and other evidence for a retrial, or securing the same verdict in a changed social climate.

Furthermore, extreme tactics of this sort are not employed against just anyone. They have a historical pedigree and are unleashed in a particular sociological context. Lynching and other forms of vigilantism filled gaps in the formal justice system in the southern and western parts of the United States. Mobs acted when a community desired swift, often bloodthirsty, resolution of a grievance against a person in their midst. But community members were prone to seek rough justice against racial or religious minorities because they already found certain undesirables suspicious and because they did not believe there would be any consequences for circumventing the legal process.

In fact, perpetrators of mob violence believe they are engaged in the expression of moral outrage and a restoration of the social order. As the Mississippi case showed, the coerced confessions were secured by lawmen acting in concert with other leading figures. The statements emerged as part of a community activity intended to send a stern warning to minorities to remember their place in the social hierarchy. In the Deep South of the 1930s, the state's relentless pursuit of these black men demonstrated that the minds and bodies of racial minorities didn't belong to them alone. Special, terrible punishments would be meted out against nonwhite offenders.

All of this means that rooting out underhanded tactics will necessarily redound to the benefit of political minorities. Procedural regularity, as much as substantive equality, can send a vital message about one's standing in the political community. This message is an inclusive one: everyone, not just the rich or members of the racial majority, deserves a shot at a fair trial.[12]

The regulatory idea contained in *Brown* is especially vital given the context in which it was vindicated, because no criminal process had yet been initiated against the men. Ellington was essentially kidnapped and beaten, then only formally arrested and charged after he agreed to confess. Brown and Shields had been arrested at the time of their questioning, but in all three situations the state's offending conduct took place before indictment. This meant that, if developed properly, *Brown* could serve as a truly innovative precedent that helped govern the interactions between the police and ordinary citizens more broadly. Even if police have no idea whether their dealings with a citizen will ultimately lead to incriminating evidence, they must abide by basic notions of fair play.

This doesn't mean that every kind of police misbehavior will result in a sanction, but it does mean that one additional set of legal arguments and justifications is available. And the more grounds that are realistically available, the more possible it becomes to do the work of equality effectively—without deferring matters of equality indefinitely or disfiguring the principle of egalitarianism.

THE ANCIENT ROOTS OF FAIRNESS

THE FUNDAMENTAL PRINCIPLE OF due process of law has an impressive pedigree. That history helps explain why it is so resonant with Americans and their leaders. The concepts associated with the ideal of fairness go all the way back to Magna Carta, whereby King John of England agreed to no longer attack his barons by armed force without some measure of legal judgment, or *legem terrae*. These barons had grown accustomed to legal protections in the courts and increasingly weary of John's ruthless and unpredictable leadership style. They had served the Crown with affection and loyalty, but John didn't play fair.

When John suffered a major setback at the Battle of Bouvines, the barons sensed a weakness and publicly renounced their loyalty to the Crown. Enraged, King John attacked the barons' castles. But when the barons captured London, John felt the need to negotiate a truce. Magna Carta, the charter that brought an end to this civil strife on

June 15, 1215, at Runnymede, satisfied the barons enough that they renewed their oaths to the king.

Magna Carta, or "The Great Charter," ended a series of royal abuses and restored to the barons a number of feudal rights, but it also guaranteed several forward-looking legal concepts "to all free men in our kingdom." The first was that the king would now be constrained by the "law of the land." To this end the king vowed to appoint "only men that know the law of the realm and are minded to keep it well." A second protection involved a guarantee of trial by modes in common usage, or "the lawful judgment of his equals." Third, the king promised to treat "right" and "justice" as matters that can't be sold, denied, or delayed. A fourth idea—proportional punishment—should be understood as a curb on royal fury: "For a trivial offence, a free man shall be fined only in proportion to the degree of his offence, and for a serious offence correspondingly, but not so heavily as to deprive him of his livelihood."[13]

Chapter 39 of Magna Carta succinctly stated this general promise of procedural regularity: "No free man shall be seized or imprisoned, or stripped of his rights or possessions, or outlawed or exiled, or deprived of his standing in any way, nor will we proceed with force against him, or send others to do so, except by the lawful judgment of his equals or by the law of the land."[14]

Practical questions of enforcement were not far from the minds of the men at Runnymede. The charter called for the barons to elect "twenty-five of their number to keep, and cause to be observed with all their might, the peace and liberties granted and confirmed to them by this charter." This last measure authorized the use of organized force to resist royal usurpations of individual rights and liberties. But a protocol would have to be carefully observed.

First, any alleged offense by the king, his jurists, or his servants had to be made known to four of the barons and be declared in a formal claim to the Crown or chief justice, with "immediate redress" sought. Second, if the king did not redress the grievance within forty days, the four barons could then refer the matter to the entire body of twenty-five elected barons, who had the power to "distrain upon and assail us in every way possible, with the support of the whole community of the land, . . . until they have secured such redress as they have determined upon."[15]

The precise words "due process" would appear for the first time in a 1354 statute of King Edward III that confirmed the key terms of Magna Carta. Legal concepts that ensured fairness for some members of English society were extended to others as the feudal system crumbled and the nation-state took its place. For centuries, due process was understood to check arbitrary actions by the state and "to guarantee full protection for property and person to every human being who breathes English air."[16]

Plucked from British political culture and transplanted in a series of state constitutions in America, due process eventually found a home in the original U.S. Bill of Rights. Today, it has come to represent a cluster of ideas: legality over brute force, judgment over irrationality, and fair play rather than ruthless domination.

There is some overlap between due process of law and "equal protection of the laws," the more specific idea articulated separately by Americans during the Reconstruction period. While an older idea of civic equality can be traced back to Roman ideas of republicanism, it is more accurate to say that the formulation "equal protection of the laws" emerged out of a plan to deal with the peculiar forms of inequality found on American soil. Those inequities arose from frictions between white citizens and African slaves, indigenous nations, low-wage foreign laborers, and religious dissenters.

Even so, the constitutional guarantees of due process and equal protection share a common text, history, and logic. Both phrases appear in the revolutionary Fourteenth Amendment, ratified in 1868. Both clauses were inspired by the same historical circumstances sur-

rounding the civic restoration of former slaves and directed toward
future problems of inequality encountered by "any person." The persistent, complex institution of chattel slavery served as the paradigmatic
example of inequality that called for ingenious, practical, and occasionally large-scale solutions.

John Bingham served as the principal drafter of the Fourteenth
Amendment. In framing that provision, he sought "a simple, strong,
plain declaration that equal laws and equal and exact justice shall
hereafter be secured within every State of the Union."

Bingham said that he had modeled the Fourteenth Amendment
on the Magna Carta. But differences in the actual words reflected a
conscious decision to take the original language in the Bill of Rights
and to broaden its application to any person within the control of a
state: "The Magna Charta 'gave the protection of the laws only to freemen' while the Fifth Amendment used 'more comprehensive words,
no person shall be deprived of life, liberty or property without due
process of law,' . . . and by the express limitation forbade the Government . . . from making any discrimination."

Over and over in debates, proponents of the Fourteenth Amendment emphasized the power of both due process and equality to help
"the humblest, the poorest, the most despised" among us. Bingham
decried the "many instances of state injustice and oppression . . . 'cruel
and unusual punishments' have been inflicted under State laws within
this Union upon citizens, not only for crimes committed, but for
sacred duty done." He emphasized that the Fourteenth Amendment
should protect everyone, whether the victim is a "citizen" or "stranger."
The litany of past abuses by state governments included making it a
crime "to help a slave who was ready to perish; to give him shelter, or
break with him his crust of bread," as well as sending missionaries to
prison for offering religious instruction to Native Americans.[17]

Closer to our own time, the ideal of fair play has proved its social
utility, especially when the prevailing methods of debating equality

lead nowhere quickly. Consider the problem of aggressive policing in many urban places, caused by a combination of overcriminalization, lopsided investment of police resources, and at times racist decisions by policymakers or policemen in the streets.

In 1972, the Supreme Court struck down a City of Jacksonville ordinance that authorized police to arrest "rogues and vagabonds," "common gamblers," "common drunks," and "habitual loafers." Laws of this sort "are nets making easy the roundup of so-called undesirables." But the difficulty under the equality approach was twofold: first, many people had trouble distinguishing between policies based on status (usually, a no-no), and those that put certain kinds of conduct off-limits (the prototypical criminal law); and, second, few wanted to recognize any of the activity involved as valuable social goods (drinking, living off the income of others, sitting around).

Rather than find discriminatory treatment, Justice Douglas's opinion for the Court declared the law a violation of fair play. The city ordinance was unduly vague, he concluded, because it did not give fair notice to citizens about what was being criminalized. "The poor among us, the minorities" would have an especially hard time figuring out the law's commands.[18]

The malleable quality of the vagrancy law led to a second problem: a risk of arbitrary or discriminatory enforcement. Though *Papachristou v. City of Jacksonville* was not an equality decision in the formal sense, the Justices acknowledged the proequality effects of striking down the law through other means. It deprived the state of a tool by which to oppress "poor people, nonconformists, dissenters, idlers" simply because of their appearance, reputation, or a police officer's subjective judgment about what kinds of lives were valuable to society.

Justice Douglas insisted that enforcing the ideal of fairness could do some of the work of equality because "the rule of law implies equality and justice in its application." Vague laws had to be wiped out in a free society because they wrongly "teach that the scales of justice are so tipped that even-handed administration of the law is not possible." Echoing the framers of the Fourteenth Amendment, the Court declared that the rule of law must be "evenly applied to minorities as well as majorities, to the poor as well as the rich."

What makes fair play such an adaptive concept is that we can curtail the use of unjust laws or policies in complex situations where more convincing proof of actual discrimination may be very hard to come by. This is our sense about policing, which involves many large-scale decisions, overlapping laws and policies, and innumerable smaller, sometimes split-second, decisions in the field. In some ways, policing is like a system, and in other ways, like a series of sprawling and loosely connected actions. Bias operates throughout such complex spaces in nefarious ways, but it can be exceedingly difficult to expose it as the work of intentional discrimination by specific people.

Edward Lawson's odyssey is instructive. Lawson, a black male who wore his hair in dreadlocks, was detained or arrested by San Diego police fifteen times over a span of twenty-two months under a law that required anyone loitering to present "credible and reliable" identification to police and account for his presence. This looks like a compelling case of racial profiling until we realize that each of the fifteen stops could be treated as a separate encounter.

Would that alarming pattern hold up if it turned out that different officers stopped him each time and that some officers who stopped him were not white? Racial discrimination in one or more of the stops would be challenging to prove, even if we had a nagging sense that Lawson's race played in a role in making him seem more suspicious. Unlike the law of equality, fair play trains our attention on the risk of discrimination rather than proof that it has actually occurred. The realistic possibility that a law or policy could be become a "convenient tool for 'harsh and discriminatory enforcement'" is enough. Evidence of past abuse helps illustrate a potential for future abuse, but is unnecessary.[19]

Consider, too, Chicago's anti-gang loitering law from the 1990s, which allowed a police officer to disperse any gathering "with no apparent purpose" that included known gang members. Over the course of three years, police issued 89,000 orders to disperse and arrested 42,000 individuals. The vast majority of the individuals targeted by the law were people of color, but was that simply because more minority gang members happened to violate the law or because officers were selectively enforcing the law against minority populations?

There was another stumbling block: the law itself didn't overtly use racial or ethnic categories so it was harder to characterize as part of a secret plan to harm minorities. Oral argument confirmed that about half of the black aldermen in the city voted for the law, while the rest opposed it—further complicating claims of intentional bias.[20]

Once again, the Court deemed this type of law to be deeply unfair and corrosive because of its open-ended terms: "Under the Ordinance, the City need not prove any act of intimidation or obstruction, or any intent to intimidate or obstruct, or indeed any wrongdoing or wrongful intent of any kind by anyone." It allowed law enforcement to cut corners when they had no evidence of wrongdoing.

The benefits to equality from disarming the police in this way should be acknowledged. Because the law allowed police to designate certain young people dangerous due to their affiliation, and to deprive them of their rights on that basis while in public places, it became the latest strategy to zone the despised from our midst. Perversely, these aggressive policing tactics were being used in communities that already felt victimized by zealous policing. In fact, the sweeps interfered with entirely innocent people who worked with wayward youth, trying to get them off the streets and away from the intoxicating influence of gangs.

At all events, the basic ideal of due process, then and now, serves many of the same ends of democratic justice as the principle of egalitarianism, especially where it comes to curbing more outrageous forms of governmental action and ensuring notions of legality and fairness.

WHY FAIR PLAY IS SOMETIMES MORE ATTRACTIVE THAN EQUALITY

MANY ACTIVISTS, LAWYERS, AND judges have opted for the principle of fair play when discrimination might have more accurately described an act of injustice. Certainly, using the principle of egalitarianism in its full glory can make a strong moral statement. Bypassing that rationale means missing out on sending a message that prejudice is unacceptable and that those who have expressed it or condoned it are worthy of condemnation. And yet, sometimes it makes sense to accept this as one of the costs of doing justice here and now.

What makes fair play occasionally more appealing than equality as a consensus rationale? The place to start is that the concept of fairness is based on widely shared intuitions about how crucial decisions should be made. Those intuitions are that we should have some ground rules (not too many but not too few), that the rules must allow for a broad range of autonomy to take risks and make mistakes, that people should deal in good faith with one another, and that scarce resources should be allocated in a way that allows everyone a fair start but does not dictate anyone's destiny. So fairness is appealing because it fuses together a variety of values and priorities we instinctively find to be important.

Now here's the kicker: while all of these connotations are associated with the principle of fair play, most of our attention is actually focused on the rules themselves. When we invoke procedural justice we necessarily say *something* about these things, but it's not necessary to say *a lot* about them or even to take them up explicitly. We don't have to decide up front what kind of autonomy is involved or what its full scope should be in this context. We don't even have to agree about every single element that would make something truly fair and equitable, as if we were designing an ideal process from scratch. It would be helpful if we did, but it's usually good enough if we just have a rough sense of the things that are really unfair.

Those are exactly the terms on which *Brown v. Mississippi* was decided, by asking whether a practice "shocks the conscience" or "offends" our nation's history and legal tradition. It is not the only way to decide what kind of process one is due. Another method is to ask whether certain kinds of methods not being offered are crucial to our modern understanding of "fundamental fairness." Whatever the approach to implementing the principle of fair play, the basic insight holds: it's possible for people with different conceptions of morality or equality or autonomy to reach agreement on fairness grounds because the rationale papers over these differences.

It's worth noting that leading political philosophers have even developed theories of justice that depend on these intuitions. Questions of justice can be converted into questions of how valuable social goods, including legal rights, are allocated by a society. This is why philosophers like John Rawls insist that the initial assignment of "basic liberties" must be done on an equal basis. Everyone should have the same access to the rights of speech, liberty, equality, and so on. He treats the distribution of wealth and income to implicate justice, too, but these are questions of a secondary order subject to a different rule. Reflecting this sense that some matters of equality can be redescribed as matters of fair play, Rawls would later describe his approach as "Justice as Fairness," which enables citizens to participate in "a system of fair cooperation for mutual advantage." Rawls insists that his theory draws upon "basic intuitive ideas" embedded in a democracy's political institutions and public traditions.[21]

Rawls isn't the only one who believes that some notion of fairness plays a central role in justice. Libertarian theorist Robert Nozick, who comes to very different answers about what a just society looks like than the redistributionist Rawls, also talks about justice in terms that evoke a popular belief in fair play. For Nozick, each person is endowed with a set of basic rights over life, health, liberty, and possessions. If one accumulates goods legitimately each time according to rules established in advance, those holdings are justly held, even though it may result in some people having more possessions in the end than others. Nozick employs the example of Wilt Chamberlain, who maximized his natural gifts to make millions of dollars as a basketball player. If Chamberlain signs a contract that gives him a share of ticket sales, and fans consent to give him money, then he is entitled to the giant pile of money that he gains. Government redistribution of Chamberlain's wealth interferes with his property and disturbs the natural pattern of his choices based on his investments and hard work.[22]

The point here isn't whether Rawls or Nozick is right about what constitutes a just society, but instead that they, like so many ordinary people, assume that fairness is a fundamental idea for organizing a community. The idea of fair dealing encompasses ideas of autonomy or dignity, as well as an expectation that everyone will play the game in good faith according to the rules. Even Plato, who expressed skepticism of democracy and social equality, insisted that the state must treat its citizens fairly. Where conservatives and liberals seem to agree is that there exists a point at which the concept of fairness can be a close substitute for equality. Whether we call it the "initial conditions that permit fair play," or "formal equality," or "preserving equality of opportunity," there is a vast intellectual space where ideologies meet and mix. Out of this philosophical overlap, it is possible to reach common ground to solve real problems.

For instance, Nozick says, "Every individual does have the right that information sufficient to show that a procedure of justice about to be applied to him is reliable and fair (or no less so than other procedures in use) be publicly available or made available to him. He has the right to be shown that he is being handled by some reliable and fair system. . . . No one has a right to use a relatively unreliable procedure in order to punish another."

This is a description of fair play many others share. That a conservative libertarian like Nozick embraces the basic idea of procedural regularity helps explain why *Brown v. Mississippi* could be such a strong, unanimous decision. Coerced confessions are unreliable, they rob an individual of his dignity, they violate a person's bodily integrity, and it is a means of cheating one's way to a verdict by stacking the deck ahead of a trial. By the time lawyers are appointed for the suspects, there isn't much that can be done. Good liberals, faithful conservatives, and suspicious libertarians can all find something to like in the decision.[23]

At the same time, practical egalitarians should see that a fairness argument can prevail in situations where proof of a bad motive is hard to muster. These gains from using a more flexible instrument can offset some of the losses from avoiding a more direct approach. When a debate becomes intractable, the question for practical egalitarians becomes: is it better to do nothing and stand pat, cognizant that inequality may worsen, or to embrace fairness as a close substitute for equality, knowing that improvements can create conditions for future action?

Another aspect of fairness that makes it capable of breaking an ideological logjam is that it is less morally judgmental than the idea of equality. The power of egalitarianism, as we saw earlier, comes from its ability to root out prejudice by judging wrongdoers in explicitly moral terms. The bureaucrat who denies all Chinese applicants a permit to run a laundry in San Francisco acts "with an evil eye and an unequal hand." Legislators who prohibit people of different races from marrying do so "to maintain White Supremacy." Those who pass laws barring same-sex marriage "demean" sexual minorities, and "stigmatize" and "humiliate" children raised in those relationships.[24]

Any deterrence effect flows from the power of equality as a legal discourse to call out a truly illiberal motivation and to stigmatize those who act out of bias. And once someone is satisfied that animus of some sort motivated the state's course of conduct, flexibility disappears over what to do about it: there is simply no reason that can ever justify animus of any sort. A policy animated by bigotry must be stricken.

Such moral conclusions mark a wrongdoer in ways that are essential in a liberal democracy, but it presumes people can agree that this level of censure is justified. And so the very facet of equality that makes it distinctive is also what can serve as an impediment to a consensus decision. Remember that all matters of justice are collective decisions. A politician must make policy decisions with constituents in mind, and one eye on reelection. A trial judge is subject to review by a higher court. An appellate judge must find rationales that gain the assent of other members of the tribunal, and might also have to stand for reelection. For a judicial order to be effective, other members of society must be willing to enforce it.

To say fair play is less morally judgmental than equality isn't the same as saying there is no moral content whatsoever. But it does shift the focus of moral outrage in an important respect, away from the motivations of actual wrongdoers and toward the inadequacy of laws, policies, and practices. The redirection of moral outrage is a subtle change but a significant one. There is a sense in which the principle of fairness takes some of the heat out of debate. It is also more constructive by nature because it re-centers arguments on what is lacking in a policy's design or operation, and on what would better promote fairness.

One can imagine due process cases that are less sensational than the facts of *Brown*, but that raise major stakes for regular folks nonetheless. In fact, most of the landmark due process cases involved utterly mundane things: turning off someone's utility service for unpaid bills, terminating disability benefits, investigating and possibly reprimanding physicians for professional misconduct, suspending misbehaving students from school. No one would get all that exercised about such matters unless they were directly involved.[25]

Another attractive feature of fair play, especially for those who are cautious by disposition, is that its reformative potential is not as sweeping as that of the concept of equality. There is something perceived to be less threatening about the *consequences* of saying that the principle of fair dealing has been transgressed. In contrast, a finding of inequality feels more dangerous because it means that access to a valuable social good must be granted to everyone. In case after case, from public schools to marriage to the franchise, we are reminded that equal access is the default rule.

For many, the remedy compelled by egalitarianism transforms the nature of an institution or experience before their very eyes. This sense of cultural disruption is enhanced if there are strong feelings of traditionalism, nostalgia, affection, or other social benefits tied to the status quo.

Violations of fair play can sometimes lead to major reformation, but they don't have to have that kind of impact. The goal, after all, is to restore an activity to its natural state, where players can engage in give-and-take and make strategic decisions. Such solutions leave a great deal of wiggle room for public servants to act. In the wake of the *Brown* case, Mississippi prosecutors could retry the three men, if there was sufficient evidence without the tainted confessions. After *Papachristou*, the police could still arrest people if they had probable cause that a crime was being committed or detain someone temporarily if suspicions warranted further investigation.

Looking beyond the defendants themselves, police and prosecutors can still aggressively solve crimes. Trial judges retain the ability to manage their courtrooms. Neither *Brown* nor *Papachristou* requires police to do anything more. They just have to resist using outrageous and unreliable methods. The state can't railroad a suspect, i.e., "permit an accused to be hurried to conviction under mob domination," or rely on shortcuts like overly vague laws. Special and brutal methods raise concerns, while regularized methods of making important decisions, especially those with "a long and consistent application," allay worries. And claims of exigency by the state can always alter the calculus in terms of what kind of procedure makes most sense.[26]

The comparatively less disruptive nature of fairness leads to a final observation: decisions on this ground are somewhat less likely to generate major blowback. Because fair play needn't mark others as bigots nor erect permanent obstacles to political goals, resistance is harder to generate. Contrast this lighter touch with *Roe v. Wade* and *Brown v. Board of Education*, both of which created far more significant obstacles to local objectives through a recognition of substantive liberty and equality rights, provoked major political resistance, and even generated second-guessing by progressives that other priorities were overlooked. Where the idea of fair play is used merely to trim the edges of a policy, leaving discretion in place, the easier path for a grumbling policymaker may be to do the damn thing over, rather than waste energy trying to gin up popular anger.[27]

WHEN BIGOTRY IS HARD TO ADMIT

FAST FORWARD TO JANUARY 27, 2017, when President Trump moved to fulfill his campaign promise to ban Muslims from entering the country. In his first week in office, he signed an executive order that dramatically reduced the number of Syrian refugees that could be admitted to the United States and indefinitely barred travel from seven Muslim-majority countries. Scenes of widespread confusion accompanied the rollout of the administration's new policy, with unknown numbers of travelers detained all over America, officials in the administration complaining publicly that they had not been consulted beforehand, and travelers pulled from planes and left stranded in other countries.[28]

State officials in Washington, Oregon, California, New York, and elsewhere complained about the order's effects on their economies. "There is a sense of bewilderment, as well as a sense of injustice" over being included on the list of targeted countries, lamented Trita Parsi, president of the National Iranian American Council. Foreign governments registered their dismay at the disruptions, with the Iraqi parliament voting to retaliate by enacting "reciprocal measures."[29]

Within hours of the executive order's announcement, volunteer lawyers and activists descended on airports, offering assistance to detained travelers and distraught family members. Protests of the executive order were broadcast on television and social media, and even supporters of the president's action lamented how things were handled.

The first lawsuit to reach a decision on Executive Order 13769 was brought by the attorney general for the State of Washington on behalf of university students and faculty, who argued that the order interfered with their ability to study and work. A federal trial judge in Seattle entered a temporary restraining order, and the federal government appealed that order.

Despite the fact that a "Muslim ban" had been a signature proposal of Trump's campaign, members of the appeals court could not agree that the president acted out of religious hostility. At least one judge had trouble concluding that President Trump had discriminated against Muslims. During oral argument, Judge Richard Clifton wondered aloud whether they should ignore the president's inflammatory campaign statements and focus instead on the fact that the order talks about country of origin rather than religious affiliation. He also struggled with the fact that the restrictions affected only a handful of countries, or roughly 12 percent of the Muslim population worldwide. "I have trouble understanding why we're supposed to infer religious ani-

mus when in fact the vast majority of Muslims would not be affected."
If this was really the fulfillment of his campaign pledge, the judge
inquired, then why didn't President Trump exclude all Muslims, or at
least many more than he did?[30]

Now, there are some excellent answers to the judge's line of questioning. One need not discriminate against all members of a group
before a finding of animus should be made, for it is just as much a violation if even a single member of a group is affected. The key is whether
there is enough evidence to say that the government intended to discriminate on the basis of religion. That other predominantly Muslim
countries like Saudi Arabia and Egypt did not appear on the list may
suggest that other matters factored into the government's calculus as
well, but should not diminish the fact that religious hostility was a
motivating factor in restricting Muslim travelers.

The undeniable fact remained that the travelers singled out for the
ban came from countries where 97 percent of the population belong
to the Muslim faith. A coincidence? Highly unlikely, given the administration's comments about the ban and the general ethnonationalist
tenor of President Trump's candidacy. Moreover, the administration
offered no reason to believe that travelers from the targeted countries
presented any more of a security threat than travelers from other countries. These facts offered more than enough evidence from which to
infer that hostility to Islam prompted the ban. Still, the panel struggled to make that finding.

Remarkably, the judges did not allow a disagreement over the
equality issue to paralyze them. Instead, they concluded in *Washington v. Trump* that the administration had violated the due process
rights of aliens, whether their connection to the United States was
"lawful, unlawful, temporary, or permanent." Despite his qualms over
the equality claim, Judge Clifton joined his colleagues on the fairness
argument to make it a unanimous decision.

The judges denounced the "shifting interpretations of the Executive Order" by the administration's own lawyers and officials. They found three kinds of procedural irregularities. First, the Executive Order failed to provide green-card holders sufficient notice and an opportunity to be heard before altering the benefits of lawful permanent resident status. Second, the order deprived lawful residents and nonimmigrant visa holders of their liberty interest in traveling abroad and reentering the United States. Third, the policy violated procedures established by Congress for handling asylum claims.[31]

This decision was a textbook use of alternative means to promote equality. It is hard to know why the judges refused to address the religious equality claims. Perhaps they differed over whether the evidence of bad motivation was strong enough. Maybe the judges didn't like the prospect of tarring a president with the inflammatory label of religious bigotry so early in his tenure. They might have worried that applying the principle of egalitarianism to decisions involving border security and immigration would tie a president's hands, especially when the individuals affected have weak or no ties to the United States. Whatever the reasons, the key is that jurists simply could not reach consensus under stress about the meaning of equality in the dispute at hand.[32]

To their credit, however, the judges' hesitation over the equality argument did not lead them to reject that rationale decisively and thereby make bad law. Rather, the court found a way to avoid saying anything definitive about the scope of equality. The panel merely "reserved" the equality claims and noted that they raised "serious" concerns.

Most important of all, the rationale endorsed by the panel—due process—helped promote equality norms. Some travelers and lawful permanent residents associated with these mostly Muslim countries had initially been treated differently than other travelers and immigrants. This was also true of refugees, who were not allowed to apply for asylum if they came from one of the seven affected countries, and this practice deviated from how other asylum seekers were being treated under federal law. The panel's ruling suggested that all of these forms of differential treatment could also be understood as forms of procedural injustice.

A victory based on the plaintiffs' due process claims entitled them to a nationwide injunction against the president's order, just as if the panel had found that President Trump harbored religious animosity against Muslims. As a result, the ruling immediately stopped harms from being inflicted on a vulnerable population and forced the government to rethink its policy.

It also forced the administration to give its policy a sober second look, and even a third. After the decision, President Trump decided to revise his executive order to retain a country-based suspension of travel, but reduce the number of people affected by his policy. The second order excluded all lawful permanent residents and visa holders from the travel ban. Only about half of the immigrants from these countries had become naturalized U.S. citizens, so this change alone made it easier for this population to travel unmolested. The new policy dropped one country, Iraq, from the list. Iraq had the second-most number of lawful entries to the United States since 2006—some 254,483 people who came to study, work, or see family and friends. So even this change significantly reduced the disparate impact of the ban on Muslims.[33]

Additionally, the revised executive order fixed another source of unequal treatment. It deleted a provision that had given immigration officials discretion to exempt asylum seekers who are members of "a religious minority" in those countries "facing religious persecution." President Trump had earlier touted this measure as a means of helping Christian refugees "unfairly" kept out of the United States, but critics cited it as additional evidence of animus against Muslims. Rather than continue to defend this differential treatment of asylum seekers based on religion, the administration opted for a new procedure that treated them all the same.[34]

President Trump gave several reasons for the new suspension of travel: each of the six countries had been a sponsor of terrorism, had been "significantly compromised by terrorist organizations," or contained "active conflict zones." These uncertain conditions prevented the United States from obtaining necessary information from these countries about travelers and increased the chances that terrorists or sympathizers could exploit the situation to threaten national security.

Almost immediately, the revised travel ban encountered a fresh wave of legal challenges across the country. A federal judge in Hawaii and another in Maryland separately ruled that the changes did not alter the main tenor of the policy, which remained infected by anti-Muslim sentiment. A third federal judge in Virginia, however, treated the new executive order as no longer facially discriminatory, finding that it was not accompanied by "contemporaneous statements suggesting discriminatory intent." The president's broad authority over national security, Judge Anthony Trenga wrote, required courts to defer to policy judgments in this area and to not "disable" a president's authority by holding his past statements against him forever.[35]

Eventually, the Trump administration withdrew each of the previous two versions of the travel ban and issued a third order in late September 2017, dropping one more country (Sudan, 97 percent Muslim) from the list and adding two others: Chad (where about 53 percent are Muslim) and North Korea. The trend of reducing religious inequities continued.

That judges and policymakers continued to disagree over the scope of equality is not surprising, but it is possible to draw a few lessons. To begin, fair play can be preferable to equality, but it is not a complete substitute. In this situation, it took care of some of the inequities created by the original travel ban, but President Trump stuck with country-based restrictions rather than moving toward a more nuanced approach to screening out potentially dangerous arrivals from all countries. At that point, the only way to force him to deviate from that path would be to secure a finding that the specific country-based solution amounted to invidious discrimination or lacked a rational basis.

Americans got their answer on June 26, 2018: A divided Supreme Court approved the travel ban 5–4. According to Chief Justice Roberts, immigration law gave a president "broad discretion to suspend the entry of aliens into the United States." He rejected the religious equality claim because the ban itself "says nothing about religion," and "the policy covers just 8% of the world's Muslim population and is limited to countries that were previously designated by Congress or prior administrations as posing national security risks."[36]

Then in a cynical move, the majority denounced *Korematsu* as "gravely wrong the day it was decided, [and] has been overruled in the court of history." While long overdue, we shouldn't make too much of this statement. This is because the reasoning of *Trump v. Hawaii* made many of the same mistakes as *Korematsu*: it failed to probe the government's claim of national security and ignored strong evidence of anti-Muslim hostility. As a result, the Justices simply replaced one despised and faulty precedent with another. They even left in place an internment-era case called *Hirabayashi v. United States*, which had approved a race-based curfew, and can still be used to cause all kinds of mischief.

As disappointing as this ruling may have been, it doesn't detract from the valuable lesson that a strategy of practical equality repeatedly forced the administration to modify a deeply unequal policy. In fact, the Justices pointed out the various changes spurred by fairness arguments, including the fact that three Muslim-majority countries had been dropped from the original ban, and that "significant" exceptions and waivers for "humanitarian" reasons had been created. The Court expected the administration to implement these conditions in good faith. If they were a sham, more legal challenges could sniff that out.

From that point on, judges might require officials to tinker with the policy. But for wholesale changes, it's up to social activism and elections to show the foolishness of these measures. Judges can't stop ethnonationalist agendas on their own. Only politics can give us those assurances.

HOW FAIRNESS CAN AVOID TRAGEDY

LET'S NOW TURN TO a third scenario, a missed opportunity to do the work of equality through other methods. By a 5–4 vote, the Supreme Court rejected a claim of racial discrimination in the application of Georgia's death penalty. Sadly, advocates and judges might have done more harm than good by pressing the equality claim to a final resolution. Not only did the Justices end up distorting the principle of egalitarianism in a close case, they also established a tragic precedent. That 1987 decision, *McCleskey v. Kemp*, left the impression that black lives were expendable and white lives were more valuable. The author of the opinion, Justice Powell, later disavowed his own ruling. Everyone might have been better served if the principle of fair play had been used to address some of the inequities identified in the criminal justice system.[37]

The case involved Warren McCleskey, a black man convicted of murdering a white police officer in a robbery gone wrong. McCleskey had grown up in a home filled with domestic violence, but he maintained good grades as a student and played football to stay out of trouble. Whenever he struggled to make ends meet, he turned to armed robbery, which landed him in prison. Once released, he alternately tried to get his life together and fell back on his old ways. On the fateful day he became eligible for Georgia's death penalty, McCleskey and three other ex-cons decided to rob a furniture store. An officer who responded to a silent alarm was shot in the face during the crime, and one of McCleskey's compatriots later fingered him as the shooter.[38]

After a jury convicted McCleskey of murder and sentenced him to die in the electric chair, experts got involved and conducted a statistical study of 2,000 murder cases in Georgia since the 1970s. What they discovered underwrote the equality claims made by McCleskey's lawyers. Strong statistical disparities emerged. According to the study led by David C. Baldus, black and white defendants were treated differently when it came to death cases, and those differences were most pronounced in cross-racial killings when black defendants were accused of killing white victims. After running multiple regressions that took account of 230 nonracial variables, the following disparities remained: black defendants accused of killing a white person received the death penalty 22 percent of the time, whereas whites charged with killing blacks accounted for 8 percent of death sentences. Defendants accused of killing white victims were 4.3 times more likely to receive a death sentence than those who killed a black person.

Drawing on this sophisticated study, McCleskey's lawyers offered two possible explanations: first, people who murder whites are more likely to be sentenced to death than those who murder blacks; alternatively, black murderers are more likely to receive the death penalty than white murderers. Either way, they argued, the state had violated the principle of equality.[39]

The evidence proved to be alarming, but things got complicated when it came time to assign blame—a central function of egalitarianism. Who exactly was doing the discriminating? It was unlikely to be Georgia legislators, who enacted a race-neutral law. One couldn't simply say "the system," at least not without dramatically altering the way that equality questions had long been resolved. For as long as anyone could remember, those cases required that a particular state actor be identified as having intentionally treated others differently. It wasn't "purposeful discrimination" if one person, or several people, accidentally created a condition of inequality. Thus, the Justices stumbled over the moral dimension of the principle of egalitarianism. If they couldn't settle on who was acting maliciously, then they would have no one to single out for their outrage and they couldn't deter future wrongdoing. So in *McCleskey v. Kemp*, five members of the Supreme Court threw up their collective hands and found that no one was responsible for these racial disparities.

What this case illustrated was a basic flaw of today's equality approach. It proved incapable of dealing with problems of pervasive inequality when multiple actors are involved, each possessing a measure of discretion that can be abused. A little bit of racism here and a little more over there would be very hard to flush out if you were discreet about it. Equal protection jurisprudence did not help and, as we shall soon see, could make matters worse. That McCleskey needed judges to overhaul how they generally thought about inequality, so they could see violations in structural terms, meant that he faced an uphill battle from the get-go.

If this weren't bad enough, next came a move of calamitous proportions. It happened because the Supreme Court feared the reformative power of egalitarianism. Faced with the possibility that a victory for McCleskey might call into question death sentences in other states, or perhaps even other inequities throughout the criminal justice system, the Justices tried to shut down these kinds of grievances.

Prosecutors from other states urged the Supreme Court to reject McCleskey's equality claim because it "strikes at the heart of the judicial system." Victims' rights groups even raised the absurd specter of affirmative action in sentencing, warning that if he prevailed, "the jurisprudence of racial and ethnic proportionality will be carried to unprecedented extremes in the governance of this nation."[40]

The sky-is-falling argument worked. "What if one accepts the study as reflecting sound statistical analysis?" Justice Powell wondered aloud in internal memos to his colleagues. "Would this require that no black be sentenced to death where victim was white?" Other correspondence showed that Powell saw the ramifications of McCleskey's equality claim to be revolutionary: "petitioner's challenge is no less than to our entire criminal justice system."[41]

So the majority not only rejected McCleskey's equality claim, they also felt the need to insulate the criminal justice system as a whole from future allegations of this sort. "Because discretion is essential to the criminal justice process," they sternly advised, from now on "we would demand exceptionally clear proof before we would infer that discretion has been abused." The reason they gave for this new rule was a prosecutor's "traditionally 'wide discretion'" in making charging decisions and presenting cases. What's more, they turned the question of fairness to defendants into a matter of fairness to the government! It seemed unfair to "requir[e] prosecutors to defend their decision to seek death penalties, 'often years after they were made.'"[42]

There are just two giant problems with this reasoning. First, prosecutors are no different in this regard than legislators or other executive officers in our democratic system. All must justify the use of force against other human beings, and sometimes they are called upon to explain their actions years later. Even police officers, who must make split-second decisions on the street, are subject to constitutional rules that constrain their use of force. Prosecutors don't have that excuse, so what makes prosecutors so special that their decisions to authorize legalized violence should be insulated from judicial review?

Second, if there is one actor within the criminal justice system who can play an outsized role in making racial disparities worse, it is the prosecutor. That person alone determines when the death penalty will be sought and why it might later be taken off the table in a bargain for a lesser sentence. There may be sound reasons for doing so, or impermissible reasons, but we would never know which if life-determining decisions are not subject to some legal review.

Prosecutors, unlike jurors, are elected locally and therefore especially susceptible to pressure from constituents and law enforcement, and sensitive to the demands of reelection. Those pressures push prosecutors to trade in death as a way of assuring longevity in their careers. A prosecutor is accountable to local politics and cultural norms. Cross-racial killings heighten these pressures, especially where the alleged perpetrator is black.

In fact, the Baldus study confirmed this hypothesis that prosecutors are the most likely culprits in exacerbating racial disparities, either by making race-based charging decisions or because the office is highly sensitive to external politics. Georgia prosecutors pursued death sentences in 70 percent of the cases involving black suspects who allegedly killed whites and only 19 percent of the time when whites were suspected of killing blacks. Powell's opinion mentioned this finding, but then not only ignored it, but also gave reasons to insulate the decision-making process that can lead to such racially disparate outcomes.[43]

In the end, the Supreme Court identified no particular flaws in how the study was conducted. The Justices did not deny that the unexplained racial patterns appeared troubling, which in other cases involving redistricting or employment or jury selection have been enough to infer purposeful discrimination. They just found new reasons not to draw that inference. Those reasons seemed largely consequential in nature: rendering justice on equality grounds might require more scrutiny for other criminal cases, and we might be disturbed by what we see.

"[I]f we accepted McCleskey's claim that racial bias has impermissibly tainted the capital sentencing decision," Justice Powell wrote, "we could soon be faced with similar claims as to other types of penalty." People charged with crimes might even extend the argument to other "unexplained discrepancies that correlate to membership in other minority groups." He then suggested that if they didn't shut down this line of inquiry, a defendant down the road might contend that he faced discrimination because of his facial characteristics or lack of physical attractiveness. The upshot: absent smoking gun evidence that a legislature, a particular prosecutor, or a judge acted with racial malice in a particular case, it would be impossible to show bias.[44]

If *Brown v. Mississippi* had restored hope in the ideal of impartial justice, then *McCleskey* dealt that dream a devastating blow. Justice Powell advised anyone reading his opinion that racial disparities are "an inevitable part of our criminal justice system." *Brown* said so much less, but allowed people to imagine that justice was attainable. By contrast, *McCleskey*, while saying so much more, sent a bleak message: we had to choose between racial justice and legal order. But the two ideas are closely connected. Good order cannot exist without justice.[45]

A decision of this sort is reactionary: a fear of reform led those in charge to entrench their own power by any means necessary rather than to expose the use of force to the rule of law. Extraordinary rules were devised to ensure unfettered prosecutorial discretion, reinforcing a lingering suspicion that some lives don't matter as much as others. As William Stuntz puts it, *McCleskey* seemingly "allows prosecutors and judges to punish crimes that victimize whites more severely than crimes that victimize blacks" by making discrimination almost impossible to prove.[46]

It's even more dispiriting because a precedent of this sort, once established, becomes exponentially more difficult to alter. Under the common law system, judges must respect a decision of their colleagues and will not overturn a prior ruling unless it is clearly wrong or subsequent events show the ruling has proved unworkable. Stability is its own virtue, even if a past ruling is unwise or harms others. Now, the added hurdle of judicial acquiescence becomes part of the problem of racial injustice.

Prosecutors around the country cheered *McCleskey* for its defense of their prerogative, but it faced a different reception from jurists and activists concerned about racial injustice. Justice Brennan, joined by three other dissenters, described the majority's protection of discretion in the justice system at all costs as "a fear of too much justice." The ruling amounted to "an abdication" of the judicial role, they said. Likewise, the NAACP called the decision "a significant barrier to the elimination of racial inequalities in the criminal justice system." "*McCleskey* is the *Dred Scott* decision of our time," thundered Anthony Amsterdam, a NYU law professor. Amsterdam predicted that "our children's children will reproach our generation and abhor the legal legacy we leave them."[47]

Unfortunately, the Supreme Court missed the opportunity to seek common ground based on the principle of fair play. They became too caught up with trying to assign moral blame and fretting over the reformative power of egalitarianism. In fact, most of Powell's ruling focused on shielding the work of juries, lingering over not only the value of sentencing discretion but also the strides that states had made in requiring the finding of certain statutory factors before a death sentence may be imposed. "*Petitioner challenges our jury system*," Justice Powell advised in his internal communications.[48]

Instead of worrying that an equality-based ruling would impair the work of juries, the Court should have considered that more legal guidance might have been necessary at the front end: the prosecutor's decision of whether to seek death in the first place. The fairness approach would have treated human beings, even suspected murderers, as worthy of dignity and respect. Not only might this option have reduced racial disparities, it would also have left jury discretion untouched in the case. For this reason, due process might have been a better basis for consensus.

A single prosecutor making arbitrary or racially discriminatory choices can create enormous problems of justice, both when a defendant's circumstances are compared to other similar defendants within the jurisdiction, and when cases are compared across jurisdictions. To underscore how unconstrained prosecutors can create problems of comparative justice: fifteen counties account for 30 percent of all death sentences in the United States since 1976, and those counties come from only four states: Texas, Oklahoma, Missouri, and Arizona. In that same time period, three prosecutors in America put 131 persons on death row.[49]

In Georgia there are forty-nine district attorneys representing each of the state's judicial circuits, each with a different approach to handling eligible death cases. Any racial disparities in these practices are merely magnified over time. Buried on page 56 of McCleskey's brief in the Supreme Court were these facts that might have made out a due process claim:

> The District Attorney for Fulton County, where petitioner was tried, acknowledged that capital cases in his jurisdiction were handled by a dozen or more assistants. . . . The office had no written or oral policies or guidelines to determine whether a capital case would be plea-bargained or brought to trial, or whether a case would move to a sentencing proceeding upon conviction even when substantial evidence of aggravating circumstances existed. . . . These highly informal procedures are typical in other Georgia jurisdictions as well.[50]

The condemned man's lawyers didn't make much of this argument, for they had decided to push the equality claim aggressively. At best, though, the record showed that each prosecutor's office in Georgia had its own leisurely practices. At worst, prosecutors simply flew by the seat of their pants when making life-and-death decisions.

But the fair play approach would not leave a vulnerable population subject to the whims of a single local official when lives are at stake or treat them as expendable elements in someone's career. Even the worst of the worst deserve to be treated with a measure of dignity and respect. We should instead ask ourselves this question: what would someone facing the irrevocable loss of life expect as a reasonably reliable set of ground rules?

Rather than stumble over the appropriate quantum of proof to make out racial discrimination, as if it could ever be an exact science, we must train our attention on the methods that would reduce errors, minimize unfairness, and enhance the legitimacy of the justice system. This inquiry would also allow one to identify prosecutors' unbridled discretion as a source of a constitutional violation, but without the heat of moral judgment associated with equality violations.

On this alternative rationale, it would be possible to say either that a state has violated basic notions of fairness or that outlier counties have done so when policies or practices fall woefully short. Procedural irregularities that should catch one's attention include the absence of policies identifying factors to be considered when deciding whether to seek the death penalty, the absence of a local or state review process to compare pending cases to past cases, or the lack of final accountability or review of death penalty charging decisions on a statewide level. Conversely, the creation of such policies and evidence of regular usage of these policies would suggest that basic ideas of fairness are observed.

Even the U.S. Department of Justice has recognized that a greater degree of standardization and centralization over the decision to seek death is integral to equality and fairness. In the federal system, no federal prosecutor may file a notice seeking a death sentence without first undergoing a rigorous review process at Main Justice and then obtaining formal approval by the U.S. Attorney General. This process requires that such charging decisions must be justified, reduces the effects of local political pressure, marshals the expertise and historical knowledge of those involved in past uses of the death penalty, and ensures legal, not merely political, accountability for this kind of decision.

Saying that fair play requires better controls on decisions to seek the ultimate punishment simply means that death is different than other forms of punishment. The taking of a human life can't be reversed. How we punish our own people implicates the legitimacy of the rule of law as well as the morality of our political community. What's more, the concerns we have about the administration of capital punishment needn't affect how charging decisions are made in ordinary crimes.

For moderates, it can be reassuring that the principle of fair play would not lead to radical reform. Recall that one of Justice Powell's concerns about McCleskey's equality claim was that it might mean that the state's death penalty law simply could no longer be applied. More process is the better answer to his concern about the runaway consequences of equality, for the concept of fairness would instead allow the state to close the gap in system-wide racial disparities in any number of ways. Fair play doesn't seek to destroy discretion. It merely seeks to discipline discretion so it is exercised according to legal standards. The impact of changed policies might be that death is sought less frequently overall, but it could also lead to an uptick in usage of the penalty in certain kinds of cases, say when racial minorities are crime victims.

Because procedural justice does not come close to judicially abolishing the death penalty, the risks of political resistance or blowback are not as severe. Today's judges are sensitive to charges of overreaching, after the Supreme Court's brush with political backlash to its death penalty jurisprudence in the 1970s—and activists should pay attention to this same lesson. The Court briefly flirted with abolishing the death penalty in 1972. In *Furman v. Georgia*, the Court struck down Georgia's death penalty law on "cruel and unusual punishment" grounds because five of the Justices saw no rhyme or reason to why defendants received that penalty. Beyond that terse statement, however, the five Justices in the majority could not agree on why the death penalty violated the Constitution—indeed, the Court was so fractured that all nine members wrote separately.

Justice Potter Stewart likened the act of receiving a death sentence to "being struck by lightning." Others felt that, while they could not definitely prove discrimination, the lack of standards facilitated pernicious considerations like race, poverty, ignorance, or disability. Justice Douglas warned that "the discretion of judges and juries in imposing the death penalty enables the penalty to be selectively applied, feeding prejudices against the accused if he is poor and despised, and lacking political clout, or if he is a member of a suspect or unpopular minority, and saving those who by social position may be in a more protected position." He concluded that the death penalty laws on the books "are pregnant with discrimination and discrimination is an ingredient not compatible with the idea of equal protection of the laws." Justice Thurgood Marshall went the farthest that day, declaring the death penalty unconstitutional not only because it is cruel but also because it "is imposed discriminatorily against certain identifiable classes of people."

Assessments of capital punishment's diminished popularity featured prominently in two opinions. Justice Brennan came closest to predicting the demise of capital punishment: "The progressive decline in, and the current rarity of, the infliction of death demonstrate that our society seriously questions the appropriateness of this punishment today." Similarly, Justice White argued that because capital punishment "is exacted with great infrequency even for the most atrocious crimes," it had therefore lost must of its credibility as a deterrent.[51]

While many believed that the country was on the verge of ending judicial executions, the majority of states responded to *Furman* by reenacting death penalty statutes. Chastened by its misreading of the political winds, the Supreme Court hastily marked its retreat four years later in *Gregg v. Georgia* by ruling that capital punishment was not inherently cruel and unusual. That decision validated the "long history" of capital punishment in America and expressed a keen "awareness of the limited role to be played by courts"—an obvious acknowledgment that judges should not issue rulings that can't be supported by the citizenry. "[W]hile we have an obligation to insure that constitutional bounds are not overreached," the Justices reminded the American public, "we may not act as judges as we might as legislators."

The anti-death penalty side of the debate lost Justice Stewart, who wrote the main opinion which signaled that the court had heard the people's desire to retain capital punishment. "The most marked indication of society's endorsement of the death penalty for murder is the legislative response to *Furman*," he observed. "The legislatures of at least thirty-five States have enacted new statutes that provide for the death penalty for at least some crimes, . . . all of the post-*Furman* statutes make clear that capital punishment itself has not been rejected by the elected representatives of the people."

So long as a state provides "guidance to the sentencing authority," the Supreme Court assured that it would not be deemed cruel and unusual to execute someone. In essence, the Justices wound up reading the Eighth Amendment's anti-cruelty provision in a way that mirrored existing due process jurisprudence, which emphasized predictable policies.[52]

This entire sequence of events suggests that a recommendation of more procedure can be a second-best response to concerns of political backlash. A judge or policymaker who fears the power of egalitarianism might be swayed by the fact that fair play does not encroach on democratic prerogative or policy discretion in the same manner that other principles do. Doubts about the fairness of the legal system can then have a principled outlet, to help do justice in concrete terms.

Such a solution is both principled and pragmatic. It is principled because the emphasis remains an overriding obligation to do justice. Worry that decisive rejection of a legal principle might harm its effectiveness in the future is a reason to avoid that rationale, but it's not a reason to avoid other rationales. Refraining from solving a problem of inequality is justified only if other methods are tried to mitigate the pain and suffering of a vulnerable population.

Doing equality by procedural means is also pragmatic because it takes seriously ongoing injuries. It entails solving problems realistically, taking account of philosophical differences and coming up with solutions that a society will support. These answers are often second best for reformers, but might be first-best or second-best preferences for others (for whom doing nothing will sometimes be more tempting than electing the most far-reaching option). Strategic flexibility of this sort is good for justice because it expands the plausible range of outcomes—each of which can advance the ball.

Fairness can be a close approximation of equality in many situations, even if it's not exactly the same. Enforcement of that idea in *McCleskey*, as well as in other scenarios characterized by unbridled discretion, can lead to new guidelines and standards. In turn, requiring that crucial government decisions be justified can reduce some of the inequities caused by unprincipled or prejudiced enforcement decisions. *Trump v. Washington* teaches that defending norms of procedural justice will disrupt unorthodox policies and can lead the government to abandon plans that target vulnerable populations or fall on them the hardest. The state employed violent and unreliable methods to solve crimes in *Brown*. Saying that the poor, black defendants didn't get a fair shake vindicates the ideal of impartial justice. Doing so benefits everyone formally, but especially people most likely to suffer at the hands of callous officials.

CHAPTER 3

THE RULE OF REASON

What need is there for reason? Very much:
both for the enlargement of our knowledge,
and regulating our assent.

—John Locke, 1690

The popular saying "Let's be reasonable!" can be a powerful rejoinder to those who wish to exclude some people from valuable opportunities or otherwise treat them differently. American jurisprudence is saturated with the principle of reasonableness, from common law rules that impose duties of care we owe our neighbors to constitutional doctrines governing when the police may stop or search us. In fact, notions of equality are embedded in the rule of reason. This means that taking rationality seriously can promote egalitarianism in some tangible ways, especially when traditional methods of debating equality fall short.

In 1980, the Cleburne Living Center applied for a special permit to operate a group home to serve thirteen individuals with intellectual disabilities in the city of Cleburne, Texas. A local ordinance allowed hospitals, sanitariums, and nursing homes to be built, but barred homes for the "feeble-minded." The city council rejected CLC's plea for an exception after neighbors organized a petition against the group home.[1]

On appeal, federal judges found that people with intellectual disabilities often experience "unfair and grotesque treatment." They noted that thirty-two states had laws providing for the sterilization of the "feebleminded" or insane, at one point or another. An interest in social control of intellectually disabled people was hardly limited to outraged voters. Many academics and public officials subscribed to eugenics, the belief that socially desirable traits and antisocial characteristics—even criminal tendencies—were heritable and that public policies should be adjusted toward "the elimination of the defective strains."

The infamous 1927 Supreme Court decision *Buck v. Bell* facilitated procreative experimentation on people with intellectual disabilities. Justice Oliver Wendell Holmes explained that the compelled sterilization of a Virginia woman with an intellectual disability raised no constitutional difficulties whatsoever: "It is better for all the world, if instead of waiting to execute degenerate offspring for crime, or to let them starve for their imbecility, society can prevent those who are manifestly unfit from continuing their kind." Doctors labeled her a "potential parent of socially inadequate offspring." Justice Holmes agreed, adding scornfully, "Three generations of imbeciles are enough."[2]

Recognizing the law's past shortcomings, the appeals court hearing the CLC's challenge decided from that moment on to treat any law that singled out people with intellectual disabilities as inherently suspicious, a presumptive denial of equality. To survive a challenge, a policy of this sort would have to be justified by substantial reasons. The city of Cleburne's ordinance failed the test, however, because its draconian exclusion of group homes "for the feeble-minded" prevented such individuals from "assimilating into and contributing to their society." All of this entailed a brave application of the law of equality—taking this step made the federal court one of two in the country to formalize judicial protections on behalf of the mentally disabled.[3]

In soaring prose, the judges warned of the corrosive effects of these kinds of laws: "The segregation of one group from the rest of society . . . perpetuates false stereotypes about the exiled group and leads to a virtual caste system built on misconceptions." They stressed that laws that fall so heavily on some members of society "are especially pernicious when the outcast group lacks the political power to resist unfair categorization."

When the case reached the Supreme Court, the Justices were swamped by arguments from every direction. Disability rights activists urged the High Court to say that the city had explicitly discriminated against people who are intellectually disabled. After all, Cleburne's ordinance had been modeled on a law that had proliferated throughout Texas, as part of a movement to reduce perceived "economic and moral losses" from the mere "existence at large of these unfortunate persons." This reprehensible history of "segregation and control, through life" of a group of people deemed "unfit for citizenship" and a "nuisance to the community" evoked the terrible practice of racial apartheid in America. Understood in this light, the local ordinance threatened to create a permanent underclass, something the Fourteenth Amendment forbade. A few critics even claimed that the city's handling of the matter violated international law.[4]

The attorneys general of Arkansas, California, Louisiana, and West Virginia presented a unified front. They recommended that the Justices ratify the lower court's approach and treat intellectual disabilities like sex, something to be examined carefully but not as rigorously as laws that depended on race or religion. Doing so would give this vulnerable population a more consistent expectation of equal treatment.[5]

But not everyone wanted egalitarianism to do more. The Reagan administration filed one of the more influential briefs warning of equality run amok. In his brief, the Solicitor General urged the Court not to afford intellectually disabled people any "special protection of the judiciary." The administration rejected any parallels between racial minorities and people with intellectual disabilities because the latter had "distinctive needs and abilities" which required leeway to address. While the use of race always implicated the "moral imperative of the unity and equality of all mankind," the Solicitor General said, taking into account a person's disabilities did not necessarily reflect "invidious and derogatory aims."

There could be valid reasons to consider a person's intellectual capacities in making decisions about employment, public safety, and government benefits—but exacting scrutiny of the laws tied everyone's hands. Equality in this context didn't call for equivalent treatment across the board, the administration argued, but instead meant something closer to individualized assessment of each person's needs.[6]

Government lawyers also urged caution because extending formal protection based on intellectual function could have an enormous effect throughout the country. "Mental retardation is among the most common of human handicaps," they informed the Justices. "Approximately 125,000 persons born each year will be mentally retarded. As many as 6,500,000 individuals now living in the United States may properly be classified as mentally retarded."

So what should be done? It would be obtuse to ignore the fact that individuals with an intellectual disability had been victimized by discrimination in the past or that they remained politically vulnerable in the present. Surely some sort of baseline of equal treatment was necessary to guard against wholesale mistreatment.

And yet, were we really prepared to treat intellectual capacity like race, religion, or even sex? If so, we might be able to detect discrimination more readily, but we might also put at risk programs that benefit those who face intellectual challenges. That's because by saying that mental ability is off-limits, we would make it harder for the government to allocate social goods on that basis.

Faced with these concerns, the Supreme Court decided that a

more rigorous, one-size-fits-all legal standard would be too confining. But to the Justices' credit, they neither ducked the case nor permitted intellectually disabled people to be consigned to second-class status. Instead, they practiced equality by other means, disapproving what happened under the general rule of reason. As Justice Byron White cautioned, "Our refusal to recognize the retarded as a quasi-suspect class does not leave them entirely unprotected from invidious discrimination. . . . The State may not rely on a classification whose relationship to an asserted goal is so attenuated as to render the distinction arbitrary or irrational."[7]

The rule of reason became common ground when Justice William Rehnquist, a more conservative jurist, said "it would not bother me greatly" to resolve the controversy in this fashion, and Justice Powell, who often gravitated to practical solutions, urged his colleagues to resolve the case decisively rather than return it to the lower court with open questions. Together, the Justices found that the city's refusal of a permit "appeared" to rest on "irrational prejudice"; not animosity so much as preconceived notions about intellectual disability. The ruling showed remarkable unity, with all of the Justices agreeing with the outcome. Only those who would have gone further in the name of equality wrote separately.[8]

Justice White's opinion for the majority scrutinized each of the city's arguments for denying the permit and found all of them inadequately supported by the evidence. City officials pleaded that they were merely preserving "the serenity of the existing neighborhoods" and "protecting elderly neighbors from harm," but they had acted on no real problems but rather "mere negative attitudes." They could cite only a single incident where a person with an intellectual disability had taken someone's mail and later returned it.

Community leaders also claimed to be protecting intellectually disabled people from being bullied by schoolchildren across the street, but it would be perverse to deny anyone a place to live on the mere possibility that someone might behave rudely. Shifting strategies, the city pointed out that the proposed group home would be located on a 500-year floodplain, leaving its residents exposed to danger should the raging waters come. This last argument was downright silly—other at-risk populations were allowed on the floodplain, such as the elderly, the injured, and the sick, while the likelihood of a flood was remote.

All of these justifications seemed so flimsy that they might even have been fabricated to hide more nefarious sentiments. But the High Court never went all the way there. It was sufficient to say that the government's arguments could not be supported by the facts. Weak justifications produced by hasty deliberation, or offered with utter contempt to the empirical reality of a situation, violate the rule of reason just as if the city council had acted out of malice.

Resolving this dispute through the rule of reason, while not perfect, had several benefits. To begin, the solution left room for disagreement on the abstract question of whether making policies based on intellectual differences was morally wrongful and therefore generally to be avoided, without allowing that squabble to stall justice. This particular policy could not be countenanced, leaving open the possibility that another situation involving a different kind of home or business might be handled differently.

On the broader philosophical question, egalitarians could even dream that one day new information might lead society to revisit how all intellectually disabled people are treated. Severing the more intractable debate over the long-term effects of an equality decision on vital social goods from the more immediate hardships suffered by such individuals helped facilitate consensus. It also elided disagreements over the causes and degree of disabilities that might be encountered. The possible benefits of greater formality were theoretical and difficult to calculate, while the gains from taking action immediately could be more readily measured.

The rationale—"vague, undifferentiated fears"—appeared more

inviting to those who doubted that hatred operated as the true motivation of city officials. The historical evidence of malice surrounding the law's origins in the 1920s felt powerful to some, but probably seemed too attenuated for others, especially when the council members' refusal to grant an exception some sixty years later was not accompanied by evidence of a desire to do harm. The middle ground—and one that won the day—was that "irrational fears" simply could not be given credence.

Critically, the rationale substituted for egalitarianism was nearly as good. Striking down the law for singling out the "feebleminded" might have been preferable as the stronger move. That way, the ordinance would be erased completely and present no more risk of harm. But what the Court did was the next best thing, by converting what appeared to be a categorical restriction on where intellectually disabled people could live into a rule that required case-by-case treatment unless good reasons emerged for treating the disabled as a group. In doing so, the Justices protected equal opportunity to make lifestyle choices.

Moreover, they placed discriminatory action based on damaging cultural stereotypes off-limits. Going forward, bureaucrats couldn't violate a person's liberty merely by gesturing toward harmful assumptions about his mental capacities. There has to be something concrete: past misconduct attributable to the person being restrained or a realistic probability of future harm to himself or others. That's a principle whose value extends well beyond the issue of group homes or even intellectual capacity. It's an idea that can be employed to ameliorate harms against any social group that encounters oppression because of overwrought fears.

These same dubious generalizations often underlie overtly discriminatory actions. In fact, a straight line can be drawn from *Cleburne's* concern with harmful stereotypes about intellectually disabled people to Justice Ginsburg's efforts in the VMI decision to root out pernicious assumptions about women. In both controversies, the government drew upon problematic generalizations about a social group's talents and capabilities. People with intellectual disabilities were presumed to be dangerous, incapable of living in an integrated environment, and helpless in an emergency. For female applicants to VMI, policymakers made negative judgments about how the so-called fairer sex would fare under grueling training conditions. Each time, someone made sweeping judgments that artificially limited the rights or opportunities of others. In terms of the solutions, two different paths led to the same place: freedom from timidity, ignorance, and paternalism.[9]

Of course, it's impossible to go through life without using generalizations. We rely on categories every day to decide whom to befriend and how to keep loved ones safe. Sometimes we are right, occasionally we are wrong. But reaching personal, snap decisions isn't the same as creating policy based on erroneous generalizations. The costs to society of being wrong are exponentially greater when we enact pernicious assumptions about other people into the law.[10]

Some generalizations are worse than others. Those based on a group's propensities and abilities are caustic to social bonds because there isn't much we can do to change how others perceive us and what groups are found to be salient to a policy problem. Such culturally received notions act as a drag on the trajectory of an individual's personal growth, drastically reduce some citizens' prospects, and can impinge on fundamental rights.

Consider a death penalty case from 2017. Duane Edward Buck claimed that his court-appointed lawyer had failed to provide effective representation because he introduced damaging evidence against his own client. A psychologist employed a dubious statistical method for predicting whether the defendant posed a threat to the community. The witness testified that he didn't think Buck would be dangerous if kept in prison, but also conceded that under his model being male and black increased the likelihood that someone would commit a future crime.[11]

Striking down the death sentence, Chief Justice John Roberts said that the expert's testimony "appealed to a powerful racial stereotype—that of black men as 'violence prone.'" Because of the presentation of such "potent" but irrational evidence in the guise of expertise, the jury could have sentenced Buck to die merely because he was black. That risk of discrimination on the part of jurors, even if it could not be proven to a certainty, was enough to call the sentence into question. Defense counsel had improperly made "race directly pertinent on the question of life or death" and courts could not be complicit in injustice by ratifying it later.[12]

Regardless of the tools we use, we combat the problem of inequality whenever we reduce the state's usage of damaging or outdated cultural ideas. A practical egalitarian shouldn't fret about whether justice is done through a complex mechanism that treats intellectual disabilities as a disfavored category or accomplished through some other tool. If a hammer isn't available, pick up a chisel. So long as there's a principled basis for acting, and consensus is within reach, doing something to improve the lives of the less fortunate will be better than doing nothing.

COMPARING BATTLE SCARS

THE RULE OF REASON can be a productive way to break out of our predictable pattern of debating equality: comparing battle scars. We often try to talk about inequality by starting with the experiences of people whose suffering under American law is well established as a matter of history—the paradigmatic examples are religious and racial minorities. We ask ourselves: what is it about their experiences that has made it easy to discriminate against them and has rendered their suffering so persistent? Our answers are that such groups are politically vulnerable to majoritarian decisions that leave them consistently worse off, that they are relatively easy to identify and harm, and they are saddled with a history of oppression. Whether differential treatment is morally justifiable thus depends on whether someone has discriminated against a "discrete and insular minority."[13]

When another group comes along with a grievance, we demand that the new group justify its claim by paying homage to past injustices before entertaining its complaint. Is being gay in America like being black or being a woman? Has a particular trait been used to keep some people underfoot? Show us your scars, we say.

In other words, we try to understand someone's grievance by reference to another, more familiar kind of pain. We do this in life, as in law, and there are both good things and bad things about trading war stories. Making decisions this way is beneficial in that it builds bridges between people and their struggles, fosters empathy for others, and helps keep the law coherent. Drawing analogies also reminds us of past injustices—such as the generations of black Americans who suffered broken families and lost opportunities under slavery and Jim Crow, or the Chinese who were victimized by racist immigration and property laws, or the Catholics or Mormons, who all had to flee angry mobs.

Ultimately, comparing battle scars isn't a satisfying way to decide questions of justice. It forces us to say—and therefore to accept—that some people are more worthy of equality than others. It also wrongly implies that justice is a scarce resource. That's the approach taken by the well-meaning Justice Harlan when he dissented in *Plessy*. "There is a race so different from our own that we do not permit those belonging to it to become citizens of the United States," he pointed out. They were the Chinese, whom Louisiana allowed to ride on whatever trains they wanted. What an insult to black citizens, many of whom "risked their lives for the preservation of the Union," to be treated worse than "the Chinaman"!

At the very least, this ritual can't be allowed to dominate the conversation. There are those who will take umbrage at the very thought of trying to equate historical experiences, as if a people's pain can be reduced to so many bullet points on a worksheet. They will refuse to play this game.

But the real problem is that it's just too easy to get caught up in the minutiae of social differences so that one becomes paralyzed by inaction. It is tempting to be dismissive of someone's grievance because his suffering hasn't been as severe as our own, or because he has endured oppression in obscurity rather than in plain sight. We might be tripped up by the fact that a group demanding justice is more numerous than another group, or because it enjoys more political clout than one might expect.

Today ten million Americans—roughly 4 percent of the U.S. population—identify as LGBT, but neither taking pains to hide one's sexual identity nor throwing oneself into political activism has been enough to make anti-gay discrimination stop. There are currently 3.3 million Muslims living in the United States, but in the Age of Terrorism broad, and sometimes erroneous, assumptions about Islam will shape public policies. While Americans have always been a religious people, in a recent poll nearly 50 percent of respondents felt that Islam is anti-American, and viewed Muslims as suspiciously as they do atheists. Despite the fact that African Americans make up 13 percent of the population and enjoy professional success in many fields, they remain the overwhelming subject of zealous policing: blacks are more likely to be searched than whites, their neighborhoods are more frequently targeted by aggressive policies, and they are incarcerated at five times the rate of whites. Demographers say that Hispanics comprise the fastest-growing ethnic group in America and project it to reach nearly a quarter of America's population by 2065, but this development has merely exacerbated unease about the country's cultural identity and economic opportunities. We could go on and on.[14]

Oppression can't be reduced to a simple formula. Some people might stand out because of their physical characteristics or behavior that visibly manifests their identity—say, wearing a head covering or a crucifix. But repression can also be stoked based on the unknown: whispers about mysterious practices or beliefs that lie well beyond the mainstream. Such a dynamic plagued early Christians in the Roman Empire and Jews throughout Europe, and vexes Jehovah's Witnesses in America today. Efforts to exclude or discipline an outsider group can certainly arise because it is relatively powerless and oppressors know they can get away with bad behavior.[15]

But sometimes discrimination comes down like an iron fist just when a group has acquired real political power. Dominant factions in society decide to gang up and put that group in its place. That happened in the immediate aftermath of the Civil War, as slaves suddenly won their freedom and posed a threat to the vestiges of white supremacy. Efforts to dilute black voting power happened once again at the turn of the twentieth century as many progressives sought to assure white workers that reforms would be driven primarily by their interests.

Let's not lose sight of the main point: it is just so easy to draw fine-grained but ultimately meaningless distinctions among the lived experiences of America's many groups. If that's what the work of equality becomes, then we are doing little more than maintaining a hierarchy of suffering—a towering monument that will be glorious to some, but foreboding to others. Anyone who does not qualify for the law's protections might even feel resentful. And while we dither, communities can fracture and cherished institutions be decimated.

Thus, the question of who constitutes a vulnerable population might be a decent way to begin a conversation about equality, but it can't be the main thing that matters when we decide who deserves the law's protection. Even those who are comfortably among the majority most of the time aren't permanently in the majority for all things in all places. They can find themselves outnumbered and treated suspiciously in certain situations. They, too, deserve the benefit of equality.

Fortunately, jurists have never said that fixing points of overlapping suffering is the only way we can debate inequities in society, and no political thinker worth her salt has ever felt boxed in by such rituals.

Reason can operate as a fallback justification when we end up talking in circles as to who deserves equality. In theory it's always part of the deliberative process. Most of the time, reason's workings are unobtrusive, filling gaps between the formal justifications we give, the perceptions we hold, and the older bodies of cultural knowledge that we invoke. Once in a while, though, it can serve as the explicit mechanism for bridging disagreements over what equality requires. When we use such second-best solutions, we've stopped polishing monuments and have rededicated ourselves to solving real problems.

HOW REASON CAN PROTECT THE VULNERABLE AND DESPISED

MOST INTELLECTUALS DISTINGUISH BETWEEN reason as the human capacity for complex thought and reason as a public ideal for politics. The first sense of reason refers to the "faculty whereby man is supposed to be distinguished from beasts" as a higher-order creature. A second concept is that of public reason, meant to capture our best sense of how law and politics should work in a well-functioning democracy. "But it is the reason, alone, of the public, that ought to control and regulate the government," *Federalist* No. 49 explained. "The passions ought to be controlled and regulated by the government." Compliance with these debate-enhancing norms, in turn, gives us confidence about the outcomes, so that we might accede to them even when we disagree.[16]

When it comes to law, the two ideas fit hand in glove because legal and political processes are not machines that would go of themselves but instead are operated by fallible human beings. Before we treat their decisions "as law," we need the people in charge to make principled decisions and to care about justice, all of which requires that they use reason to solve society's most pressing problems. For when irrelevant and pernicious considerations intrude, or regular protocols are violated with impunity, we begin to worry that some people might be granted special favors at the expense of the weak, or that outsiders among us will be unfairly maligned.

This suggests that when we reason correctly about the Constitution, we must do more than just use our brains or rely on intuition. First, the maxim: power must always be justified. We must present valid reasons for our actions. The democratic practice of reason giving rejects arbitrary decisions, and calls on "each person to defend his power without declaring himself intrinsically superior to any other citizen." It forces each of us to think carefully before asking the state to use force in the service of our hopes, dreams, and worst fears. We must hone our arguments knowing they are public and will be tested by others. The exercise exposes secret processes or hastily constructed rationales to the light of day, and in doing so makes the law accountable to our basic values.[17]

There's more. By policing the rationality of the law—or what we might call the range of reasonable solutions—we are also subtly doing the baseline work of equality. Forcing decision makers to give valid explanations ensures that the powerful don't prevail simply because they are wealthy, or have greater access, or have more at stake in a dispute. It's not enough for privileged people to just show up and be recognized for who they are; like the rest of us, they still have to justify what they want in terms of the public good.

Second, reason is largely an empirical activity, concerned with marshaling information acquired through observation and experience, calculating probabilities when knowledge falls short of certainty, and drawing inferences from established propositions. John Locke is quick to admit that reason is always incomplete because it is inherently limited by our perceptions and that reason can fail "where our ideas fail."

So it is with the law, which is a subset of the sum of human knowledge, directed to political ends.[18]

Ensuring that the law is grounded in empirical reality is another way of protecting vulnerable minorities. This is because inflamed voters and demagogues will seek to cut corners by appealing to our worst emotions, exaggerating concerns of public safety, or conjuring flawed but pervasive stereotypes about strangers in our midst.

Some justifications will be out of bounds simply because they are very bad goals: hostile to the basic design of our Constitution or damaging to rule-of-law values. Other explanations might disintegrate because they fail empirical testing in one important respect or another. A concern for probabilities and consequences offers a basic safeguard to the politically vulnerable, for every society has oppressed some of its members based on superstition, jealousy, revulsion, or hysteria. When these elements figure prominently in an important decision, you will almost always find someone has been treated inequitably.

If we've learned anything at all from the shameful segregation of African Americans and the mentally disabled, it has to be that preserving the creature comforts of those in the majority should not be a strong enough reason to justify extreme measures.

Third, the explanations given to authorize the assertion of state power over human beings must be truthful in the sense that they are addressed to real problems rather than fabricated crises, the reasons can't be ginned up after the fact, and the solutions should be fairly well suited to the problem that has been identified. Justifications must rely upon one's best sense of the truth about the world: settled facts, observations, and other sensorial information. Excluding falsity from the range of reasonable solutions helps prevent domination of the less educated, the intellectually challenged, the overworked, and those with inadequate access to reliable information.

A demand for blind faith or the assertion of raw power won't cut it. This is not only because such appeals would permit oppression by the strong over the weak, but also because such arguments insist on the assent of fellow citizens not "by the deductions of reason, but upon the credit of the proposer."

In every society there will be individuals or communities who claim special closeness to absolute truths, whether they are religious leaders or political prophets. When we insist that only reasonable arguments are to be entertained in the law, we are also insisting that no one has any greater claim on political morality than anyone else, and that the law remains grounded in our shared experience.[19]

Enforcing the rule of reason can become an attractive basis for consensus because it doesn't require shared precommitment to, or even intense affinity for, a particular ideology, worldview, or party platform. It requires only that people agree there is epistemological value in the truth, even if that truth is complicated. At the same time, the concept of reason is culturally sensitive—that is, the range of reasonable answers to a problem can expand or contract with the times, encompassing solutions that were once unimaginable or infeasible (e.g., lethal injection, public education, same-sex marriage) and excluding practices that now seem beyond the pale (e.g., forced sterilization, drawing and quartering, bans on interracial marriage).

But the most attractive gridlock-busting feature by far is that people can agree to disagree about the extent to which malice is involved in a problematic practice. If egalitarianism seeks to identify well-developed moral baselines and enforce rules of conduct vigorously across the board, the rule of reason offers a vehicle for shaping a necessary, ongoing conversation about equality's value and its limits without laying down unmovable markers.

Seen this way, when we argue over what reason requires, we are acknowledging space for future debate. That feature of the approach makes solutions less likely to provoke a backlash. In theory, a defect in the record or the state's arguments means that committed lawmakers can try again to hone arguments or develop sufficient evidence for their plan. It doesn't tie their hands in the way that the traditional approach to equality does.

A charge often leveled against this approach is that different people will disagree about whether a course of action is reasonable. That's true, but that's also true of any concept—the play in the joints is just more visible with this one. And despite the criticisms, we've always tinkered with the approach but have never abandoned it. Belief in its utility reflects a deep preference for moderation and consensus that operates as a basic structural feature of American law. If we appear to shy away from equality, it might be because not enough of us are there quite yet, and it makes sense to look for other ways to do justice while keeping the conversation going. The rule of reason is one way to do that.

When we turn to the Constitution, we see that the Framers doubled down on reason as a strategy for protecting rights and liberties. The Fourth Amendment protects us against "unreasonable searches and seizures." Likewise, the Eighth Amendment forbids "excessive bail" and "cruel and unusual punishments" from being imposed, indicating that a range of reasonable sanctions is permitted. A dependence on empiricism to ascertain the truth and protect rights is a built-in feature of the Constitution. Before the state may use force against human beings and property, it must comply with these requirements. Every warrant must be "supported by" an oath or affirmation "particularly describing the place to be searched, and the persons to be seized." These requirements of justification, necessity, and veracity are extended elsewhere: the right to an "impartial" jury, the right to be informed of "the nature and cause" of any accusation, the privilege against self-incrimination, and the right to confront witnesses and to have the aid of a lawyer.[20]

The 1973 case of *United States Agriculture v. Moreno* shows us how the rule of reason can protect the poor as well as those with unorthodox lifestyles. The dispute involved the federal Food Stamp Act. Regulations issued by the Secretary of Agriculture made ineligible any household whose members were not "all related to each other." Although this restriction was defended in court later as an effort to deter fraud, the Justices concluded that it "simply does not operate so as rationally to further the prevention of fraud." In "practical operation," the rule excludes from the food stamp program not those most likely to abuse the program but rather "only those persons who are so desperately in need of aid that they cannot even afford to alter their living arrangements so as to retain their eligibility."[21]

While much of the discussion revolved around legislators' distaste for hippies, the general approach had wider significance for the working poor. This is because it has become hard for anyone to agree on what discrimination against poor people looks like, or whether we ought to care about it. Nevertheless, the rule of reason relieved the poor from the government's anti-stranger rule, who felt its sting more than the wealthy.

Jacinta Moreno, a fifty-six-year-old diabetic, lived with another woman and her sons, sharing expenses. But the family would have to turn Moreno out of their home in order to continue receiving welfare. The Hejnys, who were indigent, took in a twenty-year-old girl with emotional problems, but doing so rendered them ineligible for food stamps. A third set of plaintiffs included a woman with a hearing-impaired child who could only afford to live near a school for the deaf by sharing a residence with someone on public assistance.

As Justice Douglas pointed out separately, laws of this sort fall heavily on "desperately poor people with acute problems who, though unrelated, come together for mutual help and assistance." They also restrict "the right to invite the stranger into one's home." Douglas would have struck down the law on the ground that it violated the First Amendment right of association. But you don't need to agree with him about the solution to believe that we need to pay attention to some of the inequities involved. Justice Douglas posed the problem this way: "[T]he Act creates two classes of persons for food stamp purposes: one class is composed of people who are all related to each other and all in dire need, and the other class is composed of households that have one or more persons unrelated to the others but have the same degree of need as those in the first class." While the rest of the Justices said that the welfare restrictions failed to serve the state's objectives, they addressed this disparate treatment without having to expand the right to association (an option that might have put other laws at risk).

Beyond remedying the marginalization of people with disabilities, the rule of reason has been deployed in situations where serious inequities were raised, but ill will was hard to prove. Judges have said that deporting someone from the country because he is a "habitual drunkard" is arbitrary; that no sound reasons were offered in defense of a referendum that wiped out all legal protections based on sexual orientation throughout the state; that a vague "distrust of private schools" is not reason enough to deny a Christian school admission to the state athletic association; and that refusing disabled state employees a hearing when they are terminated while giving nondisabled employees one can be irrational.[22]

REASON IS MORE THAN WHO DECIDES

ALTHOUGH THE RULE OF reason has traditionally contained equality-enhancing features, its egalitarian promise has been kept unfulfilled by those who would reduce reason to little more than a matter of who decides important questions. On this view, legislatures should do all the deciding, because they are closer to voters and can most accurately gauge their preferences. They can also consult experts as needs arise.

This is all correct, as far as it goes. But there are a few glaring problems with substituting deference for reason and leaving it at that. First, precisely because legislators can be so perfectly in tune with constitu-

ents, they are prone to occasional spasms of bigotry or fearmonger-
ing, and to willful blindness as to what the law and common decency
require. As a historical matter, the Constitution's framers worried about
legislatures—especially Congress—as the primary cause of "sudden
and violent fits of despotism, injustice, and cruelty." So they might
have been a little too focused on possible abuses by legislators, rather
than other kinds of government officials. As Justice Robert Jackson
famously pointed out, "village tyrants" come in all shapes and sizes.

Still, the general point holds. Even if a public official knew that
civic virtue demanded better, he might nevertheless decide to practice "the low arts of popularity" for personal profit or short-term glory
rather than exercise power for the sake of the public good. James
Madison feared "local injustices and schemes of injustice" initiated by
citizens who gained access to law to pursue "wicked projects." Vigilance by all branches of government, along with every citizen, would
be essential if reason were to prevail. For when legislators go awry,
"appeals to the people, therefore, would usually be made by the executive and judiciary departments." So complete deference to any single
branch of government, much less the legislative body, is incompatible
with the Constitution's design and spirit.[23]

Second, the fact that legislatures might have more access to expertise doesn't mean they will seek it. In fact, the very passions that can
incite officials to improve one group of Americans' standing by for-
saking the well-being of another group—the wealthy over the poor,
friends over strangers, Christians over non-Christians, corporations
over consumers—might also tempt them to ignore or suppress science
or society's collective wisdom.

Third, the extreme deference approach misstates the law. A pre-
sumption of constitutionality doesn't require that everyone who later
encounters a law fall in line. It doesn't mean that a law is automatically
reasonable because an elected official says so. It simply means that it's
a challenger's job to demonstrate that a law is problematic.

Reason, then, isn't something we just leave to elected officials and then forget about. Rather, it's a responsibility for all of us, part of a crucial public function that we must all do our best to fulfill. Just as no single person or institution has a monopoly on good judgment, so the actual practice of public reason is a never-ending process of justification, disagreement, and fitful consensus. Everyone has something to contribute and a part to play.

Carolene Products is the leading case from the 1930s that established reasonableness as the general standard for reviewing a law that doesn't target political minorities or implicate fundamental rights. Congress banned the interstate shipment of filled milk after consulting with scientists and health experts who testified that the food product, which contained vegetable oils, was "injurious to health and facilitates fraud on the public." The Supreme Court upheld the Filled Milk Act because there didn't appear to be anything irrational or anti-empirical about the law. People might have disagreed over just how serious the problem was, but there was no proof that it was a trumped-up issue.

Yet the Justices never tried to insulate laws from review. In fact, they went on to say that "a statute predicated upon the existence of a particular state of facts may be challenged by showing to the court that those facts have ceased to exist." In other words, a law's original justification might not hold forever. It's also possible to show that a law has been stretched beyond reason by those charged with enforcing it: "[A] statute, valid on its face, may be assailed by proof of facts tending to show that the statute as applied to a particular article is without support in reason because the article, although within the prohibited class, is so different from others of the class as to be without the reason for the prohibition." So much for the claim that the judgments of elected officials are to be treated as inviolate!

It's almost mind-blowing when we stop to think about just how many constitutional rules of reasonable conduct pervade our lives. Although a warrant is formally required for a search or seizure, in reality we have carved out so many exceptions from this rule that a principle of reasonableness governs most of the daily interactions the state might have with citizens on the street. A police officer needs "reasonable suspicion" of a crime before she pulls over your vehicle. If an officer has probable cause to believe a crime has been committed at some point during an encounter, a search can be conducted anywhere that contraband could "reasonably" be hidden. You can be frisked for weapons if police can cite a "reasonable basis" to believe you might be armed and dangerous. Every search and every seizure has to be conducted in a "reasonable fashion."[24]

These fraught encounters can happen anywhere, and at any time. But here's the big idea: despite the complexities involved in each encounter and the fact that law enforcement decisions implicate public safety, we don't say that anything goes. We don't defer completely to officers on the beat, whether they are making policies or split-second decisions. Rather, we take any expertise they have into account, while still demanding an objective justification for the exercise of power.

For instance, using deadly force to apprehend a suspect is "constitutionally unreasonable" when the stakes are low. Edward Garner, a black teenager, was suspected of trying to break into a house but turned and ran when seen by police. Officers saw no weapon, but shot the boy as he tried to climb a fence to escape. A bullet to the back of his head killed him. Justice Byron White, no bleeding-heart liberal, explained why the state's actions violated the standard of reasonableness: "It is not better that all felony suspects die than that they escape. Where the suspect poses no immediate threat to the officer and no threat to others, the harm resulting from failing to apprehend him does not justify the use of deadly force to do so." That is to say, it's unreasonable for the government to execute someone on the street merely to stop him. Just as it would be unreasonable to claim that every black person is dangerous, so too it's overly broad to suggest that all burglars or all fleeing suspects pose a threat to others. An officer can't rely on such generalizations to justify the use of force, but instead must point to specific facts about particular individuals to do so.[25]

During oral argument, a key exchange revealed the need for the rule of reason to have some bite, and that complete deference would not serve the ends of justice. The attorney general for Tennessee insisted that the state should have unfettered discretion to make "ethical and moral public policy decisions." But Justice Harry Blackmun asked whether a state could authorize the extrajudicial killing of fleeing individuals suspected of other crimes, like antitrust laws. Yes, the state's lawyer answered, each state should be totally free to create any kind of shoot-to-kill policies. The Supreme Court ultimately rejected this alarming position that a legislature's policy choices or even a police officer's on-the-spot decisions should be shielded from review.[26]

If the rule of reason is good enough for hot encounters in the streets, then it's the least we can demand that bureaucrats make cool decisions from their desks based on sound information. Making occasional mistakes is fine, but being callous to known risks to human life and property can't be tolerated.

In a dispiriting ruling, the Court has said that a police officer's subjective motivations—including possible racial bias—aren't relevant to Fourth Amendment questions. *Whren v. United States*, decided in 1996, is disastrous precisely because it severs the relationship between equality and the rule of reason. It short-circuits the inquiry into why an officer has decided to act and encourages pretext stops, i.e., coming up with an untrue set of reasons to explain his behavior when some other plan is really on an officer's mind. Technically, *Whren* means that evidence won't be thrown out of a criminal case simply because a police officer is biased. The only realistic remedy for overt discrimination is to sue later.[27]

That's exactly what New Yorkers did. In a high-profile lawsuit challenging the NYPD's stop-and-frisk program, a federal judge found that the city had engaged in widespread racial profiling. A Supreme

Court case from 1968 called *Terry v. Ohio* allowed a pat-down for weapons if an officer had reason to believe someone was armed and dangerous. But NYPD officers had both discriminated on the basis of race in choosing whom to stop, and had behaved unreasonably by systematically searching blacks and Hispanics more frequently than whites.

In 2011, the NYPD stopped 685,724 citizens. Eighty-four percent of those stopped were black or Latino, even though these groups made up only 52 percent of the local population. But the hit rate was terrible: in only 2 percent of those frisks were weapons or drugs ever discovered. The picture eventually came into focus: police had been targeting members of these minority groups broadly, hoping to get lucky and discover illegal guns or contraband.

U.S. District Judge Shira Scheindlin's decision once again demonstrated how two different paths can lead to the same outcome: equality, which focuses on ethical rules of conduct, and reasonableness, which emphasizes logic and empiricism. Officers systematically stopped "blacks and Hispanics who would not have been stopped if they were white," she said, frisking nonwhites far more frequently than whites, even in low-crime areas and even though searches of whites turned up weapons or contraband more frequently. There was other evidence that race played an active role in policing: officials repeatedly tried to defend targeting male blacks aged fourteen to twenty-one and "even suggested that it is permissible to stop racially defined groups just to instill fear in them that they are subject to being stopped at any time for any reason." That intentional practice to single people out on the basis of race violated the guarantee of egalitarianism.

But even if the evidence of intentional wrongdoing was insufficient, objective factors given for stopping so many more black and Hispanic citizens were unreasonable. The NYPD's policy authorized stop-and-frisks of "the right people, the right time, the right location." Who did they mean by "the right people"? The chief of police conceded this meant that officers were instructed to go after "young black males," believing this group as a whole had a propensity to commit crimes.[28]

NYPD officers frequently cited "furtive movements" and "high crime neighborhood" in their paperwork as justifications for stopping people, but incidents where officers later gave these reasons led to very few citations or arrests. To the contrary, these factors were poor proxies of criminality or dangerousness: Between 2004 and 2009, stops were 22 percent more likely to lead to an arrest if "high crime area" was not given as the reason, and 18 percent more likely if "furtive movements" was not checked. All of this evidence together suggested that officers were relying on race or race-correlated generalizations rather than legitimate, individualized behavior in making decisions on the streets. Instead, they were only citing neutral factors to cover up abusive tactics after the fact. In other words, the race-neutral explanations were post hoc rationalizations rather than accurate accounts of what actually happened on the streets of New York. The truth: police were conducting racial dragnets.[29]

To try to explain away these racial discrepancies, the city suggested that blacks residents of New York must behave more suspiciously than whites. If true, that would offer an innocent explanation for why police so often reacted forcefully to black people's movements but turned out to be so consistently wrong. These were excusable mistakes, the city's lawyers argued, rather than proof of malicious planning.

Judge Scheindlin found this entire line of reasoning not only wildly implausible, but also grounded in racist assumptions. She concluded: "To say that black people in general are somehow more suspicious-looking, or criminal in appearance, than white people is not a race-neutral explanation for racial disparities in NYPD stops: it is itself a racially biased explanation. This explanation . . . echoes the stereotype that black men are more likely to engage in criminal conduct than others."[30]

In New York, the litigants had the means to develop a wealth of statistical evidence of police practices over time showing a skewed pattern of race-based enforcement of the law. What about in a single encounter, where it is so difficult for an individual to prove discrimination? The challenges of locating proof for an equality claim makes it especially critical that we carefully evaluate the factual basis for the officer's decision to restrain or search an individual.

Hunches and overbroad assumptions simply won't do. Going with your gut, as the NYPD's stop-and-frisk program shows, can be merely exercising faulty logic rather than identifying individual behavior that is actually indicative of criminality. Such mistakes of reasoning can be worsened through aggressive policies or poor training or working in mostly minority neighborhoods. Some of the lawbreakers an officer encounters might be racial minorities, but that doesn't mean that a person presents a danger or is likely to be engaged in wrongdoing simply by virtue of being a member of a disfavored race. It's that leap from a small-sample experience to a belief that social groups have inherent traits or tendencies that is both inaccurate and pernicious.

Merely being present at a place where a crime occurs, even if it is a so-called high-crime area, can't be treated as evidence of participation in a crime. The Justices have said as much in the 1979 case *Ybarra v. Illinois*. Police officers went to a tavern to execute a warrant and frisked every patron. On Ybarra an officer felt a cigarette package, opened it, and discovered heroin inside. The Court ruled that the police had no particular reason to suspect Ybarra was armed or dangerous and didn't have probable cause: he had done nothing that justified a cursory frisk for weapons or a full search.[31]

A similar departure of reason was caught and checked by the courts when, on a different occasion, an NYPD officer observed a person speaking to known drug addicts. The officer noticed no other suspicious activity during his entire surveillance of him, but eventually called the person over impatiently, and thrust his hand inside the person's pocket, barking, "You know what I'm after." He hit the jackpot, pulling out envelopes that contained heroin.[32]

But this, too, violated the reasonableness test. "The police officer is not entitled to seize and search every person whom he sees on the street or of whom he makes inquiries," the Supreme Court reminded everyone. "Before he places a hand on the person of a citizen in search of anything, he must have constitutionally adequate, reasonable grounds for doing so."

It makes sense to assume people are innocent strangers rather than hardened criminals when all you have are misleading stereotypes. That puts the burden squarely where it should be: on agents of the state to demonstrate that a particular person has behaved in a way that poses a risk of harm before they may use force. And this principle, which applies in a public establishment like a bar, applies with even greater force in the streets. Otherwise, any racial minority could be stopped and searched simply for being in a neighborhood with more than the usual amount of crime. Race or poverty, or poverty and race together, would then be transformed into legitimate proxies for threats to public order.

These stories about policing uncover the modern incarnation of that pesky belief that certain kinds of people are natural-born criminals. When the government cuts corners in this way, its own behavior reinforces mistaken attitudes within the police force and the broader community. Crimes by whites, who are presumed to be law-abiding, don't get the attention they deserve, while crimes by people with brown or black skin have enormous resources and disproportionate punishments thrown at them. Worse, the people with the guns and the law on their side start to think their hunches are correct: that black and brown people *are* more prone to savagery and deviancy.

All of this breeds widespread cynicism that laws aren't enforced impartially in America—giving rise to rueful observations that the police have made "driving while black" and "walking while brown" illegal. Police tactics of this sort contribute to a corrosive way of thinking, a spiritually draining sense about one's real place in society. Their impact must be limited wherever possible.

TRAGIC ERRORS OF REASON

NOW LET'S CONSIDER AN episode in American history that involved egregious errors of reason: the wartime internment of Japanese Americans. After Japan attacked Pearl Harbor on December 7, 1941, Congress and the president took a series of actions that gave the military control over large sections of the West Coast. Eventually, virtually all Japanese Americans and nationals of Japan living in the United States were rounded up and taken to internment camps—some 120,000 individuals who suddenly lost homes, jobs, opportunities, and of course their liberty. Another 2,264 Latin Americans, mostly of Japanese ancestry, were seized from their homes and interned in the hope they could be traded for American P.O.W.s.[33]

"We were herded onto the train just like cattle and swine," remembered Misuyo Nakamura. "[W]e were powerless." "The government moved the horses out and put us in," Osuke Takizawa said of the Tanforan Assembly Center. "It was like a prison, guards on duty all the time, and there was barbed wire all around us. . . . I just gave up."[34]

Most of the people forcibly removed to camps in desolate parts of the United States were young adults, children, and infants. Two-thirds were U.S. citizens. The costs were enormous: beyond the psychological toll on internees from social separation and confinement, thousands of farms went uncultivated, nearly triggering a food shortage in California; net income lost came to $2.7 billion, with property losses at $1.3 billion. The sheer breadth of Japanese removal from the Pacific Coast was breathtaking, but we'd seen this strategy before in the forced relocation of native peoples and in the segregation of black Americans.

The errors that allowed internment to take place did not involve a failure to consider the possibility of racial discrimination. In fact, advocates spent most of their time advancing these arguments and the Justices spent significant energy dividing bitterly over whether wartime policies sprung from racial animosity. The Justices in the 6–3 majority, led by Hugo Black, felt that Fred Korematsu was not removed from the designated military zones "because of hostility to him or his race" but "because we are at war with the Japanese Empire."

Some Americans wanted to think of relocation camps in benign terms, like protective custody, but many acted defensively in their support of the camps. Justice Black's opinion in *Korematsu v. United States* deemed "it unjustifiable to call them concentration camps, with all the ugly connotations that term implies," as if a spiffed-up version—with the barbed wire and armed guards but without a goal of extermination like their Nazi counterparts—somehow made mass confinement of an entire race of people constitutionally palatable. President Franklin Roosevelt and his military advisors had themselves used the term "concentration camps" in discussing what to do about the Japanese in America, long before civil rights activists seized on that term to underscore the cruelty of internment.

If members of the majority emphatically denied that racial discrimination had occurred, the dissenters were equally vociferous in their belief that racial animus played a significant role in things. Justice Frank Murphy called the *Korematsu* ruling a "legalization of racism." The Court had earlier upheld a curfew for all individuals of Japanese ancestry. But the government had gone too far with race-based solutions. As Justice Jackson put it, "Now the principle of racial discrimination is pushed from support of mild measures to very harsh ones, and from temporary deprivations to indeterminate ones."[35]

This was the paradigmatic situation where the usual mode of

debating equality not only proved disastrous for the principle of equality, but also arguably closed off more diligent efforts to do justice. The dissenters were certainly right that racial hostility played some role—there was plentiful evidence that Americans blamed everyone of Japanese ancestry for the attack, while others had always wanted to do something about the country's changing demographics and seized upon Pearl Harbor as an opportunity ethnically cleanse the region—to "herd 'em up, pack 'em off." Americans backed internment by wide margins, and many wanted every last Japanese person to be repatriated to Japan, expelled from the United States, or even confined after the war, certainly never to return to the West Coast.[36]

But the crucial question is whether, in that climate, justice could be served by insisting on debating equality as we do in ordinary times. When popular desire for racially punitive measures became too powerful to ignore against people already not seen as full members of the community, we fell down on the job by not finding other answers until such destructive sentiments passed. Instead of choking over the extent of racism involved, we could have focused like a laser on the rule of reasonableness as the best way to deal with obvious inequities.

To this day, the internment of Japanese Americans remains the single largest detention of human beings by the U.S. government without any individualized findings of guilt or dangerousness. Exclusion was a radical measure, unprecedented even in a time of war. The failure of reason involved deferring completely to the government's claim that these citizens posed a real threat when the empirical record simply could not support it. Justice Black's curious choice of words—that the government acted not out of racial animosity but because of national security—implied that there could only ever be one true motivation. But that would mean the complete abandonment of any pretense of independent review. War may be hell, but it shouldn't mean that anything goes.[37]

The FBI, responsible for domestic security, knew there was "no evidence of planned espionage" on the part of Japanese Americans. More-over, the War Department had "no evidence of an imminent attack." Government officials hid these facts from the public and from judges, forcing everyone to work from a position of weakness and misinforma-tion. This distorted the debate. The worst kinds of conjecture won.[38]

Military officials not only exaggerated the immediacy of any threat, they also based their policies on unfounded stereotypes—what Justice Frank Murphy in his dissent called the problematic concept of "racial guilt." When Attorney General Francis Biddle objected to race-based removal plans, Assistant Secretary of War John McCloy, responded, "[T]he Constitution is just a scrap of paper to me."[39]

Secretary of War Henry Stimson wrote in his diary: "[T]heir racial characteristics are such that we cannot understand or trust even the citizen Japanese." Lt. Gen. John DeWitt, Military Commander of the Western Defense Command, exclaimed, "A Jap's a Jap. There's no way to determine his loyalty." In his report, which formed the basis for internment policies, DeWitt described anyone born of Japanese ances-try as "subversive," belonging to "an enemy race" whose "racial strains are undiluted." These people, he urged, ought to be treated as "over 112,000 potential enemies . . . at large today."[40]

These statements show that military authorities charged with creating emergency measures didn't care how long Japanese Ameri-cans had lived in the United States (most had lived in the country for decades) or that most were patriotic citizens—they would all be treated as inherently suspicious, enemies from within. Those in charge didn't care about the legal rights of American citizens or foreign nationals, or that more of them weren't citizens because federal law forbade natu-ralization of Japanese migrants. Just as police officers who rely upon cultural generalizations as evidence of dangerousness violate the rule of reason, so too military officers who use race or religion as proof of a propensity for lawbreaking invoke unreliable cultural fears. Argu-ments of this sort deserve no deference.

There wasn't a shred of evidence that Fred Korematsu, born in the United States, ever renounced his American citizenship or supported the war efforts of the Japanese government. It's one thing to give military officers and soldiers wide discretion to formulate strategy in the theater of war, but it's quite another to look the other way when they mistreat innocent civilians on American soil. There is plenty that ordinary citizens and judges can't do in a time of war. They can't micromanage the deployment of forces or decide how best to attack or repel enemies. But one thing they can and must do is to make sure that decisions affecting innocent civilians remain under some semblance of law and order.[41]

Instead of acting as a check on the use of pernicious stereotypes by soldiers, the Supreme Court compounded their errors of reason by embracing and perpetuating them. Justice Black's decision accepted the government's fear of a West Coast invasion and sabotage by Americans, even though they were entirely speculative. It was highly implausible that Japan could carry out an invasion without being detected. As for espionage, the opinion cited nothing more than the fact that some Japanese residents, after being mistreated by the U.S. government, refused to renounce their loyalty to the Emperor. If some expressed affinity for the government of Japan, that would have warranted further investigation of those individuals, but hardly justified indefinite detention of every member of the race. There was nothing that even remotely suggested conspiratorial acts by anyone else. After all, half of those interned were children.

Korematsu cited an earlier opinion that upheld a race-based curfew. There, Chief Justice Harlan Fiske Stone claimed that all people born to Japanese parents shared a sense of racial "solidarity." That they were less assimilated into "the white population" than some other ethnic groups was taken as proof they were up to no good. Some parents even sent their children to foreign language schools, he observed, as if that were proof of a treasonous mind. Not content to rely on the conspiratorial fantasies of others, the Justices themselves got into the act, conjecturing that social "irritation" between "the white population" and the Japanese "may well have tended to increase their isolation, and in many instances their attachments to Japan and its institutions."

Ironically, the Justices got their own classic equality formula terribly wrong. If it were true that people of Japanese ancestry comprised a highly visible and isolated community, that's supposed to tell us its members were vulnerable to prejudice and needed the Constitution's protection, not that they deserved to be put under lock and key. Just when a despised minority needed it the most, our regular habits for doing the work of equality failed them.

As Eugene Rostow later observed, these arguments had greater kinship with "folk proverbs" than empirical facts. Government officials didn't point to a shred of evidence for this wild theory that Japanese culture promoted criminality or disloyalty. To the contrary, experts in fields from sociology to political science would say there are many pressures that act on minorities to assimilate and obey the laws of their adopted country. In this instance, jurists safely ensconced in Washington, D.C., fell victim to the same logical errors made by soldiers on the streets of the West Coast.[42]

Only a concerted insistence on clear-headed thinking could even begin to curb such worries from spinning out of control. The best approach, if people didn't want to say that political leaders or their constituents were racist, would have been to work harder on behalf of the alternative rationale suggested in Justice Murphy's dissent: there was simply no reasonable basis for the drastic policy of mass internment. All the government could muster were "questionable racial and sociological grounds" rather than reliable evidence of a true threat.[43]

Lacking such information, it was unreasonable to deter espionage and sabotage by rounding up every single person that belonged to one race. To see how extreme it was to forcibly incarcerate thousands of people based on their ancestry alone, consider the many reasonable precautions the government could have pursued as alternatives to large-scale detention on the basis of ancestry. Military officers could have allocated resources to defend high-value sites: military bases, government buildings, monuments, and the like. They could have continued surveillance of any suspected saboteurs and picked up anyone for actually conspiring to act against the nation's interests.

The United States had imposed martial law in Hawaii in the hours after Pearl Harbor. While severe, that even-handed approach to restricting everyone's liberty could have been extended—though certainly at significant political cost—in parts of the West Coast if there had been a real threat of invasion. The federal government practiced selective internment in Hawaii, leaving most Japanese nationals and U.S. citizens free to work and live at home. That approach could have been employed on the mainland.

Instead of going with less intrusive measures or the broader but even-handed policy of martial law, officials pursued the more politically expedient and drastic option: maintaining civilian control demanded by most voters but allowing military officers to force people of Japanese ancestry to shoulder disproportionately the burdens of keeping America safe. The Justices noted that "hardships are part of war," yet they did nothing to ameliorate the racialized hardships based on war hysteria. What made this even more inexcusable was that judges backed internment even though they acknowledged that "most . . . we have no doubt were loyal to this country." The military authorities swept up the undesirables first, and asked questions later.[44]

On the same day the Supreme Court handed down *Korematsu*, a week before Christmas Day 1944, it issued a decision called *Ex Parte Endo*. A Japanese American woman named Mitsuye Endo had sued for her freedom from an internment camp. The Justices unanimously ordered the government to release her. Put to the test, government lawyers introduced no evidence she had engaged in any sabotage or acted to harm the United States. "A citizen who is concededly loyal presents no problem of espionage or sabotage," Justice Douglas finally declared. "Loyalty is a matter of the heart and mind not of race, creed, or color. He who is loyal is by definition not a spy or a saboteur." Moreover, the federal statute upon which the administration relied never authorized the detention of loyal citizens.

Although Endo's unconditional release vindicated the central goals of the rule of reason—taking justification and empiricism seriously— it did so too late. By then, as Justice Owen Roberts pointed out, a citizen could, "after he has suffered the disgrace of conviction and lost his liberty by sentence, then, and not before, seek, from within prison walls, to test the validity of the law."[45]

Reading the two decisions in tandem shows that the Justices had ultimately settled on the strategy of deferral as an imperfect solution to the competing demands of principle and realism: bow to popular sentiment by approving large-scale evacuation of the Japanese from their homes, but make these vulnerable citizens demand their release one by one. In fact, Chief Justice Stone delayed the release of the opinion until after President Roosevelt announced that the internment camps would be closed, so it had no real impact on the government's plans.[46]

But deferral is like a lousy rerun. We've seen it before and it never gets better. The compromise entails the sacrifice of a minority's basic rights out of convenience to government officials and to maintain the comfort of the majority. The rule-of-law principles might be useful in the future, but did the internees little good. Government officials could have acted earlier to prevent or minimize burdens on a powerless population. Regrettably, they simply chose not to do so when it mattered the most.

A number of people today share the perspective expressed by Justice Scalia: the *Korematsu* decision was "wrong" but somehow still defensible because of "panic about the war." For Scalia, "[i]t's no justification but it is the reality"—one he was convinced would happen again. But this position amounts to a capitulation to the exact passions, unfounded fears, and unprincipled acts of repression that the Founders warned against. Neither they, nor the members of the Reconstruction generation, created an emergency exception to the Constitution.[47]

Practical egalitarians would have recognized right away the impasse created by the heated debate over equality. They would have made it a priority to reduce the immediate harms from inequality rather than sidestepping those worries. Justice Douglas penned a dissenting opinion in *Korematsu* but he was convinced to file it away and join the majority. His rationale later became the basis for the *Endo* ruling. Those who opposed internment could have worked harder to keep Douglas in the fold, even if that meant swallowing the possibility there would be no ringing statement on equality. He provided the fourth vote against forced relocation. Could one more jurist have been swayed to join them if they had agreed to give up accusing military officials and the president of blatant racism?

The actual outcome: two separate and disjointed rulings, one that approved racial dragnets on an unprecedented scale, followed by a declaration of the importance of the values of individual innocence and congressional oversight in a second decision that seemed almost like an afterthought. Many Americans have heard of *Korematsu*, but far fewer remember *Ex Parte Endo*.

If Justice Douglas's draft dissent had been expanded earlier, we might have had a single decision, a unified vision of law that made clear Congress had never properly authorized mass detentions of U.S. citizens, and that without such public engagement, the administration's plan failed to rest on the kind of emergency that made extraordinary measures justifiable. In the absence of evidence of widespread criminality or disloyalty, each individual deserved to be treated fairly and given a hearing before incarceration.

When we are lax about what counts as valid justifications, that negligence hurts outsider groups more. Conversely, paying attention to reason's requirements ensures that the burdens of security and war making don't fall unequally on some people without sound justifications.

Reason's virtues don't lie merely in punching holes in terrible arguments that rationalize injustice. Its most powerful benefit is that it offers a technique for struggling against the narrative of historical inevitability. That family of arguments—bad things always happen in war, atrocities are par for the course, it's better for a few to suffer than for the majority to take any chances—is part of the authoritarian's arsenal.

Forcing everyone to slow down, to document, to justify, helps break the chain of inevitability. A rush to judgment is avoided. It also gives friends of equality time to organize and bring arguments to bear on the national security debate. This breathing space is essential because government officials have strong incentives to shade the truth during times of crisis.

Displeasing powerful people is never easy. It's harder still when they have guns. Yet that's why soldiers, like police officers, have to be restrained by constitutional norms. Someone has to call for a return to rule by reason, which is often the last hope for the friendless and despised. If not their neighbors, then activists and elected representatives; if not civic leaders, then it comes down to lawyers. It has to start somewhere.

TRANSGENDER PERSONS AS THE NEW SCAPEGOATS

IN RECENT YEARS, TWO political dynamics have brought greater attention to laws that turn on a person's gender or sexuality. The first began with the women's rights and gay rights movements, which asked us to confront the ways that policies based on sex or gender can cause lasting harm. These liberation movements have provoked an equally potent political response, as traditionalists have sought to reimpose more orderly notions of sex roles—using legal force when necessary. Those involved in these debates bring the full weight of moral and legal arguments to bear on an issue, including the memory of past causes won or lost. Each side comes to feel that civilization will end if the other side prevails.

Today, sexual minorities are caught in the crossfire, especially transgender persons. A transgender person is someone whose gender identity differs from the sex assigned at birth (which is done according to a newborn's physical appearance). On the one hand, the idea that a person's gender identity might lie on a continuum rather than a fixed binary of male-female is deeply uncomfortable. It upsets longstanding religious doctrine, some older scientific wisdom, and certainly many established social practices. The fact that transgender people comprise a political minority, are dealing with intimate matters concerning their bodies and their sense of self, and can become the subject of ridicule or violence all suggest we should make every effort to protect this vulnerable population.[48]

On the other hand, most people accept the gender identity that corresponds to their physical attributes, and wish sexual minorities no harm. They might worry that gender confusion will be exacerbated if societal norms change. Some are concerned about the spillover effects of recognizing transgender status as a constitutional idea—would this mean special entitlements? How would it affect business practices? For those holding such concerns, it is not obviously immoral to take such matters into account.

But the fact remains that transgender people exist. They deserve to be treated with dignity and respect. Increasingly, policymakers are making rules with them in mind. This new reality means it is high time to reflect on how to deal with laws that affect transgender people. Is there a way to keep in mind the material concerns of this political minority, even as they find themselves the latest flashpoint in America's culture wars? Ideally, such laws should be handled like others that implicate one's biological sex, sexual preference, or gender identity. These facets of human experience are bound up with a society's view of the good life and impact an individual's own sense of what is possible.

Even if Americans aren't prepared to agree on the broader moral question of the equal status of transgender people, we must still be ready to pursue equality by other means. For the practical egalitarian, the goal is always to try to minimize any inequities and ameliorate immediate harms while political debate over fundamental questions continues.

In March 2016, North Carolina became the first state in the country to enact a law that required individuals to use the bathroom that matched the gender listed on their birth certificate. State legislators enacted HB2 in response to the City of Charlotte's decision to amend local antidiscrimination laws to encompass "sexual orientation, gender expression and gender identity." This policy change allowed a transgender person to use whatever bathroom felt most comfortable to use, a development that alarmed a number of people in the community. The state law not only supplanted Charlotte's antidiscrimination policy, it also barred cities and counties from passing any of their own antidiscrimination laws in the future. At least twenty-four states have considered such laws. Some public schools have also gotten into the act.[49]

How should disputes of this sort be handled? The past serves as a guide. Back in 1996, the Supreme Court struck down a referendum passed by Colorado voters that amended the state constitution so as to bar legal protections for anyone on the basis of homosexuality. That ruling, *Romer v. Evans*, is remembered as a controversy about anti-gay animus. But in fact, a close reading of the case shows that it contains two independent rationales. First, heavy burdens foisted on one group must be matched by sound, rather than irrational, justifications. Second, status-based hostility is always out of bounds. Either rationale, standing alone, explains the outcome. And that also means that the case serves as the perfect roadmap for equality by other means.[50]

In a critical part of Justice Kennedy's opinion he observes that the referendum singles out some people based on a single trait—their sexuality—while broadly disabling legal protections of every kind for members of that group. Consequently, the law "inflicts on them immediate, continuing, and real injuries that outrun and belie any legitimate justifications that may be claimed for it." Colorado offered two reasons for the law: preserving the freedom of people who object to homosexuality not to associate with gays and lesbians, and conserving resources to battle other forms of discrimination. The Court rejected both of these arguments because "they were so far removed" from the broad scope of the law that it was "impossible to credit them."

The Justices could have stopped there, but they didn't. Instead, they went on to say that "the amendment seems inexplicable by anything but animus toward the class it affects." In other words, a heavy burden imposed on a single group ostensibly to satisfy poorly articulated objectives actually suggests a more nefarious motive: disgust or malice. Because it's illiberal to hate members of a group simply for who they are, and to impose an unequal burden upon them, the law was void.[51]

We now have a path forward. As with sexual orientation, people still disagree over whether the nature of the suffering experienced by transgender people is comparable to that faced by racial minorities, religious dissenters, or women. Nor have we recognized a fundamental right to satisfy basic bodily functions—at least not yet. Still, we shouldn't leave transgender individuals totally unprotected.[52]

A challenger might insist that unbridled hostility animates these bathroom laws, which would instantly doom all such laws. Yet they will almost certainly encounter those who feel that it's not hatred but rather fear that motivates these policies. The question then becomes: is that fear rational under the circumstances?

In many situations, the answer will be "no." Legislators or school officials have consistently offered two kinds of arguments when promoting "biological gender" matching bathroom laws: security and privacy. In many instances, they will not be able to point to any actual incidents where a transgender person has assaulted someone in a bathroom or otherwise poses a true threat. Occasionally, a proponent of such laws will claim that it's not about transgender people at all, but rather an effort to stop a man from pretending to be a woman in order to assault a woman in the restroom. Again, this fear can be tested to see if this is something that really happens or is instead the product of a feverish mind. Anyway, it's hard to imagine how a birth certificate–matching requirement would actually deter a person from committing assault in the john, if laws against battery already on the books aren't going to do the trick.

There are issues of practical enforcement of bathroom laws that also seem unreasonable. Since a law like this will fall more heavily on transgender individuals, they will presumably have to try get their birth certificate changed to match their gender identity, but it can be extremely difficult to get this done. And if transgender people do obtain the proper documents, will they have to keep papers on them as they navigate public spaces? If so, this type of legal regime just ratchets up one's sense of shame while raising the specter of a totalitarian gender-licensing program where our identity must be preapproved by the state before we can satisfy basic bodily needs.

As for privacy, the question is whether forcing a transgender person to use a bathroom that doesn't line up with the ideal of biological sex actually improves others' right to bodily integrity. With minor accommodations, the physical layouts and availability of multiple facilities are usually enough to take care of these concerns. Mostly, then, it comes down to some vague discomfort from sharing a small space with a transgender person. Let's be real: Would people really be more comfortable seeing transgender men in women's rooms simply because their birth certificate read "female"? That's what these kinds of policies mandate, all in the name of privacy and safety.

The absence of a sound empirical basis for policies like that of North Carolina, plus any dehumanizing comments by those in charge, will underscore that most, if not all, bathroom laws rest on stereotypes of gender nonconforming individuals as "perverts" and "weirdos." The reality is that most transgender persons are frightened and want to be let alone to use the toilet without being ridiculed. By focusing on the factual basis of perceived threats to public order, it's possible to minimize unequal harms, and even outright scapegoating of sexual minorities for broader cultural changes, while sidestepping more intractable philosophical debates.[53]

Now what about a more difficult problem: President Trump's unilateral decision to ban transgender troops? Here, the stakes are raised on all sides. As commander in chief, a president enjoys significant authority over matters concerning troop readiness. This includes the morale, safety, and privacy of soldiers. Moreover, no one has a constitutional right to serve in the military. To the contrary, everyone understands that whatever rights a soldier has are diminished while in uniform.

At the same time, the president's memorandum affects somewhere between 2,000 and 12,800 transgender soldiers, hardly a negligible number. Our notion of military service is actually more complicated as well, with many Americans who feel that military service is bound up with citizenship and civic equality. The integration of black soldiers, and later openly gay and lesbian soldiers, invoked the republican ideal of the citizen-warrior. Still, the fact that women and other sexual minorities can serve their country with minor accommodations suggests that it might be possible for transgender persons to be capable soldiers.[54]

Once again, the rule of reason might end up as the most realistic substitute for egalitarianism. The issue would turn entirely on whether being transgender is compatible with military service. President Trump has taken the view that the "disruptions" associated with transgender troops, including the costs of any necessary surgery, makes it not worth the candle. He believes that the presence of such individuals "erodes military readiness and unit cohesion." But is this determination, which categorically excludes an entire social group from the armed forces, premised on a stereotype about masculinity as a necessary component of "military effectiveness and lethality" or grounded in a set of real concerns?[55]

Furthermore, this might be the kind of decision a president shouldn't be allowed to make unilaterally. After all, policies about the composition of the armed forces also implicate Congress's powers over the military. The Constitution gives Congress, rather than the president, explicit power to "raise" armies, "provide and maintain a Navy," and to "make Rules for the Government and Regulation of the land and naval Forces." Because the question of who can serve is a judgment about civic duty and equal opportunity, it should require full public engagement.[56]

Calling the ban unreasonable wouldn't preclude political leaders from revisiting the issue, but it would raise the costs of doing so. A credible record would have to be assembled, either by military authorities or after hearings in Congress. Existing studies compiled by the previous administration indicated that disruptions would be minimal. At some point, this approach would require sifting through competing research to see if a total ban falls within the range of reasonable policy solutions. But the rule of reason might be tempting as a rationale to someone who doesn't want to impose any permanent constraints on a president in this domain, but who also thinks it unconscionable to inflict gratuitous harm on loyal soldiers.

Meanwhile, the broader national conversation about the place of transgender people in civic life can continue unabated. That debate is essential to securing more robust and lasting legal protections for sexual minorities. The Employment Non-Discrimination Act, which would clarify beyond a shadow of a doubt that the Civil Rights Act of

1964 protects against sexual orientation and gender identity discrimination, remains bottled up in Congress. In the meantime, legal and cultural changes are occurring from the ground up. Currently, twenty states plus the District of Columbia have laws that prohibit employment discrimination on the basis of sexual orientation or gender identity; another four hundred or so cities and counties have added such protections. About seventeen states and two hundred cities and counties explicitly protect gender identity in public accommodations laws, and several more jurisdictions have interpreted existing laws that ban sex discrimination to include mistreatment on the basis of gender.

The rule of reason doesn't end this conversation but shapes it in important ways. This approach pushes that conversation to be more fact-based and less ideologically polarizing. The attitude it fosters—an unswerving commitment to facts—can be exactly what is needed to cause a reset and help create conditions for compromise with justice as the object.[57]

Debates over national security or public order conducted at the highest levels of abstraction tend to overwhelm concerns about individual dignity, which can seem trivial by comparison. What's the value of poor people or disabled individuals being able to live together or in an integrated society? When the state is trying to solve crimes or prevent the next attack, what is the value of being able to stay put? Empiricizing the state's resort to legal force encourages us to home in on actual threats and probabilities rather than presumed tendencies based on broad social categories. Perhaps most important, it allows us to notice how discriminatory policies create an array of injuries, all of which can undermine the legal system in the long term.

Enforcing the rule of reason can reduce disparities in the government's treatment of citizens. Proequality gains can be achieved whether we are concerned with the unfair hardships of waging war or the costs of maintaining social order falling on some segments of society more harshly than others.

CHAPTER 4

NO CRUELTY

Looks like a dog, walks like a dog, smells like
a dog, must be a dog.

—"Agent Robert" to a
Guantanamo Bay detainee

"Power might be tempted to cruelty," observed Justice Joseph McKenna in 1910. He was right. The worst among the worst create special problems for the vision of a community of equals. A suspected terrorist captured in a foreign country, a convicted murderer awaiting execution, a sexual offender about to be released—all have done something so despicable that many will insist they have forfeited the right to be treated as full members of society.

At the same time, it's hard to imagine such individuals successfully using the political process to protect themselves. Calls to separate and humiliate belligerents, sweep away the homeless, and indefinitely monitor the convicted felon have led to the creation of new classes of people subject to novel forms of social control by the administrative state. Their plight raises grave concerns of inequality.[1]

At times, appealing to a related idea—the principle against cruelty—can do as good a job of dealing with inequities in how the irredeemable are treated. We can avoid intractable debates that require us to determine who is worthy of recognition and focus attention where it should be: the inhumanity of government policies and the damage it can do to a community's reputation.

Take the controversy over what locals called the "Queue Ordinance" in San Francisco—a law passed in the late nineteenth century requiring all men held in county or city jails to have their hair cut to an inch from their scalp. Ho Ah Kow, a Chinese national, was jailed for failing to pay a fine after being caught sleeping in a place that had less than 500 cubic feet of space for each occupant. That state law had been enacted as part of a series of regulations designed to drive out Chinese laborers. One prominent leader of the Working Man's Party of California accused China of sending its "meanest slave on earth— the Chinese coolie" to America so as to "degrade white labor." "These cheap slaves fill every place," said the activist with disgust. "They hedge twenty into a room, ten by ten."[2]

While in jail, the sheriff cut off Ho Ah Kow's queue, a long single braid of hair kept according to the custom of his people. He sued, contending that he had been denied equal protection of the laws based on his race and subjected to cruel and unusual punishment. He argued that the loss of his hair was "a mark of disgrace."

Supreme Court Justice Stephen Field agreed. The actual language of the hair-cutting law didn't single out the Chinese. Even so, he found that it was "understood by everyone" that the law's "purpose is to reach the queues of the Chinese, and it is not enforced against any other persons." Because the law amounted to "hostile and spiteful legislation," its usage denied equal protection of the law.[3]

But Justice Field wasn't finished. He pressed on to find the sheriff's actions overly cruel, declaring it a form of "torture" gratuitously added to get the Chinese to pay fines or flee the region. Thus, the law inflicted "suffering altogether disproportionate to what would be endured by other prisoners if enforced against them." This ground was particularly appealing because others saw the law the same way. In fact, the mayor had vetoed an earlier version of the pigtail ordinance, declaring it "a special and degrading punishment inflicted upon the Chinese residents for slight offenses."[4]

This controversy demonstrated, once again, there can be more than one path to justice. There is overlap in what the idea of equality demands and what the anti-cruelty principle forbids. Justice Field put it this way: "[N]o charges or burdens shall be laid upon him which are not equally borne by others, and that in the administration of criminal justice he shall suffer for his offenses no greater or different punishment."

Whichever solution one preferred, an entire community was saved from humiliation and differential treatment. As an influential figure riding circuit in California, Justice Field might have felt freer to look beyond the actual language of the statute to discern a singular motive to harm the Chinese. Yet in other situations, where multiple people are involved and there is less obvious evidence that a law is a barely disguised effort to hurt one group, the equality route might be foreclosed. Then anti-cruelty might be the best flanking maneuver available.

This enlightened spirit of mercy is codified in the English Bill of Rights, state constitutions, federal law, and the U.S. Constitution's Eighth Amendment, which prohibits "cruel and unusual punishment." It can also be found in international law, which forbids "cruel, inhuman or degrading treatment." The goal of the anti-cruelty principle is to discourage "inhuman and barbarous" practices among the citizenry. Philosophically, this maxim of ethical treatment reflects Kant's famous injunction to act so that each person is an "end" and "never merely as means."[5]

Precisely because the American people placed their hope in popular sovereignty, the risk of official atrocities remains omnipresent. The "practical and sagacious" men who framed the Constitution knew that "[w]ith power in a legislature great, if not unlimited, to give criminal character to the actions of men, with power unlimited to fix terms of imprisonment with what accompaniments they might," the law could be easily transformed into a "potent instrument of cruelty."[6]

The range of state policies that can be described as cruel necessarily changes with the times, as the government's own capacities for inflicting needless suffering also expands. "Evolving standards of decency" establish the outer boundaries of acceptable punishment. Certain kinds of penalties—drawing and quartering, maiming, torture— pass into obsolescence as "public opinion becomes enlightened by a humane justice." In 1890, the Supreme Court found the electric chair to be more acceptable than hanging, but by 2001, punishment norms had changed so much that the Georgia Supreme Court retired "Old Sparky" under its own state constitution, saying that "the specter of excruciating pain and its certainty of cooked brains and blistered bodies" exceeded modern standards.[7]

In the queue-cutting dispute, the judge compared that penalty to caning the soles of the feet, crushing fingers or toes with a thumbscrew, stretching someone on the rack, or whipping the body. He found it just as excessive. Shearing the hair of the Chinese was "not creditable to the humanity and civilization of our people, much less to their Christianity."[8]

Over time, two factors have expanded the state's ability to cause physical or psychological pain, or to enforce social isolation: technological advancement and political bureaucratization. Together, these additions to the government's repertoire allow it to exert, when it wishes, a more totalizing control of space and time.

Technological advancements can alter the government's capacity to inflict suffering exponentially. Think of the advent of electricity, lethal chemicals, or drone missiles that have made it possible to kill more human beings at great distances while diffusing responsibility across many individuals and institutions. The rise of electronic surveillance and predictive models permit a small group of people to keep tabs on a larger population. Medications mandated by the state can keep a person in an altered state of mind, inhibit aggression or sex drive, or diminish fantasies.[9]

Sprawling bureaucracies and faceless staff facilitate the efficient delivery of new punitive forms but also raise unimagined problems of accountability by adding layer upon layer of powers and practices. Today, the policeman is joined by the correctional officer, the soldier, the ICE agent, the sheriff, and the probation officer in the enforcement of America's laws. These agents of the state wield enormous everyday discretion to decide how much force to use in a given situation and which legal processes to set in motion.

There are two main ways of arguing that a practice violates the ban against cruel treatment. One method is to say that society has firmly rejected a particular form of punishment. The question is whether a measure subjects a person to "a fate forbidden by the principle of civilized treatment." We typically ask how many states employ a specific practice, with an eye toward detecting declining practices as well as very peculiar ones. We might even see how other countries handle similar matters, though this remains a controversial tactic in certain quarters.[10]

This is precisely what jurists did when they declared it draconian to burn someone alive, or to execute people with intellectual disabilities, or to use force sadistically to restrain an inmate. In the political domain, it is the same argument made by those who seek to abolish the death penalty, pointing to a declining willingness among most jurisdictions to carry out the sentence as well as America's relative isolation in the world as a bloodthirsty nation.[11]

Beyond cultural rejection, a sanction is also extraordinary if it violates our collective sense of proportionality. The key is whether the severity of a sanction is grossly out of line with an offense or particular state objective. Under this approach, prolonged or acute pain can be relevant but is not decisive. Humiliation and the loss of personal security might be enough. Justice Powell, for instance, once suggested that punishing a person for up to twenty years in prison for engaging in a single consensual act of anal or oral sex would be inhumane.[12]

The harsh effect of a punishment proved decisive in *Trop v. Dulles*, a 1958 Supreme Court ruling that a U.S. citizen could not be stripped of his citizenship for desertion. During World War II, some 7,000 American soldiers lost their citizenship in this fashion. While such a punishment involves no physical violation, or any physical pain at all, it inflicts permanent injury by effecting "the total destruction of the individual's status in organized society." An intolerable sense of uncertainty about what the future might hold exacerbates the loss of civic security, "a fate of ever-increasing fear and distress."[13]

This situation also raises the specter of future equality violations. Rendering a person stateless, a foreigner in his own country, means that he has "lost the right to have rights." This legal limbo is worse than the usual infringement of equality. Such a denuded condition makes it far more likely such individuals will be singled out for even harsher treatment down the road. "He knows not what discriminations may be established against him, what proscriptions may be directed against him."[14]

These observations can be generalized. *Any* time individuals are placed into special legal categories (or exceptions to egalitarianism), they are exposed to greater risk of unusual harms. We should expect the political pressures to treat some groups consistently worse to carry over to how such categories are actually managed, so that exemptions grow ever larger to include more situations, more human beings, more pain. When we don't hold the line on the creation of a special category, we make it exponentially harder to reduce subsequent barbarity. If we aren't willing to get rid of the legal exception, we have to be open to a larger quiver of techniques to deal with the inequities that are bound to follow.

BUILDING A CULTURE OF EQUAL DIGNITY

WHEN DEBATES DWELL FOR too long on disparities between groups, conversation about equality can grind to a halt. This dynamic is most pronounced when it comes to the role of race in criminal justice, where conversation can become "racialized" to the point that it saps energy for reform. Research suggests that when blackness and penal institutions become closely associated in the minds of average citizens, support for criminal justice reform goes down. A diminished willingness to enact change takes over, even when people believe that a situation is unjust.

One study conducted in 2012 by Stanford psychologists Rebecca Hetey and Jennifer Eberhardt asked voters in the San Francisco Bay area whether they would support a ballot measure to reduce the severity of California's three-strikes law. Before they made a choice, one set of participants was shown slides of inmates where 25 percent were black, mirroring the actual California prison population. A second set of participants was shown images with more black inmates (45 percent). Members of the second group, exposed to a blacker prison population, were significantly less willing to sign the petition (27 percent versus 52 percent) even though both groups found the law severe. Notably, both groups perceived the array of images to be "blacker" than they actually were. Hetey and Eberhardt concluded that perceptions of black criminality increased popular acceptance of harsh punishments.[15]

The researchers tested their hypothesis a few months later on the East Coast and got similar results. This time, they told New York City residents about the racial demographics in the prisons rather than showing them photos. Again, one group of respondents was given a "blacker" set of numbers. Then the groups were asked to read about the federal judge's ruling that the NYPD's stop-and-frisk program had been struck down as unconstitutional. Although both sets of residents found the policy punitive, the group given the statistics with a higher percentage of black inmates became measurably less willing to sign a petition to end the stop-and-frisk program (12 percent versus 33 percent). Once again, the blacker that voters believed the criminal population to be, the more likely they feared crime. These perceptions then dampened their enthusiasm for political change—this time, even after they were told a judge had weighed in and found the policy problematic.

If the dynamics detected by researchers hold true more broadly, then reformers face a terrible conundrum. The law of equality requires fine-grained analysis focusing on group-specific injury (race, religion, sex, etc.), and a history of oppression. What's more, political mobilization always commences by rallying affected communities. But the very steps necessary to advance equality in the criminal justice system might simultaneously create new psychological and political roadblocks to legal change.

What lessons should we draw? It can't be to give up the game. Instead, if we are concerned with justice, we'll have to be cognizant of how racial perceptions are being manipulated in presentations about crime. Exploitation of erroneous racial stereotypes has to be called out. Racial assumptions are often overdrawn even when we have accurate information. Perhaps even more important, the research confirms the need to develop an array of techniques for attacking inequality in the justice system and the virtue of being nimble in choosing among them.

Anti-cruelty rhetoric can help. A practical egalitarian ought to see that this approach can keep attention trained on systemic inequities while avoiding the traps of an overly narrow discourse.

The sad reality is that egalitarianism routinely fails society's castoffs. Equal protection claims are frequently rejected if they don't impair a fundamental right or access to a valuable social good. But a great deal of degrading treatment endured by the underclass escapes remedy simply because certain indignities haven't been made priorities by mainstream

Americans. Most people haven't had to face extreme deprivation. That means we haven't had to think hard about why access to food, shelter, air, clean water, sunshine, exercise, or healthcare might be worth protecting as basic rights. The absence of such deep and sustained reflection means that American constitutional law won't view these as high-stakes controversies unless federal law or state law has already done so.[16]

Don't many groups suffer in the same way that already recognized groups are said to have suffered? Some certainly do, but others pale by comparison. Convicted criminals comprise the classic group that deserves reduced civil rights. Their own wrongdoing plus a legitimate need to reduce the likelihood of reoffending justify a reduction in liberty, sometimes even after a prison term has been served. Even foreigners, whom we have recognized as a group that has faced historical discrimination, are treated as less than full members of the community. Many kinds of restrictions on migrants are founded on this difference in status. Individuals who take up arms against the United States also fall into this category. In other words, for some categories of people, a distinctive kind of suffering can be justified. They are the exceptions to the rule that egalitarianism ordinarily requires all persons to be treated as equal members of the community.

Now it's true that even legitimate distinctions between groups can be taken to a destructive extreme. For example, the idea that prisoners are defective members of the community has been deployed to rationalize the disenfranchisement of felons. This has had a disastrous result, with over six million people losing the right to vote this way. In four states—Florida, Virginia, Kentucky, and Tennessee—more than one of every five African Americans can't vote for this reason. But the point remains: because we are talking about convicted felons, their status serves as a major stumbling block in debates over equality. If we don't want to consign whole groups of people to legal limbo, where abuse can be heaped upon them with impunity, we'll have to find other ways to address their concerns.

Many of these inequities will evade egalitarianism's hunt for nefarious motives. This is because cruelty can come from popular "zeal for a purpose, either honest or sinister." City officials who outlaw panhandling or sleeping in public say they mean the downtrodden no harm, and wish only to preserve the aesthetic beauty of a neighborhood and keep the sidewalks free. Those who demand the perpetual monitoring of sexual offenders insist their goals are to warn fellow citizens of potential danger, not encourage vigilantism. A police officer or soldier always believes she is acting to keep innocent people safe when a suspect is handled roughly.[17]

Whereas equality discourse obsesses over the intent lying behind one's actions, the anti-cruelty debate trains attention on the objective nature of a practice (is it punitive in form and function?) and its relative place among possible punishment practices (is it an outlier or not?). In a time when we use the criminal law to express moral outrage and creative incentives to behave in all sorts of socially desirable ways, it has great potential to relieve individuals from unjust policies.

There's some overlap with the principle of fair play. Both concepts can help curb practices that violate a community's shared sense of ethical treatment. Beating a suspect to extract information can be understood as a deeply unfair practice that undermines the integrity of a legal outcome. That same behavior could be reimagined as an excessively punitive act. These are both alternatives to how egalitarianism traditionally handles a situation, by wondering if the state is treating like people alike.

The anti-cruelty principle poses a moral question, but one that's different from the kind raised by the usual way in which we talk about equality. Like the fair play strategy, the question is not so much whether certain kinds of people deserve full equality but instead what a particular sanction says about a community. Because it deemphasizes *who* deserves a particular right, this approach gives individuals marginalized for good reasons an opportunity to avoid inhumane and selective treatment. Indeed, the concept of dignity presumes that all individuals are born unique, and are entitled to be treated in a civilized fashion.

That conversation revolves around undesirable consequences to be avoided: the possibility of degradation or serious physical or psychological injury, exposure to other downstream harms, deterioration of social relationships, the damage to the community's reputation for justice.

History also reminds us that equality and anti-cruelty are interlocking values. Enforcing one principle under the right circumstances can advance the cause of the other. The architects of the Fourteenth Amendment understood inequality as a complex problem that could abridge a variety of rights: not only equal protection of the law, but also the privileges and immunities of citizenship, due process, and even the guarantee against cruel punishments.

"[M]any instances of state injustice and oppression have already occurred," John Bingham reported to fellow members of the Reconstruction Congress. "Contrary to the express letter of your Constitution, 'cruel and unusual punishments' have been inflicted under State laws within this Union for not only crimes committed, but also for sacred duty done." Bingham envisioned the Fourteenth Amendment as a multipurpose tool of justice wherever "the United States had provided no remedy." He was not choosy about how problems were classified or described. There were so many injustices to speak of.[18]

What he and other members of that generation had in mind were draconian laws and other repressive actions taken against freed persons and their supporters. In their original constitution, the people of Oregon had tried to establish a white homeland by barring free blacks from taking up residence within its borders and by making it "a penal offense for any person to harbor any of the excluded class of their fellow-citizens." Bingham called the constitution "an infamous atrocity." Indiana's constitution contained similar provisions barring any "negro or mulatto" from settling in the state, fining those who "encouraged" freed persons to stay, and voiding any contracts made with black people.[19]

Freed persons in other states were being punished "with the whip and scourge" for minor offenses, and this was seen by reformers as an incident of slavery. Heavy penalties were imposed on blacks for vagrancy, and sheriffs were allowed to hire out any detained "freedman, free negro, or mulatto" to white employers. In Florida, the children of parents convicted of vagrancy could be hired out as apprentices.[20]

Black Codes enacted by Southern states denied freed persons a host of rights, including the ability to testify against whites, own or rent property, possess firearms, or travel without an employer's permission. Alabama, Tennessee, and Mississippi all required the death penalty for any slave or freedman who raped a white woman. Louisiana barred blacks from congregating at night and preaching without permission from the local police. Many former slave states required blacks to prove they were in the "regular service of some white person or former owner." Failure to present proof of employment was taken as evidence of vagrancy.

Through the years, many have seen for themselves how ensuring cruelty-free punishments can fulfill some of the objectives of egalitarianism. In 1972 the Supreme Court struck down an array of death penalty laws because they failed to limit the discretion of juries and judges who made sentencing decisions. Untrammeled power over crucial life decisions can actually worsen structural inequality. According to Justice Douglas, "[T]he discretion of judges and juries in imposing the death penalty enables the penalty to be selectively applied, feeding prejudices against the accused if he is poor and despised, and lacking political clout, or if he is a member of a suspect or unpopular minority."

Hence, reducing merciless treatment across the board can redound to the benefit of those who tend to feel the brunt of harsh policies.

Justice Douglas pointed out that American constitutional law had evinced an abiding concern with dismantling arbitrary forms of oppression against unpopular groups. He traced this imperative from the debates surrounding the Fourteenth Amendment all the way back to the founding era. "Those who wrote the Eighth Amendment knew what price their forebears had paid for a system based not on equal justice, but on discrimination," he wrote. "In those days, the target was not the blacks or the poor, but the dissenters, those who opposed absolutism in government . . . [and] recurring efforts to foist a particular religion on the people."[21]

The promise of cruelty-free treatment can engender respect for individual dignity, a value that's also an essential component of equality under the law. As Chief Justice Earl Warren put it, "The basic concept underlying the Eighth Amendment is nothing less than the dignity of man." Dignity as an idea shares religious and secular origins, which lends it potency as a common language. Christian documents speak of "the dignity of the person" and promise "immunity from coercion" in order to foster equality and religious freedom. And the Universal Declaration of Human Rights announces, "All human beings are born free and equal in dignity and rights." Kant's own humanity formula yoked together the concepts of dignity and equality to demand respect "as much in your own person as in the person of every other, always at the same time."[22]

The opposite is also true. Vindicating the principle of equality promotes dignitary interests. In *Obergefell*, the Supreme Court defended its same-sex marriage decision by grounding it in "equal dignity"—a phrase that evokes a culture where equality and dignity are both valued. A strong dose of anti-cruelty flavored the ruling: the outcome ensures that gay people are not "condemned to live in loneliness" and perpetual "exclusion from one of civilization's oldest institutions." The children of same-sex couples, too, have dignitary concerns, for laws denying recognition to their parents' marriages caused children to "suffer the stigma of knowing their families are somehow lesser."[23]

When a certain behavior is declared off limits because of its barbarity, a new baseline is established. The constitutional rules necessarily change in response to that new baseline. For instance, when the High Court declared it excessive to execute a person for a crime committed while under the age of eighteen, it drew a protective circle around youthful offenders.

One can be forgiven for thinking that application of the anticruelty principle in *Roper v. Simmons* is at odds with equality. After all, equality requires that similar people be treated in the same way, and here the Court was saying that young offenders were categorically different from adult offenders. A closer look reveals the equality-enhancing effects of this decision. The practical effect was exactly the same as if someone had said that the death penalty unfairly singled out the youthful out of malice or for some other inappropriate reason.[24]

In fact, advocates convinced jurists that some young offenders tried as adults were, in fact, being wrongly disadvantaged. They argued that "adolescents as a class 'face a special risk of wrongful execution'" and that "immature" and "vulnerable" kids were being sentenced to death. Former U.S. Solicitor General Seth Waxman, arguing on behalf of the death row inmate, pointed out that psychiatrists are precluded from diagnosing a person with antisocial personality before the age of eighteen because of the inherently volatile nature of a juvenile's development. If experts have trouble identifying the most hardened juveniles, then jurors would have an even more challenging time correctly ascertaining the worst of the worst. Instead, Waxman argued, jurors "frequently equate maturity and psychosocial development with race and with physical appearance."[25]

His implication was unmistakable: without the additional safeguard of a bright-line rule, key actors in the criminal justice system might identify young black males as more deserving of death. The answer to an equality problem, Waxman suggested, just might be the enforcement of the ban on cruelty.[26]

In the end, Justice Kennedy's opinion agreed that juveniles "cannot with reliability be classified among the worst offenders." Their lack of maturity and underdeveloped sense of responsibility make them generally less culpable than adults who commit the same crimes. Adolescents are also "more vulnerable or susceptible to negative influences and outside pressures." A heinous crime committed by a juvenile isn't conclusive evidence of an "irretrievably depraved character."

Worse, a young defendant's age wasn't predictably used to offset the gravity of an offense, but was more often portrayed as a reason to impose the ultimate punishment. That's exactly what the prosecutor did in *Roper v. Simmons* trial. "Seventeen years old," he told the jury. "Isn't that scary? Doesn't that scare you?"

Intended or not, the Supreme Court's descriptions of the typical juvenile offender pushed back against a destructive stereotype of a new breed of "superpredators" that drove mass incarceration in the 1990s and beyond. The term, coined by Princeton criminologist John DiIulio, conjured a fearsome image of "tens of thousands of severely morally impoverished juvenile super-predators. . . . perfectly capable of committing the most heinous acts of physical violence for the most trivial reasons." He claimed that "juveniles are doing homicidal violence in wolfpacks."

This fearsome image became forever fixed in the public consciousness after a brutal attack in New York City led to the coining of the term "wilding." In 1993, the Oxford English Dictionary actually defined the term as "the action or practice by a gang of youths of going on a protracted and violent rampage in a street, park or other public place." Hillary Clinton, too, lamented certain "kinds of kids . . . with no conscience, no empathy."[27]

By the mid-1990s, others had piled on, joining DiIulio in predicting a "bloodbath when these kids grow up." The inflammatory predictions proved to be wrong—violence by children fell by two-thirds from 1994 to 2011. By the time DiIulio renounced his own views, admitting that "[d]emography is not fate," it was too late. Federal and state laws, thousands of charging decisions, and untold sentences were reached in anticipation of a crime wave led by rampaging youths.[28]

Critics have shown there is a noxious, racist quality to this generalization, which was often explicitly linked to the inner city to stoke a moral panic about black criminality. That stereotype suggested this new breed of violent youths simply can't be rehabilitated, so they must be dealt with in the harshest terms. Insofar as enforcing anti-cruelty norms created an opportunity to chip away at this overly broad generalization, that solution promoted the egalitarian agenda.[29]

It turns out that two-thirds of all teenagers under sentence of death were racial minorities while two-thirds of their victims were white. Since 1973, over half of all teenagers executed have been black or Latino. The U.S. Department of Justice has found that "[b]lack juveniles are overrepresented at all stages of the juvenile justice system compared with their proportion to the population." These racial disparities run from arrest to being charged as adults, the severity of confinement, and the length of their punishments. Because teenagers are highly suggestible, they face a greater risk of false confessions. In fact, one study found that 90 percent of juveniles who were later exonerated were African American or Latino.[30]

But the way we currently think about equal protection of the law can't reach most of these pervasive disparities because we can't always uncover specific people in the justice system who desire to hurt black children. By contrast, a substantial risk of systemic cruelty is enough to violate the Eighth Amendment. An "unacceptable likelihood" that immature and vulnerable adolescents might be executed put an end to the juvenile death penalty in America. In one fell swoop, its demise also took care of racial disparities in punishment practices for that group of offenders.

A similar dynamic occurred when the Justices placed the "mentally retarded" as a group beyond the reach of capital punishment. In "the aggregate," they said, such individuals "face a special risk of wrongful execution." They are easily manipulated into giving false confessions, aren't able to give meaningful assistance to their lawyers at trial, and "their demeanor may create an unwarranted impression of lack of remorse." In other words, there was a real possibility that such individuals are put to death not for what they do, but for who they are.[31]

People with reduced capacities kept slipping through. In the Texas case of Oliver Cruz, the prosecutor urged the jury to impose a death sentence because the fact he "may not be very smart" made him "more dangerous." Cruz had an IQ of 64 or 76, could barely read or write, and failed the seventh grade three times. Experts estimate that as much as 10 percent of the 3,600 inmates on death row could be "mentally retarded." It is believed that thirty-four individuals with severe intellectual disabilities have been executed since 1976. In 1995, Florida executed Mario Marquez, who had severe brain damage and an IQ of 60. Ricky Ray Rector, executed by Arkansas in 1992, was so brain damaged from a self-inflicted gun wound that he no longer understood what it meant to die. On the way to his death by lethal injection, he told a guard to set his pecan pie aside since he was "saving it for later."[32]

Invalidating death sentences across the board for people with severe intellectual disabilities and for juveniles based on dignitary reasons served as another way of doing the work of equality. Just as the guarantee of egalitarianism can aid chronically disadvantaged groups, so too the promise of cruelty-free punishment can help reduce the disparate treatment of vulnerable social groups. Its emphasis on dignity, vulnerability, proportionality, and unacceptable risk renders us more open to confronting systemic inequities.[33]

Anti-cruelty grounds can emerge as the ground for action even though we continue to disagree about how children or people with intellectual disabilities should be treated in the criminal justice system. We can overlook differences of opinion over why they get into trouble—is it because they are less able to evaluate consequences, or is it due to situational factors like the tendency to give false confessions? We can also put aside differences over long-term solutions, long enough to deal with glaring injustices here and now.

BEHIND PRISON WALLS

PEOPLE CONVICTED OF CRIMES serious enough to warrant imprisonment face the loss of personal space, reduced control over nutrition and exercise, a diminished sense of health and well-being. They experience indignities and inconveniences on a daily basis. This is all par for the course. There is even a euphemism for all this suffering: "the ordinary incidents of prison life." But just how bad do conditions have to get before it can be said that incarceration practices dehumanize an inmate?

Traditional egalitarianism does little good behind prison walls, where "the government's power is at its apex." We presume that inmates are locked up for what they did rather than for who they are. That distinction justifies their general suffering behind bars. They have a set of fundamental rights, such as the right to speech and religious worship, but even those can be curtailed for penological reasons.

The principle of fairness is also at its ebb in the prison context. Prisons already severely constrain an individual's liberty in two senses: first, in the sense that any additional action might only marginally increase the general suffering an inmate already experiences; second, in the sense that constraints on liberty are justified by the inmate's previous wrongdoing as well as any legitimate penological interests. As a result, a prisoner has to show he faces an "atypical and significant hardship" before he can even cry foul.[34]

What passes for fair play in prison isn't what we would tolerate on the outside. Demont Conner learned this the hard way inside the Halawa Correctional Facility, a maximum-security prison in Oahu. A guard subjected him to a strip search on his way to a religious session, including an inspection of his anal area, and he reacted angrily, swearing at the officer. He was written up for two offenses: "high misconduct" for allegedly interfering with a correctional function and "low moderate misconduct" for using foul language. A disciplinary committee heard the matter but denied Conner a request to call witnesses and sentenced him to thirty days in solitary confinement. The inmate argued that this deprived him of due process.

His case reached the Supreme Court, where the Justices seized the opportunity to create fresh roadblocks to due process claims by inmates. Normally, we would examine prison regulations to see whether they created an enforceable expectation. Now the Justices went a step further, requiring an inmate to show that he has been subjected to "a dramatic departure from the basic conditions" of his existence before he could claim an unfair deprivation of his (already reduced) liberty.

Chief Justice Rehnquist, who wrote the opinion, then made a sweeping application of this new constitutional rule. He looked around and found a variety of regulations that allowed prison authorities to clamp down on inmates, mashed them all together, and concluded that the prison had broad discretion to use force on inmates. To deal with a breach of order, correctional officers could use administrative segregation or protective custody, or even put the entire population on lockdown. So an inmate's punishment in disciplinary segregation "did not work a major disruption in his environment."[35]

The upshot: although Conner faced a sanction behind prison walls, that sanction didn't make his already miserable existence markedly worse. For that reason, prison authorities didn't have any obligation to treat the inmate fairly.

Whatever way you slice it, the Justices got it wrong. Solitary confinement is qualitatively more dehumanizing as a form of suffering. Lost human contact with others, the inability to attend educational events, and a negative impact on parole are all consequences that flow from that kind of discipline. These factors make disciplinary segregation different from other liberty-restricting actions that can be taken by prison officials.

By making it harder for prisoners to make fairness arguments, the Justices insulated most administrative and disciplinary actions from outside review. Why the callous decision? Judges had grown tired of prisoners who "comb over" prison regulations in search of legal rights. They were fed up with hearing challenges to disciplinary decisions, believing inmates were "squandering judicial resources." For our purposes, making due process mostly a dead letter inside the Big House also short-circuited the capacity of fairness arguments to deal with inequitable treatment.

Because egalitarianism and fairness have limited potency in the prison context, anti-cruelty is left to do the heavy lifting. There's no society of equals to be made behind bars, but we can try to put a stop to wanton and degrading forms of treatment that corrode the bonds between us all.

Isolated acts of brutality can violate the Eighth Amendment. When Keith Hudson, an inmate at the state penitentiary in Angola, Louisiana, got into an argument with a guard, he was taken from his cell in full restraints: handcuffs, waist chains, leg shackles. Two officers then beat him savagely while he was immobilized. They kicked and punched him repeatedly, loosening his teeth and cracking his dental plate. A supervisor watched the physical reprisal, reminding the guards "not to have too much fun."

Before the Supreme Court, government lawyers argued that the Eighth Amendment allowed guards to inflict beatings as long as they were "isolated incidents" that didn't cause a "significant injury." Since his beating arose from "a personal dispute" between a prisoner and a guard, just officers "venting their impatience, their anger on him," it wasn't an authorized punishment. Hudson had some bruises but no broken bones, they also pointed out, so we might treat this as such a low-level harm that it doesn't implicate the ban on cruelty.[36]

The Justices did the right thing by rejecting the state's invitation to look the other way. Seven members of the Court agreed that the anti-cruelty principle can be violated without "significant injury." Justice O'Connor's opinion commanded five votes for the proposition that "unnecessary and wanton infliction of pain" is enough. Where guards "maliciously and sadistically use force," no additional "significant injury" must be shown. Justice Blackmun wrote separately to underscore the importance of rejecting the more rigorous rule offered by Louisiana, which might have then permitted certain kinds of torture "ingeniously designed" to cause pain but without a telltale trace of lasting injury. He mentioned several tactics that left few marks, including whipping inmates with rubber hoses, administering electrical shocks, exposing them to heat or cold, and causing asphyxiation short of death.[37]

By ensuring that the anti-cruelty principle has some teeth, the Justices gave with one hand what it had taken away with the other. For instead of calling egregious acts unfair or unequal, we can sometimes gain traction by emphasizing their corrupting nature. Individuals who stand out among the prison population—not just dangerous people, but nonconformists of all stripes—face a greater risk of corporal punishment. Young offenders, sexual minorities, racial and religious minorities are more frequent victims of prison violence. Occasionally, the guards themselves inflict the pain, sometimes fellow prisoners are permitted to handle discipline while guards look the other way. In such encounters, it can be incredibly hard to show that an inmate was mistreated because of some disfavored trait. But the inhumanity of an event might be undeniable.

Now consider a practice that has its origins in the racist past, but whose modern usage is hard to describe as intentionally singling out someone on the basis of race. In 2002, Larry Hope challenged the practice of Alabama correctional officers tying prisoners to a hitching post for violations of social order, big or small. Hope said that he had been left tied to a post for seven hours in the hot sun for refusing to work on a chain gang. At one point, guards brought over a cooler of water near him, let dogs drink from it, and kicked the cooler over, allowing the water to spill in his direction.

"They had me chained . . . up to the hitching rail like I was a dog," one inmate said. Most prisoners were shackled to a post while standing, with two hands close together at face level. Some said tall people were tied to shorter posts while shorter people were tied to taller posts to increase the pain and discomfort. At times, a person would be kept on the post until work crews returned to the prison or after dark, "whichever was longer."[38]

Food, water, and bathroom breaks were routinely denied. At least two prisoners complained that they had defecated on themselves, while other prisoners and guards ridiculed them. Observers compared the hitching post to the pillory or the stocks, once used to punish and humiliate wrongdoers. The posts were placed in prominent locations, such as near the back gate, where guards, inmates, and visitors could heap abuse on the vulnerable figure.[39]

Six Justices declared Alabama's use of the rail an "obvious cruelty." Justice John Paul Stevens's opinion found that Hope "was treated in a way antithetical to human dignity," left "for an extended period of time in a position that was painful, and under circumstances that were both degrading and dangerous." It was "not done of necessity, but as punishment for prior conduct."[40]

The state argued that the post wasn't used maliciously or as a form of punishment, but rather served valid penological needs. But it wasn't used only for serious security breaches; it was also deployed for routine infractions. One inmate had injured his back and couldn't work, so guards tied him to a post for several hours. Another didn't have proper boots to work in so he was tied to the post for six hours.

In a related lawsuit, prison authorities admitted they used the hitching post to coerce inmates to participate in the state's "unpopular work program" and to deter work strikes. But this justification was far worse than any claim about maintaining security, for it exposed their own motives to use inmates as merely the means to an end: creating a ready supply of unpaid labor.

As evidence that concern for human dignity can cross party lines, the Bush administration's Department of Justice took the inmate's side in the dispute. Government lawyers argued that "no reasonable officer" could have thought the "prolonged, painful, and punitive use of the hitching post" was lawful. It made an impact: the Court repeatedly cited DOJ's prior investigation of Alabama's use of the restraining bar as proof that the state had ample warning of constitutional rules but ignored a substantial risk of harm. At oral argument, the state's lawyer tried to urge the Justices to defer to "split-second decision" by guards, but Justice O'Connor would have none of it. "We're not talking about split seconds," she corrected. "We're talking about seven hours."[41]

Outlawing the hitching post for its cruelty amounted to equality by another name. At the time, Alabama was the only state in the Union that employed a hitching post. In this respect, Alabama prisoners had been treated worse than inmates in every other state. The humanitarian approach resolved that particular inequity. Alabama ranked fifth in terms of the rate at which it incarcerated its own citizens and more than half of its prison population was black, so the state's nonwhite population had faced greater exposure to injury and dehumanization from this type of discipline.

While the Supreme Court didn't delve into the history or sociology associated with the hitching post, it wasn't an isolated tool. Rather, it operated as the cornerstone of a broader system with darker roots that arose after the Civil War. The Southern work camp model controlled the black population, deterred the migration of freed persons to the region, and provided cheap labor for state work projects and privately run coal mines, lumber mills, and farms. Those seriously injured or killed on chain gangs were disproportionately black. Former Alabama governor Thomas E. Kilby once acknowledged that his state's convict-lease practice was "a form of human slavery." For many observers, the sight of mostly black chain gangs on the side of the road was the return of a racialized social order.[42]

Taking away an integral component of chain gangs helped disable that troubling practice. The anti-cruelty concept by itself can't put an end to mass incarceration. But it shines a light into the darkest corners of our punishment practices, and it can take the edge off the unnecessary suffering some inmates but not others must endure.

MEAN STREETS

MASS INCARCERATION ISN'T JUST the problem of a burgeoning prison population—it also encompasses the aggressive oversight and discipline of undesirables. As of 2013, there were 2.2 million Americans incarcerated in federal prisons, state prisons, and local jails, but there were a whopping 4.8 million under some form of community supervision. One out of every fifty-one adults was on probation or parole. Georgia led the nation with 536,200 under supervision, followed by Texas (515,100), California (390,100), and Florida (245,100). New York City alone had 31,000 individuals on probation, of whom 47 percent were black.[43]

A crucial player in the modern carceral state is the probation officer, who investigates a defendant's background to assess his risk to the community for sentencing purposes. The probation officer later might monitor many facets of a person's existence. An individual on probation or parole might be required to get a job, stay sober, resist unsavory habits, participate in certain kinds of programs, avoid spending time with disreputable persons, limit social media activity, submit to random drug tests and searches of his belongings, take a lie detector test, and give a DNA sample. A violation of any of these terms of release, at the discretion of the probation officer, might lead to reincarceration or the imposition of added terms.

Most of these conditions in the abstract seem perfectly reasonable. They will only appear outrageous, if at all, once enforced in particular circumstances. Because their terms are written so expansively, subjecting them to the idea of fair play can ensure that a probationer has a better sense of what can get her in trouble, sometimes years down the road.

The truth is that there aren't enough probation officers in the world to monitor all of the people under community supervision. Only a fraction of persons on probation ever has that status revoked. So the real problem is how broad discretion is being exercised. Questions have been raised about racial disparities in the imposition of probation terms and in their enforcement. Thirty percent of all people on probation are black, though African Americans comprise 13 percent of the population. One study found that probation was revoked at a significantly higher rate for blacks than whites or Hispanics in New York City and Dallas County, Texas. A separate study of Wisconsin probationers found that African Americans had their probation revoked at three times the rate of whites, especially for drug offenses.[44]

In theory, community supervision is intended not to impose additional punishments on offenders but rather to facilitate their reintegration into the community and reduce the likelihood of recidivism. Yet in practice the actual enforcement of probation terms could be arbitrary, bizarre, or onerous. At some point one of these conditions, or several of them in tandem, will create a regime that's so severe, or give faceless bureaucrats so much authority, that the situation ought to transgress the anti-cruelty principle.

When that line is crossed, it shouldn't matter whether a defendant has consented to a restriction. Defense lawyers will always place a premium on getting as little jail time as possible for a client and underestimate how stringent conditions of release might be. If a practice is extreme, the mismatch between offense and sanction or the damage to a community's reputation won't be any different when an individual willingly participates in his own degradation.

An area worthy of attention involves sex offenders, since many people are willing to go to any lengths to prevent this type of recidivism. Besides serving prison time, an offender will have to remain under community supervision. In eight states, a person who commits a serious sex offense won't be released unless he is surgically or chemically castrated—raising major concerns about whether these methods are effective and humane.

Once out of prison, information about an offender's crime, his photo, and his current address are collected and made available to the public. Some jurisdictions bar sex offenders from going near certain places, such as schools or childcare facilities. Zoning strategies are dubious ways to deter future crime of this sort and, if taken too far, can interfere with efforts to reestablish some semblance of normalcy. Worse, onerous or stigmatizing regulations might turn out to be counterproductive if they end up encouraging offenders to disappear rather than comply with their conditions of release.[45]

If a sex offender is deemed too dangerous to release, several states have established procedures for committing them against their will, just as we do with the mentally ill. In Minnesota, over 720 individuals have been confined this way, but only one person has ever been released unconditionally. The rest have never been deemed cured enough to take the chance. Nationwide, there are roughly 5,400 individuals who committed a sex crime who are being held indefinitely.[46]

The legal fiction used to justify ongoing confinement is to call it a civil process for preventing future harm rather than a punishment for a past offense. But we've always given the definition of "punishment" a functional understanding. The moment that civil confinement looks and feels like a life sentence is the moment we need to call it what it really is: the use of force to seize and discipline the body and mind.

This is especially true now that children are thrown in among adult offenders. At least thirteen states allow a juvenile to be designated a "sexually violent predator" and involuntarily committed. The youngest person to be so held was eleven at the time of his offense and thirteen when he was sent to a juvenile detention facility in South Carolina. At age seventeen, just before he was to be released, he was labeled too dangerous to release and committed.[47]

We need to know whether existing procedures take into account a youthful offender's reduced development and capacity for rehabilitation. If not, the principle of fairness can guarantee regular evaluation to determine whether there is an ongoing threat. Studies suggest that predictions about the future behavior of a juvenile are less accurate than for an adult, that many child offenders have themselves been abused, and that a young person who commits a sex crime is far less likely to reoffend. If decision makers consistently fail to separate the worst from the redeemable, or if indefinite commitment is really just another way of giving up on juveniles, then a categorical safeguard like the one adopted in *Roper* might become appropriate.[48]

Now consider the plight of the homeless. On any given night, a half million people could be sleeping in the streets or in emergency shelters. About 2.5 million children experience homelessness each year. Like the probationer, someone who is homeless is subject to all manner of regulations seeking to reform, and if reform isn't possible, then to push him out of sight, out of mind. Unlike the probationer, however, he usually hasn't already committed serious offenses. Rather, the down-and-out are caught in a web of low-level laws enacted to minimize inconveniences to citizens with jobs and homes. The sight of homeless people around can create a sense of social instability, hurt property values, and depress tourism or economic investment.

To these ends, cities have enacted laws that criminalize urban camping, sleeping in public, begging, or sitting in one place for too long. At least twenty-two cities have also cracked down on advocates and church groups by banning the feeding of homeless people. Other measures, such as those prohibiting loitering, open containers, public drunkenness, and disorderly conduct, are often enforced more vigorously against the poor. But herding the impoverished from one place to another, or seeking to make life on the streets even worse than it already is hasn't ended homelessness. It's just made criminals out of the poor.

In 2012, Atlanta's City Council enacted an ordinance that would have made a first-time offense of "aggressive panhandling" punishable by up to 180 days in jail. The mayor vetoed that measure as overly "punitive," but signed a compromise measure that required community service for a first offense, thirty days in jail for a second offense, and ninety days for a third violation. It also prohibited asking for alms within fifteen feet of any entrance to a building or event, ATM, parking lot pay box, taxi stand, bus, rail, or subway station—making large swaths of public space off-limits to the needy.[49]

Egalitarianism has few answers for those living on the edge. That's because we haven't been able to agree that poverty ought to be treated the same way as racial identity or religious affiliation. We have collectively decided that considering race or religion is a no-no, but we haven't reached the same conviction that distinctions based on income or economic class are illegitimate.

Part of the problem is that we are conflicted about the nature and causes of poverty. Many believe that mental illness, serious injury, unstable home life, the lack of affordable housing, and the unforgiving structure of our economy together create deep poverty. At the same time, others have a nagging feeling that the suffering of the homeless is qualitatively different from that of other groups. Is it really a permanent condition? For some, things might get better if only the impoverished would get sober, acquire useful skills, and try harder to get off the streets.

This is a debate we won't finish anytime soon. The role that class plays in constraining opportunities and rights is an important question, so we should continue talking about the morally destructive problem of income inequality. In the meantime, the idea of human dignity can make some of the progress that the concept of equality can't accomplish alone.

To the extent that laws punish the down-and-out because of their status, they could violate the anti-cruelty principle. This route would avoid the need to recognize a protected group or invent a new right out of whole cloth. We don't have to get into silly arguments about whether a particular person or even an entire community hates poor people.

A case called *Robinson v. California*, which reaffirms the overlap between dignity and equality, can bridge some of this gap when debate over equality turns into inaction. There, the Supreme Court struck down a state law that made it a misdemeanor "to be addicted to the use of narcotics." One evening during a car stop, a police officer noticed Lawrence Robinson's arm, which had scar tissue and bruising consistent with intravenous drug use in the past. But he observed no actual drug activity. He still arrested Robinson under the law and a jury convicted him.[50]

The Supreme Court threw out the case, finding it cruel and unusual to convict someone merely for a "chronic condition" or "status." Justice Potter Stewart, writing for the majority, compared the law to laws that criminalized mental illness, having leprosy, or being afflicted with a venereal disease. How one acquired the condition was irrelevant, he said. It was cruel "in the light of contemporary human knowledge" to use the criminal law to penalize a condition that one could acquire "innocently or involuntarily."

Justice Douglas concurred with the outcome, but wrote separately to flesh out in greater detail why the law violated the ban on barbaric punishments. He observed that an addict "causes alarm and often leads to punitive measures." But the "addict is a sick person," while the purpose of California's law "is not to cure, but to penalize." He warned: "We would forget the teachings of the Eighth Amendment if we allowed sickness to be made a crime and permitted sick people to be punished for being sick."[51]

Robinson was an instructive example of practical egalitarianism. The law obviously treated drug addicts differently from other offenders, perhaps out of fear or disgust. But rather than get bogged down in whether drug addicts deserved to be treated like other kinds of people, conversation immediately centered on the nature of the abuse. This logic has been extended to other contexts, such as criminalizing chronic alcoholism or being a vagabond or a "habitual loafer."[52]

Any law that makes being homeless a crime can be seen in the same vein. Homelessness, too, is a condition that can be thrust upon an individual or even an entire family through no fault of their own. Putting human beings in jail for fulfilling their basic bodily needs— eating, sleeping, urinating, defecating, pleading for help—doesn't relieve any of the underlying problems. The tricky matter here is that most lifestyle ordinances are written in general terms based on conduct. So you'd have to rely on public debates about the homelessness problem as evidence that targeting the poor is what's really going on.

Appeals to common sense can work. Does anyone truly think a no-feeding law would be enforced against a middle-class family having a picnic, that a suited businessman catching a snooze in the park would be hauled off to jail for violating a no-sleeping law, or that Girl Scouts would be cited for violating an antisolicitation ordinance?

Advocates pursued the anti-cruelty strategy in challenging the City of Los Angeles's antihomeless laws, called "one of the most restrictive municipal laws regulating public spaces in the United States."

Together, city laws barred sitting, lying down, or sleeping in a public space at any time of day.

In 2006, judges for the U.S. Court of Appeals held that the Constitution prohibited Los Angeles from making criminals out of homeless people for "acts that are an integral aspect of that status." They said that the actions put off-limits—sleeping, sitting, or lying down—were "universal and unavoidable consequences of being human."

Notably, the judges didn't strike down these laws. They simply found it cruel to enforce those laws when there are a greater number of homeless people than there are available beds. As a result, the judges said that these laws couldn't be enforced at certain times, such as during the evening and early morning hours. They assured city officials they were not telling them how to make policy, or even requiring a certain number of beds be made available, but only reducing the unnecessary suffering caused by their allocation of resources and enforcement policies.[53]

Switching gears as needed to deal with injustice is consistent with the lessons of history. Initially, the poor and the sick were treated warily during the colonial period. For fear that they would become public charges and overwhelm fragile states, the Articles of Confederation explicitly carved out "paupers, vagabonds, and fugitives from justice" from the privileges and immunities enjoyed by free citizens. Giving each state the power to deal with this segment of society reduced friction between jurisdictions and instead fostered "mutual friendship and intercourse among the people of the different states."[54]

Then we thought better of such categorical exclusions from the rights of citizenship. To Bingham, the Framers of the 1787 Constitution rejected the possibility of a formally stratified society and instead created a new body politic comprised of all "the people." Because the Constitution's provisions made no exceptions, as the earlier compact had, "All the free inhabitants of the United States" now encompassed social undesirables: the itinerant, strangers, lawbreakers. The founding was on Bingham's mind because he believed the Reconstruction Amendments created new tools to implement existing rights and freedoms.

By then, states and local governments were seen as sources of great injustice. The end of slavery had created major social dislocations and economic disruptions. You had former slaves migrating to the North and the West, leading to friction in new regions. Some states tried to recapture economic losses and restore a racialized legal order in practice, if not always in name. That often entailed using criminal law to create a permanent underclass that could then be disciplined and managed.[55]

The lesson from this period is twofold. First, the Fourteenth Amendment specifically barred states from impairing the rights of all persons. Second, special attention must be given to the condition of society's worst-off, such as migrants and the poor, who will often find themselves the casualties of major economic and political changes.

BEYOND BORDERS

THERE'S A BIG WRINKLE. The egalitarian potential of the anti-cruelty principle can't be realized if national norms against horrifying forms of mistreatment are watered down. Today, the biggest danger to that principle comes from American antiterrorism programs and efforts to control the country's borders. If we aren't careful, we'll become so used to using extraordinary force against human beings that we simply won't be able to recover from the damage to America's moral standing.

"No sleep was allowed," Mohamedou Ould Slahi recalled of his time in Guantanamo Bay, Cuba. "I was given 25-ounce water bottles in intervals of one to two hours . . . 24 hours a day." The effects were "devastating," he said. "I couldn't close my eyes for ten minutes because I was sitting most of the time on the bathroom." He started to hallucinate and hear voices. When he prayed to God to relieve his suffering, soldiers ordered him to stop. During call to prayer, soldiers often sang along and mocked the detainees. Some guards called them "sand niggers."[56]

A guard described what happened to one detainee who refused to drink a can of Ensure for fear of being poisoned. Already handcuffed to a cage, the man tried to turn his head away. Another guard opened the Ensure can, "grabbed the detainee by the neck, and started to pour it down his throat." The medic "punched the detainee twice on the left side of his face." He was then hog-tied and left on the ground "in this position for a couple hours."[57]

As these experiences show, large-scale detentions of undesirables haven't ended. We've just become more sophisticated in how to accomplish it. The scale of operations has also changed: we've gone global.

In this Age of Terrorism, we might classify detainees as "enemy combatants" and hold them at black sites in foreign countries or the U.S. base in Guantanamo, which has so far housed 780 individuals. The goal is very simple: hold such persons outside of the United States, where they are invisible and the power of any allies, the press, and American law is stretched to its formal and practical limits. Some detainees may eventually be charged with crimes, but others could be held for months, or years, until hostilities end. And since antiterrorism on a worldwide scale has few definitive beginning or end points, who's to say when emergency power comes to a lawful end?[58]

In the weeks after 9/11, lawyers in the Bush administration helped lay the foundations for an aggressive conception of state authority over human beings. In a memo dated June 27, 2002, John Yoo, Deputy Assistant Attorney General, presented the Office of Legal Counsel's position that a president possessed inherent constitutional power to detain citizens and noncitizens alike as "enemy combatants." OLC legal opinions are binding on all executive-branch officials and employees. Yoo argued that presidential authority to detain belligerents was not affected by a federal law that provided that "no citizen shall be imprisoned or otherwise detained by the United States" without congressional approval.[59]

Yoo read the law not to touch the president's prerogative, but his grounding of emergency power in "the president's constitutional status as Commander in Chief" was as broad as it was breathtaking. It meant that if Congress ever tried to limit that power to act unilaterally, a president would be within his rights to resist and no one else was entitled to check his actions.[60]

A key passage of Yoo's memo tried to distinguish the internment of Japanese Americans, which he called "civilian detention camps." He never actually said whether internment is good or bad precedent; it was just something that happened. The Japanese "were not held as enemy combatants," Yoo reasoned, "and so any decision to prevent similar forms of detention in the future would not reach the President's Commander in Chief power on that score."

Whatever we think about the wartime detention of the Japanese, Yoo meant, there exists yet another special category of human beings that could be justifiably treated worse: enemy belligerents. That group consists of individuals suspected of having taken up arms against the United States. The administration argued that we had to accept the administration's designation of a person as a belligerent and that courts had no power to second-guess such labels.[61]

In theory, enemy combatants are treated differently from individuals within the law enforcement paradigm based on what they have done and not because of who they are. But as soldiers and intelligence officers on the ground push the limits, they might gather up individuals who are simply in the wrong place at the wrong time, who appear dangerous because of the color of their skin or the god they worship, or who have expressed anti-American attitudes. Some have family members or friends who behave suspiciously, so it makes sense to see them as valuable sources of information. Normally, these things might get you investigated, but now they could lead to capture, rendition, and interrogation. Once certain kinds of people are subjected to different kinds of force according to special legal rules, we have the makings of a situation that may be rife with inequities.[62]

These difficulties, in turn, are exacerbated by the lack of transparency. It's so hard to figure out what's going on in foreign lands or inside detention centers run by the military. Information is hard to come by, some of it will be classified, and military officials will only grudgingly comply with legal obligations to share details. Ordinary problems of proof in making equality claims are magnified when it comes to decisions of whom to capture and how detainees are treated.

For Yoo, the power of military detention was unreviewable in part because he characterized it as nonpunitive, and instead "exclusively preventative." This was an exceedingly slippery point. After all, the Japanese Americans forced into internment camps weren't being formally punished for anything, since they were never given hearings or charged with crimes. Both involve the forceful capture of human beings, detention without consent, and the deprivation of various rights and liberties.

So whether the government's actions are punitive in nature shouldn't turn simply on how a president's lawyers describe the use of force. We can't just take their word for it. Instead, we have to look to all the circumstances, including the government's claim of urgency. Here, the rule of reason promotes some degree of political engagement, but more will have to be done to deter abuses and provide remedies when they occur.

Reliance on this special category of people who can be held with less accountability has other predictable consequences. After a category has been established, authorities will rely on the exception to justify harsher treatment. That's exactly what happened next. In a flurry of secret memos, government lawyers relaxed any and all constitutional rules, federal laws, and international obligations that governed the treatment of detainees.

One memo authorized a variety of "enhanced" or "aggressive" interrogation techniques that would easily violate the ban on cruelty or federal law against torture: forced nudity, covering the head with a hood, manipulating diet, grasping or striking the face and abdomen, forcing someone to sit in stress positions to cause muscle fatigue, placing a subject in a confinement box, sleep deprivation, and waterboarding (which simulates drowning). These measures were admittedly "coercive," placing a detainee under "physical and psychological stress."

Even so, DOJ lawyers counseled how the tactics could be carried out so interrogators could later claim in "good faith" that they didn't lead to "severe" physical or mental pain. A separate legal memo authored by Jay Bybee—then Assistant Attorney General and now a federal judge—advised that interrogation methods weren't torture unless they caused "long-term mental harm," or physical injury "so severe that death, organ failure," or "loss of significant body function will reasonably result."[63]

Lawyers advised that sleep deprivation could be used alone or in conjunction with other things, as long as there's no "lasting mental harm." Not to worry, lawyers assured, any hallucinations should recede if a subject later gets some sleep. The clinical discussion made some of the most degrading behavior seem altogether routine: "If a detainee subject to sleep deprivation is using an adult diaper, [make sure] the diaper is checked regularly and changed as needed to prevent skin irritation."

Their legal advice became so detailed about how to get away with each torture technique, and their reading of every applicable law so forgiving, that government lawyers became one with the spies and soldiers, enabling their actions rather than trying to constrain them. At this point, internal checks utterly failed, and accountability for those actions could come only later because of their clandestine nature.

An investigation later revealed that certain figures in the administration knew the legal positions were "very aggressive." Patrick Philbin, Deputy Assistant Attorney General, asked Yoo to delete broad assertions of a president's unilateral power from the legal memos, but he refused, saying "[T]hey want it in there." Philbin probed Yoo's expansive theory, inquiring whether it would encompass an order for "a village of civilians" to be "massacred." Yoo replied, "Sure." Despite misgivings about the unprecedented breadth and inhumanity of their legal advice, top lawyers in the Justice Department signed off on these documents. In fact, counsel for the CIA had requested "maximum legal protection for its officers" against future prosecution.[64]

What the CIA and military actually did was far worse than what they told their own lawyers. Detainees were stripped naked, hooded, and kept in the cold. Interrogators threatened violence against the family members of detainees. Acts of sexual humiliation, including unwanted sexual contact, also took place. Individuals were thrown against the wall. They were shackled most of the time, and left in painful positions. Interrogators regularly disparaged detainees' religious beliefs or tried to capitalize on their senses of modesty and shame. These tactics weren't undertaken separately, but instead piled one on top of another, magnifying the abuse.

Thoroughly dehumanized, detainees lashed out. The situation had been deteriorating for a while. Some people went on hunger strikes. Others tried to kill themselves. In 2014, roughly sixty-five captives who had been held for a decade or longer banded together and took over one of the compounds. They covered cameras, jeered at their captors, waved makeshift weapons, and threw feces. A riot squad was sent in to put down the uprising with rubber bullets.[65]

All of these practices were shielded by the administration's view of military detentions as a category of policy that's simply ungoverned by law. Government lawyers argued that federal law, international law, and constitutional rules don't apply to enemy combatants in the same way, if at all. One memo for the Defense Department asserted point-blank that constitutional protections, including the Eighth Amendment, "do not extend to alien enemy combatants held abroad."

Another document tried to short-circuit the rule of reason by advising that search-and-seizure law no longer restrained the government, even within the United States. Yoo asserted that a president's authority "to use whatever means necessary to prevent attacks upon the United States" encompassed warrantless searches. As if that weren't enough, Bybee's memo sought to shield anyone involved in torture. He claimed that prosecution of interrogators "would represent an infringement of the President's authority to conduct war." Expanding these defenses considerably, Bybee also claimed that if prosecuted, interrogators could invoke necessity and self-defense to escape legal responsibility.[66]

In none of these legal documents did the president's lawyers bother to compare the military's preferred interrogation techniques with any of the ones already ruled out of bounds for other agents of the state. Rather, they broadly assumed that soldiers and intelligence officers were entitled to administer more suffering in the cause of war. Nor did they show much concern for the vulnerable state of captives. To the contrary, the entire exercise was to exploit a state of legal limbo—the very type of situation *Trop v. Dulles* had warned about. Indeed, it's the latest wrinkle on that strategy, carried out by making a person stateless by manipulating time and space and consigning that individual to a place where few laws of any particular country, or concerns of justice, can find purchase.

For the most part, the men and women responsible for the inhumane treatment of suspicious strangers were not bereft of humanity themselves. Instead, they were thoughtful, patriotic, tireless, and idealistic. Their convictions—the idea that perfect security was attainable, a beautiful theory of an all-powerful leader as the surest vehicle for defeating a nation's enemies—led them inexorably down the path to authoritarian conduct. They illustrated Isaiah Berlin's observation that idealism can deteriorate into raw instrumentalism, which "invariably leads to coercion. And then to destruction." To keep Americans safe, members of the administration from the top to the bottom saw "an infinite number of eggs, human lives, ready for the breaking."[67]

Fortunately, intervention by the political branches and the courts has restored some semblance of public reason and the guarantee against inhumane treatment. In 2004, the Supreme Court ruled that a U.S. citizen has the right to challenge his designation as an enemy combatant. As a matter of fair play, a citizen detained is entitled to notice of the facts underlying that label and a "fair opportunity to rebut" the government's assertions. It's noteworthy that Justice O'Connor's ruling quotes this line from Justice Murphy's *Korematsu* dissent: "[T]he military claim must subject itself to the judicial process of having its reasonableness determined and its conflicts with other interests reconciled." What's more, some of the worst legal memos were withdrawn by the OLC itself after new lawyers repudiated the work of the old. In 2009, President Obama signed an executive order prohibiting torture by any government agency and restricting interrogation tactics to those described in the Army Field Manual. Congress codified this ban into law in 2015.[68]

Were the captives really the worst of the worst? Some certainly posed a threat. Still, of the 780 Guantanamo detainees, most were released without any charges. The age of the detainees ranged from thirteen to eighty-nine. Fifteen were juveniles. After fourteen years of confinement, Slahi was released with no charges. He hadn't been captured on a battlefield, but was seized after agreeing to answer questions by Mauritanian officials and FBI agents. From there, the CIA transported him to a site in Jordan for interrogation, and then transferred him to Guantanamo Bay.

Slahi had trained in Afghanistan to topple the Communist regime there. Slahi's cousin had been an advisor to Osama bin Laden. He had sporadic contact with other al-Qaeda members, and these contacts led to his designation as a "high value detainee." But apart from the statements coerced through torture, authorities never found evidence to tie him to any specific acts against the United States. He wasn't the active recruiter or mastermind they believed him to be. A federal judge ordered him released in 2010, finding that the government had failed to show that "at the time of his capture, Slahi was a 'part of' al-Qaida."[69]

In the end, only some thirty individuals were charged with crimes. By October 2010, 598 detainees had been transferred out of DOD custody. At the end of Obama's presidency, forty-one detainees remained. Of those, ten faced charges or had been convicted in military commissions, five were slated for release, and twenty-six were being held indefinitely after internal review designated them as continuing dangers.[70]

A new administration, with different values and priorities, can still erode our basic guarantees. As a candidate, President Trump voiced strong support for torture, promising to bring back waterboarding "and a hell of a lot worse." For five years, the Senate Select Committee on Intelligence studied the CIA's detention program and issued a scathing report finding that interrogations were "not effective" and "brutal and far worse" than anyone realized.[71] In June 2017, the FBI, the Pentagon, DOJ, and the CIA returned their copies of the Senate report, ensuring that its findings would not become part of executive branch training or policy.[72]

Whatever the future has in store as antiterror efforts mutate and expand, the biggest problem still looms: our discomfort with extraterritorial application of constitutional norms. The courts have now recognized a U.S. citizen's right to challenge an unlawful-combatant designation. What about noncitizens? An important answer was provided in a case called *Rasul v. Bush*. There, several citizens of Australia and Kuwait held for over two years at Guantanamo sought a writ of habeas corpus. Justice Stevens's opinion for the Court found jurisdiction over the base. He read our constitutional history to say that the reach of the writ "depended not on formal notions of territorial sovereignty, but rather on the practical question of the 'extent and nature'" of dominion exercised by the government. Stevens also noted that the Alien Tort Claims Act, which explicitly provides aliens a remedy for violations of U.S. treaties or the law of nations, imposes no territorial restrictions.

If courts have power over a military base overseas, it would seem logical to say that federal laws and substantive constitutional principles also apply to conditions of confinement. Certainly from the standpoint of vindicating constitutional norms, especially those involving equality and dignity, borders shouldn't be insurmountable. If the government has the power to do immense harm to human beings, there must be effective recourse for abuses of that authority.[73]

If only it were that simple. A line of cases issued by the Supreme Court holds that foreign nationals without connections to the U.S. can't complain about constitutional violations. In these rulings, the Justices worried that worldwide application of the Constitution would interfere too much with American foreign policy and flood the courts with grievances from all over the world.[74]

The first concern packs a punch, for overly vigorous oversight can interfere with strategic decisions regarding diplomacy and war making. But the second concern elevates convenience over justice and invites arbitrary line drawing. It's possible to vindicate the value of ethical treatment without calling into question the legality of a detention or interfering with operational decisions. Where that can be done, every effort should be made to preserve the humane treatment of captives—wherever they come from and wherever they are held.

Justice Kennedy, who didn't accept the *Rasul* majority's reading of relevant federal statutes, nevertheless believed jurisdiction over noncitizens at Guantanamo was proper. He stressed that the government itself had pursued a policy of "indefinite detention without trial or other proceeding," which "allows friends and foes alike to remain in detention." This same concern about not leaving human beings at the complete mercy of the state should also drive application of equality and dignity to people and places controlled by the U.S. government.

A similar set of problems is raised by overly harsh regulation of migration. In the spring of 2018, the Trump administration announced a "zero tolerance" approach at the border. That meant a host of draconian policies: criminally prosecuting everyone who crosses the border without permission, separating all undocumented children from parents, demanding that adults give up any asylum claims in order to be reunited with their children, and even making plans to warehouse migrants at military bases or makeshift "tent cities."[75]

But deterrence arguments can act as one-way ratchets leading to ever-tougher measures. Few may care to wait for evidence that would tell us whether the policies are working as intended. And quite apart from whether ruthless policies discourage desperate families from migrating, policymakers are once again tempted to justify tough measures against noncitizens on the basis of who they are and where they are seized. We need robust countervailing ideas to reduce suffering and promote equality.

In such a context, pleas to avoid cruelty and ensure fairness would fare better than straight-ahead equality arguments. Even if foreigners don't have a constitutional right to enter the country and can't invoke the full privileges of citizenship, they are entitled to humane treatment and to have their legal claims adjudicated in an orderly fashion. These approaches would also help keep the needs of children from being lumped together with that of adults, who tend to be blamed for coming to America without authorization.

Getting to the right answers will be important. Even if we can agree that individuals detained in places controlled by the U.S. government should be afforded basic constitutional rights, what about those who are held at other faraway locations? If we say that norms of humane treatment apply only in places controlled by the United States, this will encourage military authorities to make arrangements with other countries to hold individuals of interest and unwanted migrants, away from the prying eyes of lawyers and judges. Should that happen, we would merely be displacing untold cruelties from one place to another. And those other places would be even harder to police. These loopholes must be closed if we are truly committed to keeping human beings from being treated purely as means to an end.

CHAPTER 5

FREE SPEECH

Today a white man stands convicted for protesting in unseemly language against our decisions invalidating restrictive covenants. Tomorrow a Negro will be hauled before a court for denouncing lynch law in heated terms.

—JUSTICE WILLIAM O. DOUGLAS,
BEAUHARNAIS V. ILLINOIS, 1952

"THE LAW IS DISCRIMINATORY," Chief Justice Warren said of a Virginia law enacted in 1956 that restricted the work public-interest lawyers could do in the state. "The purpose of the law is obviously to circumvent *Brown*." Some of his colleagues were not so sure.

That law, challenged by the NAACP, had been enacted as a wave of public officials vilified judges charged with integrating schools for usurping democratic authority and trying to destroy their way of life. A bare majority of Americans nationwide believed that the Justices had made the right call to end racial segregation in schools, while seven in ten Southerners opposed integration. Views about race in American society were polarized and getting worse.[1]

States from Arkansas to Florida tried to stall legal progress through a variety of techniques. Some districts opted to close schools entirely rather than admit a single black child. By far the most ingenious strategy was to make criminals out of the lawyers for the schoolchildren and organizations that came to their aid. They did so by passing a spate of laws that impaired the work of public-interest groups, enforcing those laws through fines and threats of disbarment.

In Virginia, the state legislature called an extra session to denounce *Brown v. Board of Education*. Elected representatives barred the use of public funds for integrated schools. Sheriffs and other law enforcement officials wanted lists of persons who were politically active on racial matters to keep them in line. So the General Assembly also required anyone involved in promoting or opposing legislation on "behalf of any race or color" or whose activities "tend to cause racial conflict" to register with the state and disclose names, addresses, income, debts, and expenditures. On top of that, legislators redefined the professional rules that governed the practice of law to make it harder for public-interest groups to recruit clients and manage their cases.

Courts stopped the authorities from enforcing most of these rules, leaving only a restriction that barred solicitation of legal business by an organization that employs a lawyer but has no financial interest in the case itself. The problem: that described virtually all of the NAACP's work. Its professional staff took cases in a concerted effort to dismantle racial segregation whether or not a client could pay, but the organization itself had no financial stake in the cases.[2]

The NAACP attacked the remaining regulation as a denial of equal protection and due process of law. On appeal, the organization emphasized that the law was enacted in 1956 as part of a plan of "massive resistance" to racial integration. Furthermore, it argued that the law treated the NAACP differently from groups that had a financial stake in a lawsuit and "forbids the plaintiffs to defray the expenses of racial litigation, while at the same time it legalizes the activities of legal aid societies that serve all needy persons in all sorts of litigation." Subjecting the NAACP to different rules, they said, amounted to "discrimination."[3]

Behind the scenes, the Justices argued among themselves. At conference, Justice Warren staked out the equality position in the strongest terms possible. Besides reflecting an effort to undermine the Court's desegregation efforts, he argued, the law "discriminates against those who organize to protect civil rights in favor of those who have a 'pecuniary' interest." Warren said he was "willing to go on *Yick Wo*," which had held that malicious enforcement of an otherwise valid law can still amount to unequal treatment.

Like Warren, Justice Black believed that this law "was one of a group of laws designed as a package to thwart our segregation decisions." He warned, "The NAACP is finished if this law stands." Black, who hailed from Alabama, saw through the gamesmanship of Jim Crow states. Laws like Virginia's "handicap and hobble those who are trying to enforce constitutional rights by contributing their time or money." Douglas and Brennan joined this camp, making four votes to strike down the law on equality grounds.

But most of the Justices didn't see an effort to target anyone because of race. Because the law didn't mention race, they considered it an acceptable regulation of professional conduct. Pushing back against the Warren-led quartet, Frankfurter insisted "there was nothing in the record to show that this statute is aimed at the Negroes as such." Justice Charles Whittaker similarly wanted to analyze the law in the abstract, plucking it out of the racially charged context that gave it birth. When he did that, he saw an evenhanded measure. "This law, if applied to the white supremacy group, would be constitutional," he told his colleagues. "We should be colorblind on this law."

Justice Clark worried that helping the NAACP would show racial favoritism. "We would have to discriminate in favor of Negroes" for the group to prevail, he declared flatly. Adding Harlan and Stewart made five votes to uphold the Virginia law.

In a sense, the majority of Justices wanted to delay a finding of discrimination by rejecting the NAACP's assault on the law. They wanted to let Virginia have its restriction of sponsored litigation, and to force the NAACP to come up with more evidence that the organization itself was being targeted because of the race of its members or clients. But rejecting the equality argument outright would have made a racially explosive situation far worse. Lawyers would have to continue spending precious resources to fight this second front, hoping to uncover more satisfying evidence of animosity in the application of the law, just to get back in the game.

More blatant evidence of bias might never come. Hostility toward the NAACP or its black clients could be extremely hard to prove if the history surrounding passage of the restrictions weren't enough. And it would be nearly impossible to complain of unequal treatment if officials charged with enforcing the law were clever enough to mind what they said, and if they enforced the law against at least one other group. In the meantime, the law would fall hardest on organizations dedicated to enforcing constitutional rights. Desegregation matters would have to be handled by volunteer lawyers with little money or expertise. The effects of such a disastrous ruling wouldn't be limited to Virginia. If the Court approved Virginia's law, other states would surely follow.

The equality argument seemed doomed. But before work could be completed on the opinion, fate intervened. Whittaker retired, and the case was held over for reargument. Frankfurter then suffered a stroke. Their replacements, Byron White and Arthur Goldberg, proved to be more sympathetic to the NAACP's position but still uncertain about which way to go.[4]

Even so, the basic conundrum remained: how should the stakes be understood and how much weight should be given to the state's motivation? As Professor Harry Kalven put it: "If the Court ignores the motivation of the South in these cases, it risks deciding great issues in a vacuum and giving us a parody of legal wisdom; yet if it acknowledges the motivation of the South, it risks giving constitutional litigation the appearance of civil war and of giving us a parody of neutrality."[5]

Ultimately, the High Court declared the Virginia law unconstitutional, not on equality grounds, but rather for "unduly inhibiting protected freedoms of expression and association." Justice Brennan's surprising opinion in *NAACP v. Button* turned to the First Amendment—an argument the NAACP didn't originally make. What was shaping up as a disastrous 5–4 ruling narrowly rejecting the equality claim turned into a landmark 6–3 ruling based largely on the idea of expressive liberty. In fact, the opinion explicitly noted that the Court was not reaching "considerations of race or racial discrimination."[6]

That the state was trying to regulate conduct rather than status, which tripped up some of the Justices, no longer proved to be an obstacle, for the guarantee of free speech now encompassed "vigorous advocacy" as well as "abstract discussion." And because the NAACP sought to vindicate constitutional rights, this kind of "cooperative, organizational activity" would be treated as political expression.

It was a stunning turnabout. Frankfurter had been tapped to draft the Court's opinion upholding the Virginia law. His original approach would have allowed Virginia to treat the NAACP differently from other groups since the statute didn't mention any group by name. Now, under Brennan's free-speech framework, the legal activities of public interest organizations would be "privileged" as if they were political associations, accorded maximum protection under the Constitution. No one had to be singled out to enjoy that protection.

Although grounded in freedom of expression, the solution advanced the banner of equality in several ways. First, because the NAACP was dedicated to "the lawful objective of equality of treatment," knocking down barriers to the group's work empowered regular citizens to defend the principle of egalitarianism. We do that by organizing locally, asking for help from committed volunteers and experts, and lobbying elected officials and filing lawsuits.

Second, in shielding unpopular expression, the Court also necessarily protected the vulnerable groups that tend to hold those views, "[g]roups which find themselves unable to achieve their objectives through the ballot." Such a minority group might make a "distinctive contribution" to political debate even though it is not a "conventional political party." For this proposition, the decision recalled the experiences of unions and communists whose peaceful gatherings had been broken up by police and controversial speakers arrested.[7]

Third, although the Justices refused to say that Virginia had actually discriminated against the NAACP, they did find that the open-ended law "lends itself to selective enforcement against unpopular causes." The mere risk of unfair treatment could not be tolerated because the law could "easily become a weapon of oppression, however evenhanded its terms appear."

This accomplished the work of equality in an ingenious way, by developing a principle that barred discrimination against someone's viewpoint. Discriminating against a person's perspective can be just as bad as discriminating against a person because of who she is. This idea was then joined with the concept of fair play, so that the fear of selective enforcement creates tangible harms we can do something about right away. It is fundamentally unfair to subject politically active groups to so much uncertainty over whether the state will try to single out their activity for punishment. The law risked "smothering all discussion" about possible representation. NAACP lawyers, the organization's members, and sympathetic figures in the community "would understandably hesitate" to discuss subjects related to possible lawsuits.

Throughout, the approach emphasized the societal value of the group's speech rather than the status of the group relative to other groups. Nor was it essential that actual discrimination had occurred. But there can be no mistaking that the real effect is virtually identical to what egalitarians originally preferred. Ensuring that a group can engage freely in activities that are central to its mission is the next closest thing to protecting the group itself from unequal treatment.

Credit where credit is due: Warren, Brennan, Black, Douglas, Goldberg, and White all appreciated the urgency of the task at hand. Desegregation efforts across the country would have been disrupted without groups like the NAACP leading the way. Judges couldn't initiate cases on their own, they could only enforce the principle of equality in lawsuits filed by others.

Allowing states to interfere with interest-group advocacy would have been tantamount to the Supreme Court waving the white flag on the goal of racial integration itself where communities pushed back hard. There was little money to be made pursuing such cases, and no shortage of abuse heaped upon those brave enough to do so. Because citizens would be tolerant of major legal changes only for so long, throwing up obstacles was just another way of trying to run out the clock.

Sensing that rejection of the NAACP's equality claim might spell the end of desegregation, decision makers did not stay wedded to fixed positions come hell or high water. Instead, they found a way to pursue equality by other means. They remained flexible as to possible methods, and when the opportunity arose, they forged a new path using First Amendment law that broadly appealed to others.

It wouldn't just be liberal groups that found reasons to like the rhetoric and rationales of free speech to solve problems. Eventually, conservative advocacy groups, too, would come to appreciate the solution as a boon for their causes.

A COMMON TONGUE

TODAY IT'S COMMONPLACE TO think that the right to free speech clashes with the pursuit of equality. After all, prominent controversies have begun when bakers, parade organizers, men-only organizations, and even the Boy Scouts of America claimed a free speech right to be exempt from civil rights laws. Hard choices must always be made about where to draw lines, and if we don't choose wisely, we could inadvertently undermine liberty or equality.[8]

Yet *Button* shows that the two values aren't perpetually at odds. There are times when vindicating speech rights can actually promote equality—giving us two for the price of one. This makes sense because there is a deep synergy between the two bodies of knowledge. So much so that it's possible for the free-speech approach to reset the terms of debate and to serve as a substitute rationale when formal equality can't produce consensus.[9]

Cross-fertilization between equality and free speech isn't an accident. Rather, our convictions that the two ideas are closely linked have been forged through historical experience. Members of the Civil War generation were incensed that racial inequality had been unfairly reinforced through limitations on speech. They recalled that the House of Representatives from 1836 to 1844 operated under a "gag rule" that required all petitions, memorials, or resolutions "relating in any way" to the subject of slavery "be laid upon the table, and that no further action whatever shall be had thereon." At the time, John Quincy Adams had declared this a blatant violation of "the rights of my constituents, and of the people of the United States to petition, and of my right to freedom of speech, as a member of this House."[10]

As the country struggled with the spread of slavery, Representative Bingham criticized laws passed by states and local jurisdictions to restrict abolitionist speech. The Kansas Territorial Assembly joined the states of Alabama, North Carolina, and Virginia in prohibiting the circulation of any writings that induced slaves to escape or "persuad[ed]" persons of colour . . . to rebel." Any attempt to make it a crime for a U.S. citizen "'to know, to argue, and to utter freely according to conscience,' is absolutely void," Bingham thundered. He noted that it would be illegal in some states to read the words of the Declaration of Independence asserting that all men are born free and equal. "Before you hold this enactment to be law, burn our immortal Declaration and our free-written Constitution, fetter our press."[11]

During ratification debates, supporters of the Fourteenth Amendment described the right of free speech as an antidote to past injustices, when men were "mobbed" and "some even put to death for uttering abolitionist sentiments." Slavery had led to "despotic laws" that "nullified constitutional guarantees of freedom and free speech and a free press."

Some of the worst abuses occurred in New Orleans after the withdrawal of federal troops. Union sympathizers were fired from teaching posts and law enforcement jobs, replaced by those who still believed in the aims of the Confederacy. When Republicans recalled a convention to deal with the enactment of Black Codes in the state and to give blacks the vote, local opponents of equality had all delegates indicted. What started out as an effort to discourage proequality expression then turned into violent suppression of peaceful politics. Mayor John T. Monroe, a supporter of the Confederacy, organized old rebels, known white supremacists, and police officers to confront the assembly.

On the day of the convention, July 30, 1866, angry mobs attacked the delegates and police joined the fray, killing forty delegates and their supporters, and injuring another 136 people. A House Select Committee later charged with investigating the event described it as "a massacre," laying primary responsibility on the mayor, who led the "merciless attacks of the armed police." For several hours, "the police and mob, in mutual and bloody emulation, continued the butchery." Even "at distant points in the city," freed persons "peaceably pursuing their lawful business, were attacked by the police, shot, and cruelly beaten." A number of black veterans of the Civil War were killed or injured that day.[12]

Tough lessons from earlier battles over equality, such as the 1866 massacre, have shaped how we understand speech and equality as related values. Authoritarians often seek to curb one right as a way of limiting the other. It can even be a way of testing the citizenry's tolerance for repressive policies: if one kind of restriction fails to spark outrage, another oppressive policy might be coming down the pike. When contentious issues of racial injustice are raised, it is tempting to stop the momentum of reformers and preserve entrenched power by curbing the right to speak and gather peacefully.

The converse also takes place. Dehumanizing certain kinds of people, whether on the left or right, can be a technique to get voters to go along with the restriction of speech rights. That's what happened to socialists, artists, left-wing protesters, and sexual minorities for much of the twentieth century. And it's what has happened with troubling frequency to religious dissenters and traditionalists in our polarized age.

So why might practical egalitarians turn to free speech to promote the ends of equality? For starters, Americans place paramount importance on this right among all others. It has been called "indispensable" to "nearly every other form of freedom," and "the deadliest enemy of tyranny." Salman Rushdie has observed simply, "Free speech is life itself." Songs of praise for liberty can be overwrought, but they clue us in to the existence of a formidable resource.[13]

The chief function of speech is "to free men from the bondage of irrational fears"—a leading cause of inequality. Besides ensuring that equality-promoting information can circulate widely among the people, the right also facilitates innovative, and at times aggressive, advocacy.[14]

The popularity of this right produces strategic benefits. A dirty secret is that we find all kinds of actions to implicate "speech": writing, speaking, reading, drawing, listening, proselytizing, playing music, dancing, wearing black armbands, viewing pornography, marching, burning a flag in protest, refusing to salute the American flag, boycotting businesses, displaying a monument—just to name a few.

We feel intuitively more aggrieved, even personally affected, when someone's speech rights are involved. This inclination renders many of us more willing to confront injustice when there's some expressive dimension to a dispute. As the *Button* controversy also illustrates, the free- speech approach is actually more receptive to claims of systemic injustices than the traditional equality method. A pragmatist would take note of these advantages, and draw from this knowledge to advance the cause of equality.[15]

Protecting unpopular views will undoubtedly protect unpopular groups. The key to remember is that the marginalized population shifts as the political climate changes. In more fearful times, or when white interests are threatened, the person on the outs will be the migrant, the refugee, the racial minority, the non-Christian. In more liberal and diverse enclaves like urban areas and universities, oppression morphs into something different: the risk that progressive orthodoxy will lead to a purge of those who don't toe the company line on such issues as diversity, the nature of sexuality and proper relation between the sexes, and the role of religion in society. Defending free speech in such contexts can protect the religious or conservative dissenter from unjustified harms.

In fact, the free-speech method demands that each individual be treated on his own terms—not merely as part of a vast conspiracy, a movement, or a faceless element of "the left" or "the right." Each person is responsible only for his own words and actions. The bad acts of one group should not prevent another group from being able to express itself. So, for example, if a particular gathering organized by a student chapter of the Republican Party gets out of hand through no fault of its own, that shouldn't preclude the group from holding another event in the future. And it certainly shouldn't be held against a different organization that shares the same general beliefs.

That was the crucial principle laid down in *NAACP v. Claiborne Hardware Company*, a case that arose out of civil rights boycotts organized in 1966 against businesses that refused to serve black customers. The businesses targeted by the collective actions sued the NAACP, the Mississippi Action for Progress, and a number of civil rights leaders for malicious interference with their businesses—and succeeded in obtaining a whopping judgment of $ 1.25 million for lost earnings during a seven-year period. If this legal ruling stood up, it would have bankrupted many of the parties involved and discouraged this type of direct action on behalf of equality.[16]

Fortunately, the Supreme Court stepped in. Citing the First Amendment, the Justices ruled that organizing an economic boycott to change government policy was a form of protected expression. At a key point, Justice Stevens reassured that the right to associate with others "does not lose all constitutional protection merely because some members of the group may have participated in conduct or advocated doctrine that itself is not protected." If certain individuals commit crimes, they can be prosecuted for their own violations. But the state can't just seize upon "mere participation in a peaceable assembly" to claim there is a conspiracy to break the law.

Once again, on the broader level, protecting creative political tactics facilitated vigorous efforts to tackle structural inequality. And at the individual level, demanding more solid proof of illegal conduct beyond emotional speeches ensured that each person was treated the same regardless of group membership or political cause.

Our commitment to the radical inclusiveness of ideas, coupled with a belief that a person is responsible for his own conduct, performs the work of equality. "One man's vulgarity is another's lyric," shrugged Justice Harlan, as he overturned a person's disturbing-the-peace conviction for wearing a jacket emblazoned with the words, "Fuck the

Draft." Embedded in Harlan's phrase is a clue about the power of free-speech norms to preserve equality. Who's to say whether the man's choice to become a walking billboard amounted to political art or pointless profanity?

Among the most celebrated sayings from our First Amendment tradition, this statement affirms that we are all equal within the political community. Each of us enjoys an equal right to speak and listen to others. We all have different tastes, and being offended from time to time is the price we pay for living in a free society.

Every time we defend someone's right to speak freely, we make an implicit promise to defend the right of the next person who might stake out a different view. That vow of evenhanded treatment is a design feature of the speech method. It yokes together the proponent of an idea and its most vociferous opponent. As much as each despises the other, the flag burner has a right to express himself just as the flag waver does. Neither may negate the existence of the other. The libertarian enjoys the same ability to organize as the socialist. Advocates of racial equality possess the same right to work on behalf of legal change as defenders of white supremacy.[17]

There are categories of speech that are historically recognized as exceptions to the rule. Libel, fighting words, calls to violence or law-breaking, verbal threats, and obscenity remain unprotected. But we've narrowed the scope of these exceptions as we have matured as a society. The historical trend bespeaks a philosophical calculation: more speech in circulation, though some of it may be destructive in the wrong hands, is better than a world bereft of ideas.

When the speech at the heart of a dispute is unpopular, those in the majority are reminded that the tables could be turned one day. And if that day comes, those whose perspective suddenly makes them outcasts will want to be treated with the same kind of respect.[18]

What equal respect means is that we must treat each person as capable of expressing something useful. We do that by presuming that

most speech is worth protecting and by brushing aside rules that interfere too much with give-and-take. Then we leave it up to each person
to draw her own conclusions and hope for the best. Reducing the raw
power of the state to suppress minority views ensures the capacity of
each individual to read, think, and act for himself.

Because freedom of expression is a basic value in our society, it can
serve as a common tongue. For civic republicans, speech is the vehicle
for perfecting the community through virtuous, public-spirited deliberation. To liberals, self-expression is a means to reach an individual's
natural potential. That shared sense of its importance can fill gaps in
a person's argument. As we've seen over and over, the biggest hole in
one's equality claim is often that there doesn't appear to be a crucial
social good at stake. That's one way to understand why some jurists
were initially not sympathetic toward the NAACP's grievance in *Button*: there's no right to engage in unethical professional conduct or to
make one's living as a lawyer. In fact, states have long governed the
practice of law as they see fit.[19]

But by reframing the lawyers' actions as a type of political expression, practical-minded egalitarians were able to elevate the stakes of
the dispute. The right to engage in political discourse is seen as one of
the most valuable social goods a citizen possesses. If used wisely, and
under the right circumstances, this move can aid some of the most
vulnerable groups to seek out like-minded people, make an impact on
law and society, and convert citizens to their cause.

The ban on viewpoint discrimination does some of the same work
that hatred does for the concept of equality. Where a government official disadvantages a speaker because of disagreement with or disgust
for an idea, he has acted on an illiberal motivation. Doing so hurts
a person's ability "to establish worth, standing, and respect" for his
perspective. It's analogous to what happens when a government official treats someone differently because of hatred for a social group to
which that person belongs. Whenever a person is treated poorly by

the state because of what he says or what he believes, that person has been robbed of his dignity just as if he has been mistreated because of who he is. So when we protect the ability to voice one's beliefs without fear of government reprisal, we are also enforcing the principle of egalitarianism.[20]

A vivid example can be found in a dispute in New York from the early 1990s concerning the use of public school grounds after hours. The facilities were open for rent to the local community, but the school district twice rejected Lamb's Chapel's request to screen a film about Dr. James Dobson, the evangelical Christian and radio personality. School officials deemed Lamb's Chapel a "radical church" and worried that the event would be so controversial it would cause public unrest. The Supreme Court disagreed with the school's decision, finding that it had discriminated against the group's "religious point of view."

Practical egalitarians should take note. In this alternative way, the Justices required that the group be treated with the same respect accorded other civic groups when it comes to the use of public property. Since school would have been done for the day, concerns about proselytizing young children were overblown and there was no real risk of religious domination because the group wasn't asking for special treatment. By overreacting, school officials ended up treating the religious group unfairly. Though the Court relied on speech rules rather than equality rules, it still benefited the disfavored group in roughly the same way.[21]

Of course, no one has an absolute right to use government resources in whatever way he wants. Schools exist to educate children; they don't serve as a place for the rough-and-tumble exchange of ideas. But free-speech rules impose a duty of evenhanded treatment if the state chooses to make its facilities available to the community. And if a school opens its doors for speech purposes, it can't then slam the door on a group merely out of disgust for its message. It has to treat all comers the same, or else close the facilities to everyone.[22]

While mistreating someone out of disagreement with his perspective is always out of bounds, proof of actual discrimination isn't necessary to make out a violation of the speech principle. A serious threat of selective enforcement, or an unjustified burden on the ability to express ideas, can be enough to violate the First Amendment.

What's more, we won't even wait for the authorities to actually enforce a law if vital speech values are endangered. Instead, we are sometimes willing to stop a policy dead in its tracks. We even have a phrase to capture our belief that speech is so precious that we shouldn't wait for a dangerous law to be applied against someone. We are adamant that the "chilling effect" of a law must be stopped straightaway so citizens won't feel the need to censor themselves.[23]

Concerned about society-wide effects, judges have struck down laws that restrict sexually explicit material on the Internet, restrictive signage laws, policies requiring organizations to disclose membership lists, bans against expression at airports, and vague rules for demonstrations and permits.[24]

A dispute over a 1958 Arkansas law illustrates the equality-enhancing power of free speech. The law required every teacher, principal, or professor employed by a public institution to swear out an affidavit listing all organizations to which they belonged or had made monetary contributions in the past five years. Punishments included fines and the loss of a teaching license. B. T. Shelton, a twenty-five-year veteran of the Little Rock public school system, refused to disclose his associations as required by law. He was promptly fired.[25]

The Supreme Court invalidated the law, concluding that "the unlimited and indiscriminate sweep of the statute" violated the educators' rights to free association. Justice Stewart's opinion reasoned that the law had "an unmistakable tendency to chill that free play of the spirit which all teachers ought especially to cultivate and practice." The state had exceeded any legitimate need to determine the fitness or competence of teachers and instead exposed them to punishment for their beliefs or affiliations. Justice Stewart lamented "the pressure on a teacher to avoid any ties which might displease those who control his professional destiny." The temptation to "discharge teachers who belong to unpopular or minority organizations" would be especially pronounced.

Indeed, Shelton, who was African American, turned out to be a member of the NAACP at a time when employers and politicians had gotten fed up with the group stirring up trouble. So he feared, with good reason, that revealing his connection to the group would expose him to political retaliation. There was no need for him to prove that he had been singled out in any way—the mere threat that it could happen proved intolerable.

All of these advantages make the free-speech principle a formidable instrument for dealing with inequities—more so than the idea of equality can accomplish alone. In fact, it would do wonders if the proactive disposition we assume to reduce speech harms were adopted for the harms from inequality. Some might say that expression is a special right. Yet equality, too, is a fundamental value and there's no reason to always privilege one over the other. Until we are as watchful for threats to equality as we are for threats to free speech, we'll have to keep searching for other ways to reduce inequities.[26]

Talking to the Unwanted

The indifference we often feel when confronted with other people's suffering can suddenly turn into alarm when expressive liberty appears to be at stake. This is even true when it comes to individuals convicted of serious crimes. Every so often, government officials try to restrict our ability to communicate with the unwanted: sexual offenders, gang members, and migrants.

Let's start with the battle over North Carolina's law that made it a felony for a registered sex offender "to access a commercial social networking web site" where minors may be reached. Anyone convicted of a "sexually violent" offense was barred from the Internet for life, while all other sexual offenders could not go online for thirty years.[27]

At oral argument, North Carolina's attorney general repeatedly emphasized that "[t]hese are some of the worst criminals who have abused children." But the Justices would have none of it, for free speech was admittedly involved. Troubled, they peppered the advocate with questions exploring just how far the state wanted to go to impair a citizen's opportunity to interact through the Internet.[28]

The government's lawyer tried to compare the social media ban to zoning laws enacted by many states that effectively say, "[S]ex offenders can't go into the public square," and can't visit parks, schools, or playgrounds. But this didn't satisfy Justice Breyer. He mused, "Maybe those have the same problem." If the idea is to keep sex offenders from interacting with a minor, Breyer noted, then they could go "[n]owhere, really, because children are everywhere."

Some were troubled at the prospect that approving the law could encourage states to ban access to social media for people convicted of other kinds of offenses. Could a state forbid everyone convicted of a fraud from using Twitter and LinkedIn? What about other crimes that entailed taking advantage of somebody through communication? The possibilities seemed endless. As Justice Sotomayor pointed out, "The Internet could be used for almost any crime."

In the end, the sheer breadth of the law, coupled with the paramount importance given to freedom of speech and association, carried the day. The Court struck down the law because the state "with one broad stroke" had barred access to events, employment ads, political exchanges, religious information, "the vast realms of human thought and knowledge." The law criminalized all kinds of perfectly innocuous information and social interactions.

That's what happened to Lester Packingham. What got him in trouble was creating a Facebook account and celebrating that he had beaten a traffic ticket. "No fine, no court cost, no nothing spent. . . . Praise be to GOD, WOW! Thanks JESUS!"—he wrote in a post noticed by a police officer. If that innocent statement offering praise to his Maker had been uttered by anyone else, it would be obvious that punishing him for his words would violate the First Amendment. Because Packingham was a convicted criminal, however, it raised the question of how far we are willing to go to strip an entire category of people of their rights and humanity.[29]

The free-speech solution—declaring the law a "complete bar" on protected expression—allowed jurists to sidestep the harder philosophical question of where to draw the line when it comes to treating prisoners worse than ordinary citizens. That's an important, long-term issue that deserves a thoughtful answer. But we're not going to get to that answer on a single day or in a single controversy. In the meantime, the speech approach reduced serious inequities along the way.

It's one thing if careful restrictions were imposed as a condition of release, the Justices suggested, but it's quite another to put the Internet off limits to an entire group of people for such a long period of time. The restriction, which singled out one category of offenders, encompassed some 20,000 residents of North Carolina. Over 1,000 individuals had actually been prosecuted under the law over the course of nine years.

Calling a problem by another name can break through a demeanor of indifference. After describing the situation as a free-speech issue, the Justices uncharacteristically expressed grave concern about taking the idea of the convicted criminal as a defective citizen too far. "It is unsettling to suggest that only a limited set of websites can be used even by persons who have completed their sentences," they observed. The dangers of indefinite social isolation seemed to be on their minds: "Even convicted criminals—and in some instances especially convicted criminals"—might benefit from being part of "the world of ideas, in particular if they seek to reform and to pursue lawful and rewarding lives."

What North Carolina tried to do—forbidding contact between social undesirables and other human beings in the virtual world— has been tried repeatedly in the real world. Laws banning loitering, vagrancy, and disturbing the peace have historically been misused against racial and sexual minorities, political dissenters, and poor people as means of social control. At times, the free-speech principle has proved useful to push back against these kinds of zoning strategies.

When the Supreme Court struck down Chicago's anti-gang loitering ordinance in 1999, it said that the law denied people liberty and fair play. Yet it would be hard to miss the fact that the underlying problem being addressed was that of unequal social burdens. Justice Stevens's opinion gestured toward the history of American vagrancy laws, originally patterned after Elizabethan poor laws and later modified by former slave states "to keep former slaves in a state of quasi-slavery." The import of his move could not be clearer: laws like Chicago's ought to be examined with care because a common ancestry suggested a common practice of oppression.[30]

Because the Chicago ordinance was too vague, it risked criminalizing completely innocent activities by known gang members and anyone in the city who might be seen in their company. The Justices cited a prior case in which they struck down a law that made it illegal for three or more people to gather on a sidewalk in a manner that was "annoying" to passersby. "Conduct that annoys some people does not annoy others," Justice Stewart had written. Such a vague law operated as "an obvious invitation to discriminatory enforcement against those whose association together is 'annoying' because their ideas, their lifestyle, or their physical appearance is resented by the majority of their fellow citizens."[31]

The Court now applied this rationale to the anti-gang ordinance.

"Friends, relatives, teachers, counselors, or even total strangers might unwittingly engage in forbidden loitering if they happen to engage in idle conversation with a gang member." Perversely, because the anti-gang law banned loitering "without an apparent purpose," it was completely toothless against activities that might actually be socially harmful. A gang member playing basketball while waiting to complete a drug transaction would escape the law, but a gang member absorbed in a conversation with friends about the polarized state of politics could be swept up by police.

Since the law gave the police officer on the street too much discretion, the danger of discriminatory enforcement could not be ignored. Indeed, thirty-four of the sixty-six individuals involved in the lawsuit were charged simply for being in the presence of a known gang member—in other words, for merely associating with someone designated as socially undesirable.

At oral argument, these concerns took center stage. Justice O'Connor worried aloud about "the potential for arbitrariness by the police in interpreting the law," particularly in "poor neighborhoods." To reduce the risk of discrimination against viewpoints or individuals, she instead recommended a loitering law that focused on specific locations like restrooms or schoolyards rather than types of people. Underscoring her concern that the ordinance focused on certain kinds of people, Justice Ginsburg asked the city's lawyer if he thought it permissible "if the statute said, instead of gang member, reasonably suspected of being a prostitute, reasonably suspected of being a beggar?"

The city's lawyer gave a troubling answer: some people deserve fewer rights than others because they are inherently threatening. "The kind of terror to the point where law abiding people won't even be able to use their streets and are at risk of drive by shootings and other things" doesn't exist with prostitutes and beggars, he stated. That is, he compared gang members to terrorists and was willing to criminalize their status—being a gang member—and merely being in a public place.

Enforcement of the ordinance left tens of thousands of young men, mostly black and Hispanic, with a police record. It affected not only gang members but also people who worked or socialized with such individuals. Those criminal records made it harder to find jobs and housing, obtain credit, or access certain government benefits.

The point isn't that gang members deserve special rights. It's that they don't deserve fewer rights than others simply because of their designation—something the state itself is in charge of managing. Nor do those who come into social contact with such individuals deserve fewer rights. Once a person crosses the line and commits a harmful act, then that misbehavior can be punished.

A free-speech approach might be useful in another context: reducing some unequal burdens faced by undocumented migrants and individuals who comfort them. Federal law makes it a crime to "encourage" or "induce" an alien to come to, enter, or reside in the United States in violation of the law. Violation of this provision is punished by a fine and up to five years in prison.

This is in addition to provisions that already outlaw transporting or harboring an undocumented alien, engaging in immigration fraud, illegally entering the United States, or conspiring to violate the immigration laws. But why would the government need this extra tool when they already have laws on the books that amply discourage migrants themselves from breaking immigration rules? It must be to affect the behavior of the immigrant community by denying them the aid of sympathetic neighbors and friends.[32]

In common parlance, the words "encourage" or "induce" mean "to persuade or influence" or "to give courage, comfort, or hope." Thus, the federal law regulates speech and not just conduct. But this is too expansive a limitation on speech, for it criminalizes both private and public discussions about immigration matters. It seemingly reaches family members and coworkers who seek only to console one another and figure out how to keep families intact and safe. The provision might chill legal advice to clients about whether to remain and contest their immigration status or removal. It also puts at risk support services offered by religious and other civic organizations, which might involve discussions of an unauthorized migrant's residence or legal status.

Even worse, the law threatens political advocacy. One hotly contested issue is what to do about the so-called Dreamers, foreign children brought to the United States when they were young and less morally culpable for violating the law, but for whom America is the only home they have ever known. Advising a Dreamer to remain in the United States to seek legal or political relief appears to violate this provision, as would merely telling her to stay if recourse runs out.

A major defect of the law is that it turns on the perspective a person holds. If you encourage an undocumented migrant to stay in America, you have violated the law but if you discourage the same person from doing so you haven't transgressed the law. Yet skewing public debate by disfavoring one viewpoint isn't permitted under First Amendment rules. Those in power can't insulate their policies from criticism in this fashion. This law restricts the free flow of conversation and denies citizens information needed to make sound choices.

There's still another problem. Advocacy of illegal activity is protected by the First Amendment unless the risk of lawbreaking or violence is "imminent." That's why proposing revolution is protected, as is the discussion of subjects that might be illegal at the time. This includes such topics as drug trafficking, civil disobedience, and—for historical reference—escaping from bondage.[33]

This restriction of pro-immigration persuasion resembles some of the despicable laws enacted by states and territories to quash abolitionist organizing and, later, to discourage freed persons from entering and remaining in those lands. The Territorial Laws of Kansas enacted by a proslavery assembly made it a crime to "advise, persuade, or induce" any slave to rebel against his master. It was also a crime to "aid or assist in enticing, decoying, or persuading" any slave belonging to another to resist his master or to "entice" or "persuade" a slave to escape from an officer. Other provisions made it illegal to "maintain that persons have not the right to hold slaves in this Territory" through "speaking or writing," and, more broadly, to print, write, or circulate any material calculated "to induce such slaves to escape."

All of these laws prohibiting speech that might induce slaves to resist were laid on top of other laws that banned the harboring of slaves, just as the speech restrictions today bolster existing laws making it illegal to "conceal," "harbor," or "shield" undocumented migrants. And in both situations, we have concerns about the humanitarian treatment of individuals whose legal status is in flux. With slaves, as with migrants today, some denied they could ever be true citizens of the United States because they were racially or culturally out of step with the dominant society.

Merely expressing an antislavery viewpoint in Kansas got you at least two years of imprisonment and hard labor, while printing or circulating material that might "induce" escape or produce "a disorderly, dangerous, or rebellious disaffection among the slaves" was punishable by "not less than five years" of the same.[34]

The Reconstruction generation denounced these "infamous statutes" as pure "wickedness," the product of an illegitimate effort to prevent "a free and independent constituency to question the validity of that legislation." Bingham declared that the legislation "abridges the freedom of speech and of the press" and denies persons "any process but that of brute force." He condemned the laws for preventing individuals "from uttering thoughts and 'sentiments' calculated to effect and secure the freedom of every citizen of the United States enslaved in the Territory of Kansas." Bingham denounced the monstrous efforts of equality's enemies who made it "a felony to aid freedom in its flight," and "a felony to shelter the houseless, to clothe the naked, to feed the hungry, and to help him that is ready to perish."[35]

Similarly, Congressman Galusha Grow of Pennsylvania castigated the territorial assembly for exacting "unwarranted oaths" from every free person to support proslavery laws while simultaneously "destroying freedom of opinion and the right of private judgment as to the constitutionality of the laws of the country, which is the birthright of an American citizen."[36]

In yet another historical parallel, many of these restrictions on political persuasion to protect the rights of slaves were aimed at not only migrants but also their allies in the antislavery and emigrant aid societies. One of the most famous groups was called the New England Emigrant Aid Company, founded in Boston initially as a for-profit but later converted into a nonprofit association. These organizations helped citizens who opposed slavery to resettle in territorial lands and thereby change the odds of the ongoing debate.

Proslavery forces wished to shut down these groups for allegedly stoking racial conflict in new lands, while abolitionists said such societies "originated far back in the history of the country." Their defenders in Congress asserted that the groups were formed in the name of "liberty, freedom, the right of freemen to occupy free territory," and performed any political work "peaceably"—plainly evoking rights guaranteed by the First Amendment.[37]

What we owe immigrants and refugees as a matter of basic equality is on the table, but that conversation itself at times can become an impediment to practical justice. Debates over modern immigration policy, like the battles over slavery or the rights of freed persons, are complicated and emotionally charged. For good reason: deciding which human beings may become full members of our political community implicates our highest values. So does how we treat each individual as we sort out the yeas from the nays.

A country cannot long endure if it is incapable of securing its borders and making difficult membership choices. But our debates over immigration should be passionate and informed rather than artificially restricted by one-sided rules because those we are talking about happen to be strangers.

Felon Disenfranchisement

We say in America that the right to vote is fundamental. Yet we haven't truly meant it. A closer look reveals a more disturbing picture of broken and partial citizens, badly reintegrated into the community after a criminal conviction—a politically destabilizing situation about which the Reconstruction Congress had been gravely concerned. The problem comes from major disparities in how states handle the right to vote after someone runs into trouble with the law.

Over six million Americans are currently forbidden from voting due to a past conviction. This makes the United States an outlier among advanced industrial democracies. With incarceration rates lately the highest in the world (though the United States has 4.4 percent of the world's population, it has 22 percent of the world's prisoners), the rise of a permanent political underclass becomes ever more possible.

If they were alive today, the patriots moved by the spirit of equality to enact the Reconstruction Amendments would be appalled by how state officials use the criminal law to hamper civic participation and entrench partisan control of government. How can a person who has had a brush with the law ever feel like an equal citizen again, with a real shot at a future, when his neighbors won't even trust him with the vote?[38]

Forty-eight states and the District of Columbia strip a person of the right to vote while incarcerated. Thirty-five states prevent parolees from voting, and thirty-one states keep probationers from doing so.

Four states deny the vote to all persons with felony convictions, and each state has a separate procedure that allows certain offenders to apply for reinstatement. Then there are the states that impose waiting periods whose clocks don't start until parole or probation is finished. In Wyoming, an offender has to wait five years before begging officials to restore this basic right of citizenship, while in Virginia individuals who commit a drug felony must wait seven years after completing a sentence.

The unequal effects on political participation are corrosive. American citizens rendered incapable of participating in elections are overwhelmingly poor and racial minorities. At this very moment, more than two million African Americans nationwide are disenfranchised. According to one estimate, one out of every thirteen black citizens will lose the right to vote sometime during his life and possibly never regain it.[39]

This is an outrage. Virtually every theory of democracy and conception of equality rests on the franchise as a linchpin to our system of government. The right to vote is said to be "preservative of all rights." Do we mean it? When President Johnson signed the Voting Rights Act of 1965 he said, "[T]he vote is the most powerful instrument ever devised by man for breaking down injustice and destroying the terrible walls which imprison men because they are different from other men."[40]

Securing ballot access empowers members of marginalized groups to "do the rest for themselves." But a growing number of Americans can't protect themselves through the political process even if they wanted to do so. That's a recipe for permanent second-class status for former inmates and a growing threat to democracy.

While vote restrictions for felons have a long pedigree, states have gone too far in distorting the democratic process, returning to a strategy that has its roots in the Black Codes and Jim Crow. The true reason for "manipulation of the ballot" was "to establish white supremacy in this State," declared John B. Knox, as he opened the convention to amend the Alabama Constitution in 1901. But the official justifications would have to change. Stopping "the menace of negro domination" remained the paramount goal, but the public rationales for reducing black voting power would shift from "his race" to "his intellectual and moral condition."[41]

Debates in Virginia followed a similar pattern. Disenfranchisement was previously limited to "infamous crimes," but in 1902 Virginians also opted to expand the grounds to "any felony, bribery, petit larceny," and other crimes so as to preserve the political power of "the dominant race." When some legislators worried that whites could be affected, Democratic state senator Carter Glass reassured delegates that the change "does not necessarily deprive a single white man of the ballot, but will inevitably cut from the existing electorate four-fifths of the negro voters." It would be "discrimination within the letter of the law," Senator Glass promised. "This plan of popular suffrage will eliminate the darkey as a political factor in this State in less than five years."

Today, the forces of disenfranchisement hang their hat on passing language in the Fourteenth Amendment that mentions "citizens of the United States" whose vote might be abridged "for participation in rebellion, or other crime." There's no doubt this provision presumes that states have some power to restrict a convicted criminal's vote. But its language is too mild to justify all of the inequality that has been created in its name. The provision doesn't enshrine unlimited state power over the franchise. Instead, the entire point of the discussion is to penalize states that illegitimately interfere with the franchise by altering how their electoral votes will be calculated.[42]

Reading these words in an extreme "states' rights" manner would also undermine the purpose of the Reconstruction Amendments, which was to force states to respect the civil rights of the politically despised. As we have seen, supporters of those provisions drew attention to the multiple ways that enemies of equality abused the criminal law to keep political minorities underfoot. Over and over, they argued that guaranteeing equality, due process, and other rights would be crucial to a healthy civic order. These statesmen went on to enact the Fifteenth Amendment to underscore the indispensable nature of the vote.

In a reaction against equality, many states turned to the twin powers of criminal law and felon disfranchisement to flout the rights of black citizens. Florida adopted a new constitution in 1868 that expanded its felon disenfranchisement program to cover offenses such as vagrancy and petty theft. At the same time, state officials ramped up usage of such laws to throw freed blacks into the criminal justice system. The approach facilitated the twin goals of reasserting white domination of political affairs and disciplining black lives through law enforcement, judges, and their allies. It's no surprise that the nonwhite prison population in America doubled between 1850 and 1870. In Alabama alone, nonwhites at one time made up only 2 percent of the prison population but that figure leapt to 74 percent by 1870.[43]

Understanding how structural inequality came to exist may be one thing, yet overcoming contemporary obstacles to dismantling such systems of injustice is quite another. Concerns about upsetting long-standing practices, disrupting gubernatorial prerogatives, and altering partisan advantages work together to preserve status quo inequality.

If those in charge love power more than they love equality, there might be another road to justice: some restrictions can be trimmed through the Free Speech Clause. Let's take Florida, which has been among the most flagrant abusers of its authority over the vote. The state's 1868 constitution permanently deprived every man and woman convicted of a felony of the right to vote. While in 1980 only 2.6 percent of eligible voters were barred from doing so for this reason, by 2016 10.4 percent were disfranchised. The racial inequities were stark. One out of every five black citizens in Florida was barred from voting due to a conviction.

The only way to regain the franchise is by petitioning the state's Executive Clemency Board after waiting five or seven years, depending on the crime. This body meets only four times a year. Once a citizen applies for restoration, staff members review the papers and make recommendations, but they aren't binding. Florida's governor reserves "the unfettered discretion to deny clemency at any time, for any reason." In fact, the governor crowed, "We can do whatever we want."[44]

Even after saying no to reinstatement, a governor has sometimes barred individuals from reapplying for reinstatement in arbitrary and punitive ways. In one egregious case, Governor Scott's office refused to restore a fifty-four-year-old man's vote and said he could not reapply for another fifty years!

If a state official refuses to restore someone's right to vote for reasons that violate federal constitutional protections, say, against racial or religious discrimination, such a decision obviously cannot stand. But as we have repeatedly seen in other situations, it can be incredibly challenging to prove a deliberate plan to harm someone where multiple decision makers are involved. The disparities based on race, poverty, and party are striking, but could it be said which, if any, decisions are actually motivated by these grounds?

It's often too much to ask to have to isolate improper reasons in individual cases. Pervasive inequities are perpetrated by a two-step system that disables the right to vote for everyone convicted of a felony, and then subjects individuals to onerous, arbitrary procedures for regaining lost rights on the back end. The scheme itself encourages discrimination and then helps to hide evidence that it is occurring.

After hiding the ball, some of these same officials then have the nerve to say that if more black and brown people are losing their vote, they should just stop committing crimes. There's no evidence of bias, they suggest, only demonstrated criminality. Disenfranchisement regimes thus promote inequality in another sense: *rhetorically*, by distracting people from the legal architectures of power that facilitate mass incarceration, and by redirecting attention to popular but false narratives of dangerous minorities. What we then fail to see, and all too often refuse to grapple with, is that many different institutions and cultural practices work together to foster pervasive inequality.

In January 2018, a federal judge for the first time ruled that Florida's vote reinstatement scheme violated the Constitution. But the jurist wasn't persuaded that discrimination had been shown definitively. Rather, he determined that the procedure offended the rights to free speech and political association. This decision was both surprising and courageous. It should be applauded as a textbook example of equality by other means.

As the judge correctly points out, state procedures regulating voting impact "core First Amendment activity." Today, even corporations are understood to have speech rights implicated by their ability to participate in elections. If faceless corporations can speak and participate in political affairs, then why not former inmates, who are flesh and blood after all, and have material interests on the line during elections?

In Florida, high officials claimed they were restricting the franchise to "responsible voters," but that term is so malleable that it's not possible to reliably predict what would be taken into account. Not only did the scheme lead to arbitrary and unfair results, there was also a real risk that Florida's scheme facilitated viewpoint discrimination against citizens. A significant probability existed that government officials could reward former felons who are more likely to vote for their candidates or policies, or deny the applications of citizens who might oppose the party in power. But as Judge Mark Walker warned, "A state cannot yank the right to vote from a Republican felon but retain voting rights for Democratic felons."

There was other evidence that officials manipulated the reinstatement process for partisan gain. In four years under a Democratic governor, 154,000 citizens had their voting rights restored, while over a period of seven years, a Republican administration returned the vote to fewer than 3,000 citizens.[45]

During one reinstatement hearing, the governor asked about an illegal vote cast by a white man seeking restoration of his right to vote. The applicant chuckled and said, "Actually, I voted for you." The governor granted his application. At the same time, five others—all of whom were black and were also asked about illegal ballots—had their applications denied.

Judge Walker also found that applicants who criticized the government or existing laws were treated differently than applicants who didn't generate controversy. A Navy veteran who spoke out during his hearing about the unfairness of felony disenfranchisement laws saw his application denied due to traffic tickets. By contrast, several applicants who said nothing politically controversial but had traffic violations had their votes reinstated.

Others have agreed that byzantine or irregularly enforced voting procedures deny citizens a fair shake. In 1982, a black man living in Mississippi argued that a local board of commissioners targeted African Americans for disenfranchisement and that it did so to retaliate against individuals involved in politically controversial activities. Federal judges said that his allegations, if proved, would violate the Constitution. He had shown, for instance, that there were many people living in the county with a felony conviction like himself who had not been deprived of the vote.[46]

Although a speech-based outcome is not the same as a ruling grounded on equality, it is nearly as good for the good that it does. It's a defensible means of reducing systemic inequities when the equality principle isn't a realistic answer. For one thing, it's effective. The ruling puts the entire voting deprivation process on hold. Florida must then decide what to do. If the state insists on presuming that all felons are forever undeserving of the vote, then it must come up with a restoration regime that reduces the risk of impermissible considerations.

For another thing, it's an important achievement on which others can build. It might be easier to secure support for such a rationale because few states act in such openly defiant ways. In that sense, a person who wishes to do something about outlier jurisdictions like Florida but has qualms about going too far can act without threatening the power to restrict the vote across the board. Once a precedent for tackling egregious schemes is established, it becomes easier to build upon such victories.

In the best of worlds, people will push legislators to enact laws that automatically reinstate a felon's voting rights. That alone would reduce the possibility of political mischief, especially during election season when the temptation to help the party in power can be overpowering. Another solution is to reduce the sheer number of crimes that lead to the loss of the vote in the first place. Ensuring that all nonviolent offenders can vote, as Virginia has done recently with drug offenses, or repealing or reducing waiting periods, as Delaware and Texas have done for most crimes, would also reduce inequities. Better yet, a state could follow the lead of Maine and Vermont and forswear its vote-stripping power completely as utterly incompatible with a modern democracy, as a harsh measure that's unlikely to deter crime or facilitate rehabilitation, and as a power whose exercise inevitably leads to discrimination.

The Wages of Nationalism

ONE OF OUR BIGGEST challenges today comes from a resurgence of nationalism and white supremacy. There is overlap between the two projects, even if they aren't identical. It's best to diagnose each separately to see how equality is impacted, and figure out how free speech can address some of the negative effects of these phenomena, even though rights alone can't stop either from happening.

Patriotic sentiment, which can be stirred to great effect regardless of one's party or class, is harnessed through nationalistic projects for some political ends. Historically, those ends have been war, major economic reorganization, state-building at home or abroad, and the codification of new political values on a countrywide scale. Liberal nationalism has been critical to the founding of America, the reconstruction of the rights of citizenship after the Civil War, the creation of the welfare state, and the dismantling of Jim Crow. Conservative nationalism has revitalized civic institutions, ensured that discussions of duties to the community accompany claims of individual rights, and modernized the capacities of national defense.

Even so, the burdens of nationalistic projects are never borne equally. When tribalism rears its head, the hunt for common enemies of the people ramps up in earnest. In the past, special forms of misery were inflicted upon kulaks, plutocrats, socialists, and pacifists. Today, the "enemies of the people" might be journalists, non-Christians, racial justice protesters, religious fundamentalists, and foreigners.

One of the playbooks of the nationalist is the manipulation of cultural symbols, like the flag, the pledge, or the Bible. What the First Amendment can do is sever the connection between state power and ideology, so that government officials can neither completely control the meaning of a political symbol nor run the machinery of the law to punish those who resist nationalist projects.

That's exactly what the Court did when it held that a Jehovah's Witness could refuse to salute the American flag without facing discipline from school authorities. Marie and Gathie Barnet, ages eight and nine, lived in a rural area. They were raised by their father to believe that paying homage to the flag was akin to worshipping a graven image in violation of the Bible. Their teacher had no trouble with their view, but the principal wouldn't stand for it and expelled the girls. At the time, in the early 1940s, nationalist feelings ran high as America battled hostile forces abroad and worried about infiltration at home.

"One man's comfort and inspiration," Robert Jackson observed, "is another's jest and scorn." When the Justices struck down the compulsory pledge, calling it coerced expression, they also made clear that doing so would benefit those with unorthodox views at a time when many Americans were demanding uniformity of sentiment. First, while couched as an individual's "right to speak his own mind," in practice that rule benefits entire communities that hold religious or philosophical objections to political rituals.

Constitutional protections extend to members of social movements such as Black Lives Matter, who might face government-directed repercussions for taking a knee. Political leaders can certainly condemn football players and other activists who refuse to participate in the National Anthem, but they can't take any formal actions to punish their symbolic protests or conspire with others to deny their rights.[47]

Second, if the state possesses the power to compel patriotism through legal sanctions, then presumably it could take other, more forceful, measures against holdouts. "Those who begin coercive elimination of dissent soon find themselves exterminating dissenters," warned Robert Jackson ominously. Putting a stop to legal sanctions for refusing to bow before political idols breaks this cycle of state-sponsored violence before we go too far down that road.

The mobilization of national sentiment stirs unpredictable passions and begets, in the immortal words of Jefferson, "habits of hypocrisy and meanness." Nationwide, over two thousand children were expelled in the 1940s for refusing to salute the flag. Besides handing out expulsions, some local officials around the country had threatened to send children to "reformatories maintained for criminally inclined juveniles." Parents themselves had been prosecuted for causing delinquency. Police in Odessa, Texas, arrested seventy Jehovah's Witnesses for refusing to salute the flag, and then released them to a mob, which tried to stone them. In Richwood, West Virginia, religious objectors were tied up by law enforcement, forced to drink castor oil, and then paraded through town.[48]

The principle of free speech stays the hand of the highest national official all the way to the lowliest county employee. Moreover, it helps keep schools from being converted into a weapon against "any class, creed, party, or faction." That way, no child will be used by the state merely as a means to a political end.

Reducing this danger is critical during times of nationalist fervor, because it will be children who are the most likely props and casualties in patriotic narratives spun by adults. They are the athletes and other students who take a knee, who demonstrate against white supremacy or gun violence, or who give comfort or aid to friends who happen to be undocumented migrants.[49]

Third, preventing coerced participation in government rituals and propaganda programs reduces discrimination against "occasional eccentricity and abnormal attitudes"—and, by extension, the individuals and groups holding such views. When nationalism is ascendant, conscientious objectors will be lumped together with treasonous conspirators. That's precisely what happened to the Jehovah's Witnesses in the '40s: they were called spies, traitors, and "fifth columnists"—the last, a label that was even used to describe people of Japanese ancestry while America was at war.

Writing separately in the pledge case, Justices Black and Douglas underlined this point by observing that patriotic incantations can serve as "a handy implement for disguised religious persecution." The way it works: political performances of this sort publicly identify conscientious objectors without seeming to do so. Dissenters must out themselves if they wish to remain true to their beliefs. Through peer pressure, nonconformists are then easily ostracized. Any natural allies are also discouraged from lending aid because, having had to participate in the ritual themselves, they are more likely to resent the excusing of objectors from the activity as unfair.

To put it another way, nationalistic propaganda creates the appearance of equality, but it's an impoverished simulacrum of justice that elevates identical behavior along with a unity of purpose. It dissolves mutual obligations owed between individuals and weakens our commitment to limits based on legality or humanity.

The principle of free speech steps in to ensure both dignity and equality. In fact, the free-speech principle overlaps with the idea of religious freedom and equality to safeguard religious views that depart not only from majoritarian sentiments, but also from established doctrines within the religious traditions themselves. It wouldn't alter the outcome even if most mainstream churches in America had no problem with a mandatory pledge—say, on the theory that routine, outward displays of affection for their country are just something good Christians owe to Caesar. The fact that most believers had a harmonious vision of church and state wouldn't allow the dominant religious viewpoint to be imposed through civil law on sects that differ in their reading of scripture, any more than it would allow a majority of Americans generally to do so.[50]

On June 6, 1966, Sydney Street, a black war veteran, heard on the radio that civil rights leader James Meredith had been shot in Mississippi. Upset, he retrieved a neatly folded American flag from his New York City apartment, walked to the intersection of St. James and Lafayette, and lit the flag on fire. As the flag burned and a crowd gathered, he said aloud, "If they let that happen to Meredith, we don't need an American flag."

The police charged Street with malicious mischief for defiling an American flag. While there was uncertainty over whether he was convicted simply for burning the flag or for uttering defiant words, the Justices made clear that Street could not be put in jail for "distasteful" or disrespectful expression.

As shocking as Street's actions were, they conveyed a message that underscored his belief in equality. To Street and millions of other citizens battling racial segregation, the United States had abandoned, "at least temporarily, one of its national symbols." According to their shared vision of constitutional life, equality and dignity are central features of the American project.

"Isn't anyone going to help me?" James Meredith had whispered as he lay bleeding alone in the road. If the government couldn't keep safe a black man who had integrated white schools and signed up black voters, then it had failed the basic test for legitimacy. The flag of such a government no longer commanded the allegiance of the most vulnerable citizens. It might as well burn.[51]

As the exercise of the fundamental right of free speech to protest violations of equality, burning his flag represented an appeal to liberal nationalism as a remedy to white supremacy. Street demanded: Will you jail me for protesting racial inequality at the same time you allow a white supremacist to gun down a civil rights marcher in the light day? If so, his actions suggested, we might have order but we'll never have justice.

In truth, the American flag wasn't Street's target. Rather, he was assailing the kind of nationalism that worries more about maintaining appearances—keeping perfect order in the streets or burnishing the myth of an untouchable flag—than about the moral task of meeting the tangible needs of each citizen.

Vindicating Street's right to speak freely prevented him from being singled out as a protester based on the provocative quality of his approach, the substance of his proequality message, or his race. The legal solution met his defiant message with a hopeful message that rights do exist, that they are important, and that peaceful politics is the only way forward. In every practical sense, protecting unfettered expression allowed him, and the millions of other Americans outraged by the racist attack on Meredith, to continue to press the cause of civic equality.

But let's not pretend that Street's plea for equality is somehow antinationalist. It's as nationalistic as the vision of Chief Justice John Marshall, who helped establish the supremacy of federal law in early America, or John Bingham, who insisted that the rights of national citizenship trump state and local prerogatives, or even Martin Luther King, who took to the streets so that racial equality would finally be part of our inalienable rights.

If we believe in American constitutionalism, the choice can't be between nationalism and something else. Rather, we must choose between competing visions of nationalism: one that demands obedience and superficial sameness regardless of the costs, or another that esteems authenticity of sentiment and equality for all.

Love of country can't be quashed. It won't be dissipated no matter how many laws we pass or eloquent opinions judges publish. Instead, our best hope for surviving the worst is to ride out nationalism's peaks when they come, while softening its edges wherever we can.

THE CHALLENGE OF WHITE NATIONALISM

"YOU WILL NOT REPLACE us!" shouted white nationalists who descended on Charlottesville, Virginia, in the summer of 2017. "White lives matter!" From Berkeley, California, to Shelbyville, Tennessee, activists invigorated by the rightward turn in national politics have gathered openly to promote racial solidarity, chant anti-Semitic slogans, and revel in "blood and soil" imagery.

Let's be honest: feelings of racial or ethnic self-love are unsurprising as a matter of anthropology. After all, the instinct to prefer one's own is a survival technique hardwired in each person—however racism enters that process. Yet expressions of white power, closely associated with the dehumanization of racial minorities and other undesirables, conjures fears of prejudice and subjugation. The impulse to celebrate one's race or ethnicity will seem natural to some, and horrifying to others.

Where it becomes a clear and present danger to liberalism—and especially equality—is when tribal sentiments become formalized as state policies, programs, and official practices to ensure that only the people who belong to the right race or hold the correct cultural beliefs can exercise political power. At that point, history has shown that an exclusionary attitude turns into an effective means to terrify, degrade, or extinguish whole groups of people.

This is the avowed objective of white nationalism. We need to be able to see the project for what it really is, whether it is called Aryanism, neo-Nazism, or the rebranded alt-right. As a political movement, white nationalism trades in nostalgia for an imagined past of glorious self-governance by white people, writing the contributions of other peoples and cultures completely out of the story of America.

Activists have divergent ideas about how to save the white race from extinction, whether it's making living conditions so miserable for racial minorities that they depart the country of their own accord, or ramping up mass deportations, or initiating a race war. But they all agree on the same end goals: purifying the population and reestablishing government by racially conscious whites alone.[52]

Knowing that illiberal ideas can lead to murderous forms of inequality, why not allow the state to intervene a step or two earlier, to interdict racist or xenophobic speech from being uttered? We could say, as some have urged, that suppressing hate speech is being done in the name of equality. After all, white nationalists reject equality as the basis of citizenship, which they insist destroys inherent human differences as well as the capacity for excellence. They also deny the value of pluralism, which they think causes the mongrelization of the white race and the destruction of Euro-American culture.[53]

Hard-core racists are exultant when they see crosses burning or Klan members marching through Jewish neighborhoods or their followers celebrating on the campus of Mr. Jefferson's university—all of which the First Amendment permits. They think they are reaching white citizens who feel ashamed of their heritage and imbuing their cause with a sense of inevitability.

Given our promise to protect equality-enhancing speech as well as hate-producing expression, it's worth asking whether this approach also contains the means to undermine equality in the long run. Does protecting hateful expression destroy the very conditions for equality? Yes, we must be honest and recognize that such a risk exists.

This danger of democratic failure comes from the choice we have made to require the government to treat all speakers in an evenhanded way. Because it's possible that freedom of expression gives just enough breathing space for totalitarian ideas to win the day.

Antifascists—and for that matter, antiracists more generally—say that taking this sort of risk is pure foolishness. According to critics of liberalism, fascists have historically gained power lawfully, and even a handful of fascists have been able to seize authority successfully. Fascism must be confronted directly whenever possible, they say, so that the philosophy never gains even the appearance of popular approval or legitimacy.

They have a point. There's no doubt that hateful authoritarian ideas have currency at a time when citizens live disconnected existences and fewer individuals have faith in democracy. Americans scour the Internet, open to alternative forms of solidarity when traditional institutions break down. That way lies the possibility of radicalization. Oppressive programs almost always begin through political expression that dehumanizes outsiders while making insiders feel special, destined for greatness.

Antifascists make up a decentralized movement, with some anarchists mixed in among left-leaning activists. They are not united philosophically so much as they agree on the necessity of destroying fascism. Most have no patience for impediments to that goal—whether they involve legal process or respect for the rights of identified fascists. "No free speech for fascists," one Midwest antifascist group declared, and others have taken a similar hard line. To save the world from fascism, they would have us deviate from one of liberalism's most cherished tenets: that the government must strive to treat individuals based on what they actually do rather than based on who they are.[54]

What's a practical egalitarian to do? Tactically, it's possible to support certain private actions engaged by antifascists, such as participating in peaceful counterprotest, identifying white supremacists in sensitive or prominent government positions, or rushing to the aid of proequality activists in harm's way.

But philosophically, egalitarians must draw the line at dehumanizing members of the far right or denying them liberties simply because of who they are. On this point, the practical egalitarian must part ways with the antifascist. Whatever means are taken in the name of equality can't corrupt the project itself. Otherwise, the pursuit of equality collapses upon itself, becoming no more than a war of all against all.

Remember: extremism has been with us for as long as there has been political order. No one has a monopoly on the impulse to erase his ideological enemies from the equation once and for all. To the contrary, visionaries of all stripes have been tempted to take shortcuts to remake the world in their own images. Anarchists, abolitionists, traditionalists, and communists have at different times turned to guns, bombs, and beatings in an attempt to settle political debate conclusively. But turning to repressive measures has never completely extinguished love of freedom and liberty. Instead of violence to settle scores, we have made the decision to prefer never-ending dialogue.

In the late 1940s, after encountering the horrors of European Nazism and Fascism, we almost made a different choice. Robert Jackson saw the fragility of democracy up close, having served as America's chief prosecutor in the Nuremberg trials. Upon returning home, he observed that the ends of nationalism "have been racial or territorial security, support of a dynasty or regime, and particular plans for saving souls." For Jackson, speech that singled out entire groups of people for derision is so destructive that it can't be countenanced by a democratic society. He urged that we put such degrading expression outside of the Constitution's protection.

Jackson also worried about the historical strategies of "two organized groups of revolutionary fanatics, each of which has imported to this country the strong-arm technique" developed in Europe. "One faction organizes a mass meeting," he pointed out, while "the other organizes pickets to harass it." The possibility that this could descend into street clashes wasn't theoretical but real—and in some cases, orchestrated by the marchers themselves. Indeed, radicals often seek to "paralyze and discredit" democratic authority by causing chaos in the streets and sowing fear in the population. Images of disorder then pave the way for muscular acts of repression.[55]

So when Justice Jackson's colleagues wanted to overturn Father Arthur Terminiello's breach-of-the-peace conviction for whipping up a crowd of eight hundred, Justice Jackson objected. Over a thousand counterdemonstrators agitated outside the auditorium in Chicago as Terminiello warned of "the scum" and "menace of Communism," who had "murdered," "raped," and sent people into slavery.

"That is what they want for you," he said of counterprotesters. Comparing his enemies to "snakes" and "bedbugs," Terminiello bellowed, "We must not lock ourselves in an upper room for fear of the Jews. . . . We don't want them here; we want them to go back where they came from."

Despite the hateful nature of Terminiello's words, the Supreme Court protected his right to express himself. In his opinion, Justice Douglas insisted that the function of free speech is to "invite dispute," even if a person's oration "stirs people to anger." Terminiello certainly spewed racist, conspiratorial, and anti-Semitic ideas, but he hadn't called on his audience to do anything in particular to break the law.

The choice we've made collectively, then, is to place our bets on robust debate, believing that terrible ideas should be ventilated and defeated in the light of day, rather than locked away. It's not the choice that many other countries have made, but even those who have outlawed hate speech haven't been able to extinguish prejudice or extremism.[56]

Of course, our choice to take a chance on free speech won't guarantee perpetual peace. It's certainly not enough to stop bad things from happening. But it expresses hope that in the long run the approach will work better than running to and fro, trying to extinguish frightening ideas. This is the same conviction that democracy, while far from perfect, is better than its alternatives.[57]

There are several things that protecting free speech does to promote equality. Perhaps counterintuitively, when we guarantee the avowed racist's right to say what he feels and to associate with other racists if he so desires, we actually affirm the deeper values of equality and dignity. A nonpaternalistic understanding of free speech is based on the belief that an individual won't act on every fleeting thought. A person might reject a virulent message or, having been influenced by it, might change his mind before acting on it. A system of free speech is also premised on the sense that listeners, too, must take some responsibility for their actions, or else ideas can be quashed simply because someone else later behaves badly.

Just as important: a citizen is more than the worst thing he has ever said or believed. There is the chance that someone who entertains terrible, even dangerous ideas, can be turned around by friends, families, or colleagues. This won't be true of everyone. But it will be true of enough people that we shouldn't give up on those who have been associated with a horrible idea. This ideal of free speech as a redemptive value is something that egalitarians, too, can get behind.

Moreover, by empowering the extremist to speak, we are also disarming him in another, crucial way: by depriving him of the charge of bias. Every radical accuses the government of being out to get him, every man of the people asserts that elites will stop at nothing to hide the truth.

Once conspiracy theorists and extremists have said their piece, it's harder for them to claim unfair treatment. They can still make an accusation of bias, in fact they're certain to do it anyway. But the charge doesn't have the same sting as if the state had tried to suppress their point of view for fear it is too dangerous to be said aloud.

There's nothing that freedom-loving Americans hate more than efforts to silence someone. Ask a young person what will generate sympathy for a cause, and the answer is likely to be: paternalistic efforts to control what can be read or watched, or the oddball ideas that can be entertained, even experimentally. Suppressing ideas only makes them more exotic, more mysterious—imbuing them with a power they wouldn't have if they had to stand on their own. How many people, for instance, consciously choose to read works from the list of perennially banned books?

Banning ideas actually erodes the necessary conditions for equality. It breeds resentment, stokes anger, and makes citizens suspicious of law itself. Just as treating people differently based on their status damages the connections between citizens and faith in government, so too punishing some people more harshly for having unpopular ideas undermines respect for the law and the community.

What went wrong in Charlottesville and Berkeley wasn't allowing white supremacists to speak and congregate. It's that knowing the situation would be volatile, city officials failed to take sufficient precautions to keep radicals apart from one another, and ensure safe conditions for citizens to demonstrate peacefully. The risk of violence is real, but it can and should be managed for the sake of speech and equality.

Justice Jackson was wrong when he said that protecting hateful ideas renders the authorities powerless to deal with the prospect of disorder. In fact, cities, states, and universities can all impose limits on when and how expression takes place, especially at large-scale events. Speech can't be banned outright, but reasonable conditions can be placed on permits for parades and rallies. Participants can be told where they may congregate, sensitive locations can be put off-limits, durational limits may be added, and attendees may be barred from assembling with weapons and other dangerous items to ensure that an event remains a peaceful affair.[58]

When these conditions are well designed and implemented, all speakers—the opponents of equality, the antiracists, and everyone in between—can safely contribute to public discourse. How an event is managed can reinforce the equal worth of every speaker-citizen. Conversely, treating a speaker differently merely feeds the sneering message of extremists that equality and liberty are nothing but empty slogans, that those in charge will violate their own values out of sheer desperation to crush opposing views.

Allowing everyone to speak and associate on the same terms doesn't mean that the government has to stand by idly while hate-mongers flood the public arena. It means only that the state can't have one set of rules for the speech that most people like, and another set of rules for speech that is unpopular.

Each of us can exercise our own prerogative to speak freely to counteract the effect of giving white nationalists a platform. Civic leaders would be doing equality by other means when they call out illiberal ideas and denounce the efforts of groups organized to undermine civic equality. We won't always agree on who or what is being denounced, but it's better that each of us gets a chance to sort this out than it is for the state to decide in advance what we can and can't hear.

Indeed, our commitment to equality requires us to denounce illiberal ideas early and often, even though we can't suppress them. Judges and elected officials have often added their voices to those of ordinary citizens in repudiating extremism at the same time they allow enemies of equality to have their moment.[59]

Hate may get a hearing; free speech doesn't guarantee that any idea will be received as worthy or useful. Nor does the First Amendment shield a speaker from facing the consequences of his speech. So long as the government is not involved, the person who voices extreme ideas can be shunned, denied private employment, and refused other opportunities without violating the Constitution.

There's no such thing as the enjoyment of liberty completely untainted by controversy or judgment. In fact, an important way that freedom of expression aids equality is that in order to exercise the right of speech, a person must choose to associate with certain ideas. That feature of our system of rights makes it easier to identify those with far-out and potentially dangerous ideas and to monitor their actions if warranted. White separatists might get to say their piece, but in doing so, they rightly earn special attention from the rest of us to ensure that peaceful speech doesn't cross the line into criminal behavior.

And even when the government is involved, there are limits to free expression. The speech rights of government employees—such as judges, teachers, and police officers—may be properly restricted when certain expressive activities would interfere with their jobs. Holding white supremacist views or advocating for white separatism surely interferes with the capacity to enforce the law equally or to teach impressionable children about civic values.

Words do wound. Racist speech can inspire acts of prejudice. There's no denying it. Yet in the end, we must resist the temptation to silence the speech we find dangerous. Defenders of slavery, and later racial segregation, gave in to that temptation but it didn't end debate. Those of us who love equality shouldn't make the same mistake.

When slaveholders stacked the deck by banning antislavery expression, it just made abolitionists more convinced of the righteousness of their cause and more willing to take extreme measures. Ideas have a way of escaping their would-be captors—surreptitiously, if they must. Banned pamphlets are passed back and forth by true believers, words of resistance are whispered by candlelight.

Quashing expression is a cop-out, a feel-good way of gesturing toward the goal of equality, without doing anything about structural problems that allow hatred to fester and outlandish political solutions to gain traction. It feeds a false impression that inequality can be solved through simple solutions.

The truth is that equality can't be achieved that easily. Inequality won't be defeated if we prevent people from expressing inegalitarian thoughts. Overt prejudice is merely the most visible aspect of inequality in America. To make progress, the fight must be waged in the trenches, through electoral politics, civic activism, and lawsuits. Only these methods can yield durable victories.

There is hope. While the rallies in Berkeley and Charlottesville led to outbreaks of disorder and galvanized the far right, subsequent events in Boston and Gainesville occurred mostly peacefully. Exponentially more proequality forces showed up than alt-right figures.

A resurgent white nationalism accomplishes something else. No longer can anyone claim with a straight face that inequality and racism have been solved in America. The comforting thought that we had already achieved a postracial society proved to be fleeting, more of an impediment to practical equality than the impetus for reform. On the contrary, we have all had to face the uncomfortable truth that many policies voters are willing to support overlap with proposals enthusiastically endorsed by avowed enemies of equality.

It's possible that the direst warnings are accurate: we've reached the limits of democracy, and liberalism itself is in its death throes. But if that's true, it won't be because we've decided, out of sheer desperation, to abandon all of our long-held convictions.

And if those predictions turn out to be wrong, if Americans once again repudiate white nationalism and commit to tackling the injustices that plague our daily lives—then we just might have something left that's worth fighting for.

CONCLUSION

WHEN PRESIDENT JOHNSON SIGNED the Civil Rights Act of 1964 into law, he celebrated the occasion as part of the "struggle for freedom" in which each generation has "fought to renew and enlarge its meaning," and called on all Americans to "lay aside irrelevant differences and make our Nation whole." A year later he assumed a bolder stance, calling the Voting Rights Act "a triumph for freedom as huge as any victory that has ever been won on any battlefield."[1]

President Kennedy had earlier cautioned that the pursuit of equality was not the "search for charity," for that merely produces a feeling of "condescension" in people. Instead, he appealed to that "plain, proud and priceless quality that united us all as Americans: A sense of justice." LBJ himself was quick to add that "we can't legislate human dignity," but we can equip people with "potent weapons" to guarantee their own dignity.[2]

This is the right approach, but it is all easier said than done. What we've had to learn the hard way is that injustice can't be vanquished during a final showdown. Opposition to the transformative idea of equality runs too deep. As LBJ acknowledged after "Bloody Sunday" in Selma, "Experience has clearly shown that the existing process of law cannot overcome systematic and ingenious discrimination."

Enacting landmark legislation, even one valorized as "the greatest piece of social legislation in our generation," isn't enough to finish the job. Authoring the Declaration of Independence, writing the words "equal protection" into the Constitution after the Civil War, finally ending a filibuster on a civil rights bill as Americans filled the streets demanding equal treatment—these are all historic achievements in their own right. But they're still not enough.

We have to conceive of a better plan to outwork enemies of equality and bring together friends of justice. The stakes are high, given modern government's ability to destroy lives and deny opportunities. The state's expanded capability to stratify individuals along all kinds of dimensions, to sort and re-sort people in novel ways, calls for an equally crafty response to ensure equality and freedom.

So beware of purists who would lead you to glorious, spectacular defeats when everyday suffering can be reduced through less glamorous, persistent labor. I have argued that the best way to do justice in the face of manifest inequality is to become grittier in our disposition, while broadening our tactics. Instead of flying higher and higher into theory in a quest for gorgeously rendered concepts that can solve all of our problems at once, our goal should be to immerse ourselves in the squalor of human existence.

For inspiration, we need look no further than the words of Langston Hughes, who had a message for all "beauty-makers." "Give up beauty for a moment," he instructs, because it prevents us from perceiving the depths of human suffering and stifles the possibilities for true peace. "Look at harshness, look at pain,/ Look at life again." We have to be willing to relinquish, at least temporarily, perfect dreams, perfect outcomes, perfect law. Once released from the prison of the ideal, we can finally wrestle with the everyday humiliations that people experience when they are treated differently.[3]

Our struggle for equality requires a double-fisted approach. Wherever possible, we should continue to call out forms of inequality that undermine the basis of our community. But where major resistance arises and the risk of a calamitous setback emerges, the answer isn't to fight on a single front against all odds. Nor is it to take shelter in a bunker and dream of more congenial circumstances. Instead, the battle ought to be waged on multiple fronts to probe for points of weakness, and to initiate fresh lines of attack.

Pragmatic measures must be undertaken to reduce inequities even when—and *especially* when—the direct appeal of egalitarianism fails to win the day. The "moral growth of a great nation requires reflection, as well as observation," Frederick Douglass astutely observed at the height of the Civil War. But this deliberative process takes time.

While each of us plays our part in those great ethical debates, we must still meet the need for effective solutions now. Smaller agreements can be reached to lift unequal burdens and reduce social pain, even if we remain unable to agree on the big questions.[4]

Pursuing justice requires us to develop a keen historical understanding of inequality's causes, without rancor or a thirst for vengeance. It also demands effective action. We must hold fast to our convictions without being headstrong, and become skillful at managing different tactics and possible outcomes without falling for cheap victories.

By reducing the suffering of vulnerable populations through other methods, we lay the groundwork for future arguments, coalitions, and victories. Bit by bit, we can improve the social conditions that are critical to making lasting progress. These victories reinforce linkages between egalitarianism and other values, building a civic culture of equal respect. Along the way, we forge alliances between human beings with different backgrounds and priorities, across the many fault lines that separate us.

ACKNOWLEDGMENTS

THIS BOOK WAS MADE possible by the kindness of many individuals. First and foremost, my loving family: Tammy, Graeme, and Nora. My agent, Ellen Geiger, put me together with talented editor Matt Weiland at Norton, who shepherded this project from concept to print in record time. The support of Remy Cawley, Zarina Patwa, and the entire production team has been truly impressive. I am blessed with colleagues throughout the academy who support my work in too many ways to count: Bruce Ackerman, Keith Bybee, Susan Carle, Stuart Chinn, Bob Dinerstein, Lia Epperson, Willy Forbath, Megan Ming Francis, Mark Graber, Brian Murchison, Camille Nelson, Anna Law, Karen Orren, Aziz Rana, Jenny Roberts, Christopher Seaman, Stephen Skowronek, Dan Tichenor, Priscilla Yamin. A pack of diligent students rendered invaluable research assistance, including Cody Meixner, Sarah Pongrace, Jenna Ruddock, Stefanie Steinberg, Margaret Strouse, and Catherine Warren. I am grateful to have been able to bounce ideas in the book off others at Washington and Lee University's School of Law, the University of Maryland's Constitutional Law Roundtable, and at a conference jointly organized by the University of Oregon Law School and the Wayne Morse Center for Law and Politics. My heartfelt thanks to all.

NOTES

Introduction

1. Joanna Walters, "Trump's Travel Ban: Stories of Those Who Were Detained This Weekend," *Guardian*, Jan. 31, 2017; Eoghan MacGuire et al., "Trump Travel Restrictions Leave Refugees Stranded: Reports," *NBC News*, Jan. 28, 2017.

2. For accounts of pluralism and collaboration, see John D. Inazu, *Confident Pluralism: Surviving and Thriving Through Deep Difference* (2016); Jeffrey A. Segal and Harold J. Spaeth, *The Supreme Court and the Attitudinal Model Revisited* (2002).

3. Brief of Constitutional Law Scholars as Amici Curiae in Support of Plaintiffs-Appellees and Affirmance, International Refugee Assistance Project v. Trump, No. 8:17-cv-00361-TDC (4th Cir. Apr. 19, 2017), 4, 16. As the constitutional law scholars argued, this anti-animus principle is understood to be a major component of both the Fourteenth Amendment's Equal Protection Clause and the First Amendment's Religion Clauses. For further reading on their arguments, see Corey Brettschneider, "Why Trump's Immigration Rules Are Unconstitutional," *Politico*, Feb. 1, 2017; Joshua Matz et al., "A Different View of Why the Muslim Ban Violates the Establishment Clause," *Take Care*, Apr. 20, 2017, https://takecareblog.com/blog/a-different-view-of-why-the-muslim-ban-violates-the-establishment-clause.

4. Throughout the book, I use the words "egalitarianism" and "equality" interchangeably to denote a broadly shared idea that individuals in similar circumstances ought to be treated the same way. I recognize that there can be strong differences of opinion about what these ideas mean beyond this point of agreement, especially for those who specialize in political theory, constitutional law, or antidiscrimination law.

Chapter 1: Practical Equality

1. President John F. Kennedy, Speech, White House, June 11, 1963. During this televised speech, JFK introduced the bill that would become the Civil Rights Act of 1964.

2. Congressional Globe, House, 39th Congress, 1st Session (Feb. 28, 1866), 1088–1095; "Thirty-Ninth Congress, First Session," *New York Times*, Mar. 1, 1866, at 4 (publishing Bingham's remarks); Congressional Globe, 39th Congress, 2d Session (1867), 811; Kurt T. Lash, *The Fourteenth Amendment and the Privileges and Immunities of American Citizenship* (2014), ch. 4; Akhil Reed Amar, *The Bill of Rights: Creation and Reconstruction* (1998), 190.

3. Brown v. Board of Education of Topeka, 347 U.S. 483 (1954).

4. Yick Wo v. Hopkins, 118 U.S. 356 (1886). In 1882, Congress passed the Chinese Exclusion Act, which barred laborers from immigrating from China for ten years and prevented the Chinese already in the United States from becoming naturalized as citizens.

5. Ibid., 374.

6. Deborah Hellman, *When Is Discrimination Wrong?* (2008), 31–38. Hellman offers a comprehensive but "modest" theory of equality based entirely on a theory of "demeaning" action. She acknowledges that, under her approach, "it is unlikely that a norm of non-demeaning will require that people have access to some particular conception of rights or minimum level of goods." Ibid. at 33.

7. See, e.g., Church of Lukumi Bablu Aye, Inc. v. City of Hialeah, 508 U.S. 520, 547 (2013) ("upon even slight suspicion that proposals for state intervention stem from animosity to religion or distrust of its practices, all officials must pause to remember their own high duty to the Constitution and to the rights it secures"); United States v. Windsor, 133 S. Ct. 2675, 2693 (2013) ("The Constitution's guarantee of equality 'must at the very least mean that a bare congressional desire to harm a politically unpopular group cannot' justify disparate treatment of that group"). While hostility is always out of bounds as a motivation for treating people differently, it's not the only way to violate the principle of equal regard. The flip side of hatred is adoration—another excessive sentiment. When the state treats one group better than another out of special affection for the first group, that too denies the second group equal regard. This might be the best characterization of bans on interracial marriage, which states often justified out of a desire to privilege and preserve white blood lines and white culture. See Loving v. Virginia, 388 U.S. 1 (1967).

8. Obergefell v. Hodges, 135 S. Ct. 2584, 2599 (2015).

9. Ibid. at 2602.

10. Romer v. Evans, 517 U.S. 620, 634–35 (1996).

11. Thomas Aquinas, the *"Summa Theologica"* (1265–74) (Fathers of the English Dominican Province tr. 1915), Part II: Ethics, Question 92: Of the Effects of Law, 22-24.

12. Loving, 388 U.S. at 11 (quoting Hirabayashi v. United States, 320 U.S. 31, 100 [1943]). There is an important difference between government officials using their position to condemn inegalitarian actions by private parties and taking actions to disfavor them. The first should raise few constitutional problems, while the second is more likely to deny equal treatment or abridge free speech.

13. Reply Brief for Cross Petitioners, U.S. v. Virginia, 1996 WL 2023 (U.S.), 2; Brief for Respondents, U.S. v. Virginia ("The central point, however, is that it would no longer offer the benefits of single-sex education, nor would it be able to retain the adversative system. VMI would instead become nothing more than a pale shadow of the service academies, far less attractive to students . . . and indistinguishable in its methodology from the coeducational Corps of Cadets and ROTC program already available at VPI").

14. United States v. Virginia, 518 U.S. 515 (1996).

15. Amicus Brief of Coalition for the Protection of Marriage in Support of Hollingsworth and Bipartisan Legal Advisory Group, Hollingsworth v. Perry, No. 12–44 (Jan. 29, 2003), 5; Brief for Respondents, Grutter v. Bollinger, 539 U.S. 306 (2003), 13.

16. 518 U.S. at 566–67 (Scalia, J., dissenting); 517 U.S. 620, 644 (1996) (Scalia, J., dissenting).

17. Richard Kluger, *Simple Justice: The History of Brown v. Board of Education and Black America's Struggle for Equality* (1975), 584, 585–619; Del Dickson (ed.), *The Supreme Court in Conference (1940–1985)* (2001), 652–71; Philip Elman and Norman Silber, "The Solicitor General's Office, Justice Frankfurter, and Civil Rights Litigation, 1946–1960: An Oral History," *Harvard Law Review* 100 (1987): 817–52; Mark Tushnet and Katya Lezin, "What Really Happened in Brown v. Board of Education," *Columbia Law Review* 91 (1991): 1867–1930.

18. Kluger, 617–19.

19. Plessy v. Ferguson, 163 U.S. 537 (1896).

20. As Justice Brown put it, "A statute which implies merely a legal distinction between the white and colored races—a distinction which is founded in the color of the two races, and which must always exist so long as white men are distinguished from the other race by color—has no tendency to destroy the legal equality of the two races, or re-establish a state of involuntary servitude." Ibid., 543.

21. Dred Scott v. Sanford, 60 U.S. 393 (1857). The Missouri Compromise admit-

ted Missouri to the Union as a slave state and Maine as a free state, and excluded slavery from lands above the 38° 30" parallel, while allowing the people of states below that imaginary boundary to choose for themselves whether to be slave or free.

22. Two Speeches by Frederick Douglass; One on West India Emancipation . . . and the Other on the Dred Scott Decision, Delivered in New York, on the Occasion of the Anniversary of the American Abolition Society, May 1857, in John Stauffer and Henry Louis Gates, Jr. (eds.), *The Portable Frederick Douglass* (2016), 248–68; *Chicago Tribune*, Mar. 12, 1957; Paul Finkelman, *Dred Scott vs. Sanford: A Brief History with Documents* (1997); Don E. Fehrenbacher, *The Dred Scott Case: Its Significance in American Law and Politics* (1978).

23. Editorial, New Orleans *Times-Democrat*, June 9, 1890.

24. "The Separate Car Law," New Orleans *Times-Democrat*, Nov. 19, 1892.

25. 163 U.S. at 560 (Harlan, J., dissenting).

26. Dickson, 649–69; Mary L. Dudziak, *Cold War Civil Rights: Race and the Image of American Democracy* (2000).

27. § 20–54 Virginia Code, "An Act to Preserve Racial Integrity."

28. Naim v. Naim, 197 Va. 80, 87 S.E.2d 749 (1955).

29. The U.S. Supreme Court actually refused to hear the case twice: the first time, the Justices took the case as an obligatory appeal and then vacated it on the ground that "the inadequacy of the record as to the relationship of the parties to the Commonwealth of Virginia at the time of the marriage" prevented the Justices from deciding the case. Naim v. Naim, 350 U.S. 981 (1956). When the case returned to the High Court a second time, the Justices dismissed the case for being "devoid of a properly presented federal question." Naim v. Naim, 350 U.S. 985 (1956). See also Gregory Michael Dorr, "Principled Expediency: Eugenics, *Naim v. Naim*, and the Supreme Court," *American Journal of Legal History* 42 (1998): 119, 147–48.

30. Alex Bickel famously extolled "the passive values" as a way for judges to offer "guiding principle and expedient compromise." Alexander M. Bickel, *The Least Dangerous Branch: The Supreme Court at the Bar of Politics* (1962), 64. On how these rules are manipulated to govern citizen access to the courts, see Erwin Chemerinsky, *Closing the Courthouse Door: How Your Constitutional Rights Became Unenforceable* (2017); Lea Brilmayer, "The Jurisprudence of Article III: Perspectives on the 'Case or Controversy' Requirement," *Harvard Law Review* 93 (1979): 297–321.

31. Martin Luther King, Jr., Letter from a Birmingham Jail, Apr. 16, 1963.

32. Civil unions typically offered the same benefits under state law, but they were not portable to another state and were not recognized by federal law.

33. William N. Eskridge, Jr., and Darren R. Spedale, *Gay Marriage: For Better or Worse? What We've Learned from the Evidence* (2006); William N. Eskridge, "Equality Practice: Liberal Reflections on the Jurisprudence of Civil Unions," *Albany Law Review* 64 (2000–2001): 853–81. For a general defense of spare, incompletely theorized conceptions of rights, see Cass R. Sunstein, *One Case at a Time: Judicial Minimalism on the Supreme Court* (1999).

34. President Clinton penned an op-ed years later expressing his regret for signing DOMA. Bill Clinton, "It's Time to Overturn DOMA," *Washington Post*, Mar. 7, 2013; Statement on DOMA, President Bill Clinton, Sept. 20, 1996. Clinton claimed he faced overwhelming support for DOMA, and that he signed only to head off a constitutional amendment. But there wasn't a serious movement until later, and no president can stop citizens or legislators from proposing constitutional changes.

35. Alexis de Tocqueville, *Democracy in America,* tr. Henry Reeve (1840), vol. 2, ch. 10; Daniel A. Farber, "Reinventing Brandeis: Legal Pragmatism for the Twenty-First Century," *University of Illinois Law Review* 1995 (1995): 163–90.

36. William James, *Pragmatism: A New Name for Some Old Ways of Thinking* (1921); John Dewey, "What Pragmatism Means By 'Practical,'" Larry A. Hickman and Thomas M. Alexander (eds.), *The Essential Dewey*, vol. 2 (1998), 377–85.

37. On constitutional borrowing as a form of legal reasoning, see Nelson Tebbe and Robert L. Tsai, "Constitutional Borrowing," *Michigan Law Review* 108 (2010): 459–522.

38. Legal pragmatists like Judge Richard Posner have shown the way but their approaches have been criticized sharply when offered as a general theory of jurisprudence or mindset for judging. I think these concerns about consequentialism are weighty enough that any resort to pragmatism must be firmly tethered to customary methods of settling disputes, whether by judges, government officials, civic organizations, or regular citizens. Richard A. Posner, "Pragmatic Adjudication," *Cardozo Law Review* 18 (1996): 1–20.

39. Congressional Globe, 39th Congress, 1st Session, 1089.

40. Letter of Thomas Jefferson to Francis W. Gilmer, June 7, 1816.

41. Eric Foner estimates that 1,000–5,000 slaves escaped between 1830 and 1860. Foner, *Gateway to Freedom: The Hidden History of the Underground Railroad* (2015); Graham Russell Gao Hodges, *David Ruggles: A Radical Black Abolitionist and the Underground Railroad in New York City* (2010), 88–101.

42. Hall v. De Cuir, 95 U.S. 485, 489–90 (1877).

43. Brief for Plaintiff in Error, Plessy v. Ferguson, 1896 WL 13990 (1896), *22–23.

44. Shapiro v. Thompson, 394 U.S. 618 (1969); Universal Declaration of Human Rights, Dec. 10, 1948; Crandall v. Nevada, 73 U.S. 35 (1867).

45. Frederick Douglass, "Prejudice Against Color," *The North Star*, June 13, 1850, in Stauffer and Gates, 422.

46. Kenneth W. Mack, "Law, Society, Identity, and the Making of the Jim Crow South: Travel and Segregation on Tennessee Railroads, 1875–1905," *Law & Social Inquiry* (1999): 377–410.

47. Ernst Freund, *The Police Power: Public Policy and Constitutional Rights* (1904), 416. Thomas Cooley, a leading nineteenth-century scholar, similarly observed that the police power could be "pushed to an extreme that shall deny just liberty." Thomas M. Cooley, *General Principles of Constitutional Law*, 2d ed. (1998), 238–39, 310–27. Oliver Wendell Holmes similarly stressed that police regulations "must be so clearly necessary to the safety, comfort, or well-being of society, or so imperatively required by public necessity" before they should be sustained. James Kent, *Commentaries on American Law,* ed. Oliver Wendell Holmes (1873), 340.

Chapter 2: Fair Play

1. The Fifth Amendment of the U.S. Constitution guarantees due process of law when the federal government deprives someone of life, liberty, or property, while the Fourteenth Amendment's Due Process Clause expands that obligation to state governments. The Third Amendment says that soldiers may not be quartered in any house without the owner's consent or during a time of war "but in a manner to be prescribed by law." The Fourth Amendment not only subjects searches and seizures to a standard of reasonableness but also outlines a detailed process for obtaining warrants. Besides guaranteeing due process of law, the Fifth Amendment requires grand jury indictment for capital or other "infamous" crimes, prohibits double jeopardy and compelled self-incrimination, and subjects the taking of private property for public use to "just compensation." Under the Sixth Amendment, an accused enjoys the right to a speedy and impartial jury trial, notice of the charges and witnesses, and the assistance of counsel. The Seventh Amendment secures the right of a jury trial in civil suits where the value of the controversy exceeds $20 and requires that such suits be resolved "according to the rules of the common law." U.S. Constitution (1789), amends. 3, 4, 5, 6, 7, 14.

2. Brown v. State, 173 Miss. 542, 158 So. 339 (1935); Neil R. McMillen, *Dark Journey: Black Mississippians in the Age of Jim Crow* (1990), 197–99; Richard C. Cortner, *A "Scottsboro" Case in Mississippi: The Supreme Court and* Brown v. Mississippi (1986). The act of stringing up Ellington "is said to have injured his spine permanently." "Change of Venue Granted in New Trial of Mississippi Torture Case," *Chicago Defender*, Nov. 7, 1936.

3. Cortner, *A "Scottsboro" Case*, 23–24.

4. Ibid., 471. "Two Negroes Held in Meridian Murder," *Greenwood Common-wealth*, Apr. 2, 1934 (reporting that "Authorities said the pair, Ed Brown, 30, and Henry Shields, 27, admitted robbery as the motive for the attack"); "2 Negroes Held on 3 Charges," *Clarion-Ledger*, Jan. 8, 1935; "Kemper Slaving is Before Jury," *Clarion-Ledger*, Apr. 4, 1934.

5. The Mississippi Supreme Court twice upheld the convictions. In the defendants' direct appeal, the court rejected a number of claims, including that the confessions were wrongly admitted into the record, and that mistakes were made in the jury instructions. Brown, 173 Miss. 542. Justice Anderson dissented from that decision, saying that without the coerced confessions there was insufficient evidence to support a murder conviction. He also insisted that defendants were denied due process of law because counsel "had neither time nor opportunity to do their part." The justices then sat en banc, considered the arguments again, and confirmed its previous decision. Brown, 173 Miss. 542, 161 So. 465 (1935). That decision led to the U.S. Supreme Court's ruling in Brown v. Mississippi.

6. "Seek Funds to Aid Defense in Torture Case," *Chicago Defender*, Dec. 7, 1935.

7. Brown, 161 So. at 472 (Griffith, Anderson, JJ., dissenting); "Jail Two Negroes in Kemper Murders," *Clarion-Ledger*, Apr. 1, 1934 (reporting that Brown and Shields, "negroes," were held in connection with Stuart, "prominent planter of the Giles Community").

8. The *Clarion-Ledger*, the leading Mississippi newspaper, called Justice Griffith "severe in his comment upon the alleged participation of officers in the hangings and whippings." "Supreme Court Denies Final Plea of Kemper County Negro Slayers," *Clarion-Ledger*, Apr. 39, 1935.

9. Brown v. Mississippi, 297 U.S. 278, 285–86 (1936).

10. Strauder v. West Virginia, 100 U.S. 303 (1880).

11. "Negro Convictions Vacated By Court," *New York Times*, Feb. 18, 1936; "Press Favors Judgment in Cropper Case," *Chicago Defender*, Feb. 28, 1936.

12. Amy Louise Wood, *Lynching and Spectacle: Witnessing Racial Violence in America, 1890–1940* (2009); W. Fitzhugh Brundage, *Lynching in the New South: Georgia and Virginia, 1880–1930* (1993).

13. Magna Carta §§ 40, 45, 52, 55, 56, 57 (1215).

14. Ibid., § 39.

15. Ibid., § 61.

16. C. H. McIlwain, "Due Process of Law in Magna Carta," *Columbia Law Review* 14 (1914): 27–51. The English experience showed that paper guarantees were one thing, and the power to enforce those rights was quite another. For when King John later refused to abide by his promises in Magna Carta, barons led by Robert Fitzwalter waged war against the king with the aid of the French.

17. Kurt T. Lash, *The Fourteenth Amendment and the Privileges and Immunities of American Citizenship* (2014); Gerard N. Magliocca, *America Founding Son: John Bingham and the Invention of the Fourteenth Amendment* (2013); Garrett Epps, *Democracy Reborn: The Fourteenth Amendment and the Fight for Equal Rights in Post–Civil War America* (2006), 232–33 (quoting Sen. Jacob M. Howard); Michael Kent Curtis, *No State Shall Abridge: The Fourteenth Amendment and the Bill of Rights* (1986); Adamson v. California, 332 U.S. 46, 107, 116–17 (1947).

18. Papachristou v. City of Jacksonville, 405 U.S. 156 (1972); Tammy W. Sun, "Equality By Other Means: The Substantive Foundations of the Vagueness Doctrine," *Harvard Civil Rights–Civil Liberties Law Review* 46 (2011): 149–94; Anthony Amsterdam, "The Void-for-Vagueness Doctrine in the Supreme Court," *University of Pennsylvania Law Review* 109 (1960): 67–116.

19. Kolender v. Lawson, 461 U.S. 352 (1983).

20. City of Chicago v. Morales, 527 U.S. 41 (1999).

21. John Rawls, *A Theory of Justice* (1971), 53–54; John Rawls, "Justice as Fairness: Political Not Metaphysical," *Philosophy and Public Affairs* 14(3) (1985): 223–51, 225. It is telling that the most influential modern constitutional theory takes as its starting point the many procedural features of the U.S. Constitution. John Hart Ely contends that the entire Constitution should be understood as guaranteeing procedural values, which he believes should reduce worries of overreach by judges if they interpret ambiguous provisions in ways that enhance procedural values. Ely is wrong, of course, that the Constitution contains only procedural values, for many of the rights have a substantive quality. And even text that appears procedural in nature can be read to create rights with substantive content. Still, the expansive reliance of Ely's theory on fairness and its popularity among lawyers and academics offer more evidence as to the allure of process-based arguments. John Hart Ely, *Democracy and Distrust: A Theory of Judicial Review* (1985).

22. Robert Nozick, *Anarchy, State, and Utopia* (1974), 10–11.

23. Ibid., 102–6.

24. Yick Wo v. Hopkins, 118 U.S. 356, 374 (1886); Loving v. Virginia, 388 U.S. 1, 11 (1967), Brown v. Board of Education, 347 U.S. 483, 494 (1954); Obergefell v. Hodges, 135 S. Ct. 2584, 2590, 2601–5 (2015).

25. Memphis Light, Gas & Water Division v. Craft, 436 U.S. 1 (1978); Mathews v. Eldridge, 424 U.S. 319 (1976); Withrow v. Larkin, 421 U.S. 35 (1975); Goss v. Lopez, 419 U.S. 565 (1975); E. Thomas Sullivan and Toni M. Massaro, *The Arc of Due Process in American Constitutional Law* (2013).

26. See, e.g., Cooper v. Oklahoma, 517 U.S. 348 (1996) (striking down state law that required a defendant to prove incompetence to stand trial by "clear and

convincing evidence" because a "near-uniform application of a standard that is more protective of the defendant's rights than Oklahoma's . . . offends a principle of justice that is deeply 'rooted in the traditions and conscience of our people'"). For a reminder that serious exigencies can and should affect what kind of process is due, see Hamdi v. Rumsfeld, 542 U.S. 507 (2004) ("we agree that indefinite detention for the purpose of interrogation is not authorized" and "a citizen-detainee seeking to challenge his classification as an enemy combatant must receive notice of the factual basis for his classification, and a fair opportunity to rebut the Government's factual assertions before a neutral decisionmaker").

27. Justice Ruth Bader Ginsburg, who supports abortion rights, has nevertheless criticized *Roe* for its breadth, which "seemed to have stopped the momentum on the side of change." Meredith Heagney, "Justice Ruth Bader Ginsburg Offers Critique of Roe v. Wade During Law School Visit," May 15, 2013, https://www.law.uchicago.edu/news/justice-ruth-bader-ginsburg-offers-critique-roe-v-wade-during-law-school-visit.

28. "Religious Composition by Country, 2010–2050," *Pew Research Forum*, Apr. 2, 2015.

29. Executive Order 13769, Protecting the Nation from Foreign Terrorist Entry into the United States, Jan. 27, 2017; Thomas Erdbrink and Jeffrey Gettleman, "In Iran, Shock and Bewilderment Over Trump Visa Crackdown," *New York Times*, Jan. 27, 2017.

30. "Federal Judges Express Skepticism About Arguments on Trump's Travel Ban," *Chicago Tribune*, Feb. 7, 2017.

31. For this reason, the panel declined to defer to the White House Counsel's interpretation that the order should be read to exclude lawful permanent residents. Washington v. Trump, No. 17–35105 (9th Cir. Feb. 7, 2017), 22. Eventually, a district judge in Virginia did rule that the travel ban constituted "religious discrimination" against Muslims. That decision was not tested by appeal before the administration issued a revised executive order. Aziz v. Trump, No. 1:17-cv-116 (LMB/TCB) (E.D. Va. Feb. 13, 2017).

32. The courts have held that there is a constitutional right to travel, but those decisions involved traveling among states within the country and really only establish a prohibition against treating newcomers differently from a state's own citizens. See Saenz v. Roe, 526 U.S. 489 (1999); Shapiro v. Thompson, 394 U.S. 618 (1969).

33. Executive Order Protecting the Nation from Foreign Terrorist Entry into the United States, Mar. 6, 2017; Glenn Thrush, "Trump's New Travel Ban Blocks Migrants from Six Nations, Sparing Iraq," *New York Times*, Mar. 6, 2017; Phillip Connor and Jens Manuel Korgstad, "Countries Affected by Trump Travel Rules Accounted for More Than 900,000 U.S. Entries Since

2006," Pew Research Center, Feb. 3, 2017, http://www.pewresearch.org/fact-tank/2017/02/03/countries-affected-by-trump-travel-rules-accounted-for-more-than-900000-u-s-entries-since-2006/; Mona Chalabi, "How Many US Immigrants Come from Trump's Seven Banned Countries?," *Guardian*, Jan. 28, 2017.

34. Daniel Burke, "Trump Says US Will Prioritize Christian Refugees," *CNN*, Jan. 30, 2017.

35. Sarsour v. Trump, No. 1:17cv00120 (AJT/IDD) (E.D. Va. Mar. 24, 2017). Rachel Weiner, "Virginia Judge Sides with Trump Administration on New Travel Ban," *Washington Post*, Mar. 24, 2017.

36. Trump v. Hawaii, No. 17-965, 2018 WL 3116337 (June 26, 2018), *9. Justice Sotomayor, joined by Justice Ginsburg, certainly had the better of the argument as to pretextual efforts to harm minorities. She felt that the administration's "repackaging does little to cleanse" the executive order "of the appearance of discrimination that the President's words have created." She castigated her colleagues for "turning a blind eye to the pain and suffering the Proclamation inflicts upon countless families and individuals, many of whom are United States citizens." Ibid., 35 (Sotomayor, J., dissenting).

37. "Justice Powell's New Wisdom," *New York Times*, June 11, 1994.

38. Jeffrey L. Kirchmeier, *Imprisoned by the Past: Warren McCleskey and the American Death Penalty* (2015), 11–15.

39. McCleskey v. Kemp, 481 U.S. 279 (1987).

40. Brief of Amici Curiae State of California and County of Los Angeles, McCleskey v. Kemp, 1986 WL 727362 (Sept. 22, 1986); Brief of Amicus Curiae Washington Legal Foundation and Allied Educational Foundation in Support of Respondent, McCleskey v. Kemp, 1986 WL 727360 (Sept. 19, 1986).

41. Scott E. Sundby, "The Loss of Constitutional Faith: *McCleskey v. Kemp* and the Dark Side of Procedure," *Ohio State Journal of Criminal Law* 10 (2012), 5–35, 31, n.118. Justice Powell was even more openly skeptical about reliance on the Baldus study in his communications with other Justices. He argued that a win for McCleskey would "invite a system of 'statistical jurisprudence'—unprecedented in civilized history." Ibid., 32.

42. McCleskey, 481 U.S. at 296.

43. Only in 32 percent of cases involving white defendants and white victims did Georgia prosecutors seek death; when the races of the perpetrators and victims were both black, prosecutors sought death 15 percent of the time.

44. McCleskey, 481 U.S. at 314–19.

45. Ibid., 312.

46. William J. Stuntz, *The Collapse of American Criminal Justice* (2011), 121.

47. McCleskey, 481 U.S. at 320, 339 (Brennan, Marshall, Blackmun, Stevens, JJ.,

dissenting); Adam Liptak, "New Look at Death Sentences and Race," *New York Times*, Apr. 29, 2008 (quoting Anthony Amsterdam's speech at Columbia University).

48. Sundby, 31.

49. Brandon Garrett, *End of Its Rope: How Killing the Death Penalty Can Revive Criminal Justice* (2017); Carol S. Steiker and Jordan M. Steiker, *Courting Death: The Supreme Court and Capital Punishment* (2016); Angela J. Davis, *Arbitrary Justice: The Power of the American Prosecutor* (2007); Robert L. Smith, "The Geography of the Death Penalty," *Boston University Law Review* 92 (2012): 227–89; "Too Broken to Fix: Part I, An In-depth Look at America's Outlier Death Penalty Counties," Fair Punishment Project (Aug. 2016), 3–4.

50. Brief for Petitioner, McCleskey v. Kemp, 1986 WL 727359 (Sept. 3, 1986), *58–59.

51. Furman v. Georgia, 408 U.S. 238, 306–9 (1972) (Stewart, J., concurring); ibid., 256–57 (Douglas, J., concurring); ibid., 258, 299 (Brennan, J., concurring); ibid., 315, 366 (Marshall, J., concurring); ibid., 310, 313 (White, J., concurring).

52. Furman, 408 U.S. 238; Gregg v. Georgia, 428 U.S. 153 (1976).

Chapter 3: The Rule of Reason

1. The ordinance also prohibited homes for drug addicts or alcoholics, as well as "penal or correctional institutions." Cleburne Living Center, Inc. v. City of Cleburne, 726 F.2d 191 (5th Cir. 1984).

2. Buck v. Bell, 274 U.S. 200 (1927).

3. The Fifth Circuit followed the Ninth Circuit in J.W. v. City of Tacoma, 720 F.2d 1126 (9th Cir. 1983), by applying "intermediate scrutiny" to laws that singled out people with mental deficiencies. This approach, considered by constitutional lawyers to be tougher than rationality review but more forgiving than "strict scrutiny," requires the government to give a significant justification for its actions, and the means are closely tailored to the ends.

4. Motion and Brief Amici Curiae of Association for Retarded Citizens et al., No. 84–468, City of Cleburne v. Cleburne Living Center, 1985 WL 669791, Feb. 2, 1985.

5. Amicus Curiae Brief of the State of Connecticut, Joined by the States of Arkansas, California, Colorado, Illinois, Louisiana, North Dakota, Rhode Island, Tennessee and West Virginia in Support of Respondents, City of Cleburne v. Cleburne Living Center, No. 84–468, 1985 WL 669786, Feb. 1, 1985.

6. Brief for the United States as Amicus Curiae Supporting Reversal, City of

Cleburne v. Cleburne Living Center, No. 84–468, 1985 WL 669781, Jan. 2, 1985.

7. Technically, this was still treated as an Equal Protection case, but the rule of reason requires every law or policy to be rational. That requirement doesn't change based on the technical doctrinal challenges mounted against an official action.

8. For the backstory on the Justices' deliberations, see William B. Araiza, "Was *Cleburne* an Accident?," *University of Pennsylvania Journal of Constitutional Law* (2017): 621–69. The decision was written by Justice White and joined by Justices Powell, Rehnquist, Stevens, and O'Connor. Stevens wrote separately, as did Marshall (who was joined by Brennan and Blackmun).

9. As Justice Ginsburg put it in United States v. Virginia: "The justification [for using sex as a classification] must be genuine, not hypothesized or invented post hoc in response to litigation. And it must not rely on overbroad generalizations about the different talents, capabilities, or preferences of males and females." 518 U.S. 515, 533 (1996).

10. George Lakoff and Mark Johnson, *Metaphors We Live By* (1980).

11. Buck v. Davis, 139 S. Ct. 759, 768–69, 777–79 (2017).

12. Ibid. It didn't matter that the defendant's own lawyer called this witness. He should have known about the expert's unorthodox views, and putting him on the stand constituted ineffective assistance of counsel.

13. This formula, discussed at greater length later in the chapter, can be found in the famous Footnote 4 of United States v. Carolene Products, 304 U.S. 144, 152 (1938).

14. Michael Lipka, "Muslims and Islam: Key Findings in the U.S. and Around the World," Pew Research Center, Aug. 9, 2017, http://www.pewresearch .org/fact-tank/2017/08/09/muslims-and-islam-key-findings-in-the-u-s-and-around-the-world/; James Forman, Jr., *Locking Up Our Own: Crime and Punishment in Black America* (2012), 218–19; Michelle Alexander, *The New Jim Crow: Mass Incarceration in the Age of Colorblindness* (2010).

15. Kenji Yoshino, *Covering: The Hidden Assault on Our Civil Rights* (2006); Bruce Ackerman, "Beyond *Carolene Products*," *Harvard Law Review* 98 (1985): 713–46.

16. John Rawls defines public reason as "political discussions of fundamental questions" in a "public political forum." It encompasses "the discourse of judges in their decisions . . . the discourse of government officials . . . and, finally, the discourse of candidates for public offices and their campaign managers." Rawls, "The Idea of Public Reason Revisited," *University of Chicago Law Review* 64 (1997): 765–807, 767–69; *Federalist* No. 49 (Hamilton or Madison) (1788).

17. Bruce A. Ackerman, *Social Justice in the Liberal State* (1980), 359. Howard Schweber posits a spectrum of activities that includes "perception-belief-reasons-justifications." Applied to "coercive state action," he says, "the expression of a justification is an articulation of a theory of legitimacy applied in a concrete case"—one that is public and objective in nature, and subject to testing by others. Schweber, *Democracy and Authenticity: Toward a Theory of Public Justification* (2012), 75–76.

18. John Locke, *An Essay Concerning Human Understanding* (1689), Book IV, ch. XVII, par. 9, in Alexander Campbell Fraser (ed.) (1894; repr. 1959), vol. 2, 405.

19. Ibid., Book IV, ch. XVIII, in Fraser, vol. 2, 416.

20. The standards may shift depending on the context, and so the range of acceptable conduct might be broader or more narrow, but the preference for moderation in government policy persists. U.S. Constitution, amends. 2–8.

21. United States Department of Agriculture v. Moreno, 413 U.S. 528 (1973).

22. Ledezma-Cosino v. Lynch, 819 F.3d 1070 (9th Cir. 2016); Christian Heritage Academy v. Oklahoma Secondary School Activities Association, 483 F.3d 1025 (10th Cir. 2007); Romer v. Evans, 517 U.S. 620 (1996); Copelin-Brown v. New Mexico State Personnel Office, 399 F.3d 1248 (10th Cir. 2005).

23. This led James Wilson to advocate a division of the legislative power between two houses. Wilson, "Of Government," *The Legislative Department, Lectures on Law* (1791), ch. 12. *Federalist* No. 10 (Madison) (1787); *Federalist* No. 49 (Hamilton or Madison) (1788).

24. Terry v. Ohio, 392 U.S. 1 (1968) (stop-and-frisk is constitutional if based on "reasonable suspicion"). Warrants remain subject to probable cause, as do arrests without a warrant.

25. Tennessee v. Garner, 471 U.S. 1 (1985).

26. Linda Greenhouse, "Court Weighs Deadly Force by Police," *New York Times*, Oct. 31, 1984.

27. Whren v. United States, 517 U.S. 806 (1996).

28. Floyd v. City of New York, 959 F. Supp.2d 540, 586–87, 590, 603–6, 52–22 (S.D.N.Y. 2013).

29. Ibid.

30. Ibid.

31. Ybarra v. Illinois, 444 U.S. 85 (1979).

32. Sibron v. New York, 392 U.S. 40 (1968), was a companion case to *Terry*.

33. Natsu Taylor Saito, "Justice Held Hostage: U.S. Disregard for International Law in the World War II Internment of Japanese Peruvians—A Case Study," *Boston College Law Review* 40 (1988): 275–348.

34. Gary Y. Okihiro, *American History Unbound: Asians and Pacific Islanders*

(2015), 347; Eileen Sunada Sarasohn, *The Issei: Portrait of a Pioneer, an Oral History* (1983), 183; Eric Yamamoto et al., *Race, Rights, and Reparation: Law and the Japanese American Internment* (2001).

35. Korematsu v. United States, 323 U.S. 214 (1944). Technically, the case claimed to apply strict scrutiny to the wartime measures, but its permissive analysis and its emphasis on the reasonableness of internment suggested far more lax review. Similarly, in *Hirabayashi v. United States*, the Justices said that "ethnic affiliations" afforded "a rational basis" for the race-based curfew, 320 U.S. 81, 101–2 (1943). See Neil Gotanda, "The Story of *Korematsu*," in *Constitutional Law Stories*, ed. Michael C. Dorf (2004), 250–95, 262.

36. James MacGregor Burns, *Roosevelt: The Soldier of Freedom* (1970), 215. In a poll taken December 1942, a year after Pearl Harbor, only 35 percent of Americans believed internees should be allowed to return to the Pacific coast. Of the 48 percent opposed to their return, half believed internees should be sent back to Japan, 13 percent said "[P]ut them out of this country," and 10 percent agreed with the sentiment: "[L]eave them where they are—under control." Art Swift, "Gallup Vault: WWII-Era Support for Japanese Internment," http://news.gallup.com/vault/195257/gallup-vault-wwii-era-support -japanese-internment.aspx.

37. Justice Wiley Rutledge's comments from a related curfew case are instructive on the importance of resisting complete deference to the authorities. "The officer, of course, must have wide discretion and room for its operation. But it does not follow there may not be bounds beyond which he cannot go and, if he oversteps them, that the courts may not have power to protect the civilian citizen." Hirabayashi, 320 U.S. at 1392 (Rutledge, J., concurring).

38. Memorandum to the President from Attorney General Francis Biddle, Feb. 17, 1942. In this memo to FDR, Biddle described the political pressure to evacuate all Japanese people, but argued that it was "extremely dangerous" to "suggest an attack on the West Coast and planned sabotage is imminent when the military authorities and the F.B.I. have indicated that this is not the fact." He also warned that "race riots" might occur if the government tried to carry out such a massive relocation effort. Biddle closed by urging the president to "clarify the situation in the public mind." Little did he know that FDR had already given the War Department the go-ahead to intern everyone of Japanese ancestry.

39. DeWitt's original draft report never claimed that time was of the essence, it merely asserted that "an exact separation of the 'sheep from the goats' was unfeasible." All copies of that draft were destroyed by the War Department after McCloy wanted it rewritten. Gotanda, 281–82.

40. Richard Reeves, *Infamy: The Shocking Story of the Japanese American Intern-*

ment in World War II (2015), 49; Lt. Gen. J. L. De Witt, Final Report, Japanese Evacuation from the West Coast, June 5, 1943, in Korematsu, 323 U.S. at 235–36, n.1 (Murphy, J., dissenting).

41. Peter Maguire, *Law and War: An American Story* (2000); Peter Irons, *Justice at War: The Story of the Japanese-American Internment Cases* (1983). The *Los Angeles Times*, which had called for internment, expressed this view: "As a race, the Japanese have made for themselves a record for conscienceless treachery unsurpassed in history." Editorial, *Los Angeles Times*, Apr. 22, 1943.

42. Eugene V. Rostow was a professor and later the dean of Yale Law School. He served in a variety of capacities in the Roosevelt administration, and later served as undersecretary for political affairs under President Lyndon Johnson. Rostow, "The Japanese American Cases—A Disaster," *Yale Law Journal* 54 (1944–45): 505–33, 506; Hirabayashi, 99; David Cole, "Enemy Aliens," *Stanford Law Review* 54 (2002): 953–1004.

43. Korematsu, 323 U.S. at 236 (Murphy, J., dissenting).

44. On February 19, 1942, President Roosevelt signed Executive Order 9066, which authorized the War Department to designate military zones "from which any or all persons may be excluded."

45. Korematsu, 323 U.S. at 201 (Roberts, J., dissenting).

46. Irons, *Justice at War*, 344–46.

47. Matt Ford, "The Return of *Korematsu*," *Atlantic*, Nov. 19, 2015. Justice Scalia employed a Latin phrase to capture his position: "Inter arma enim silent leges . . . In times of war, the laws fall silent." Mark Tushnet (ed.), *The Constitution in Wartime: Beyond Alarmism and Complacency* (2005).

48. In fact, a number of states and local governments—from California to Minnesota to Washington, D.C.—have enacted laws and policies that protect sexual orientation broadly in a way that covers discrimination against the transgendered.

49. Dave Philipps, "North Carolina Bans Local Anti-Discrimination Policies," *New York Times*, Mar. 23, 2016. After boycotts of the state and the defeat of the sitting governor, who was an active supporter of the law, legislators repealed HB2 in March 2017. This happened as part of a political compromise that also prevented cities and counties in North Carolina from extending legal protections on the basis of sexual orientation in the future.

50. Romer v. Evans, 519 U.S. 620 (1996). In appropriate contexts, challengers have argued that Title IX of the Civil Rights Act of 1964, which bans discrimination on the basis of sex by any education activity receiving federal funds, should be interpreted to include sexual orientation. Some courts have agreed. See, e.g., Board of Education of the Highland Local School District v. United States Department of Education, 208 F. Supp.3d 850 (S.D. Ohio

2016) (rights of transgender student violated where school's concerns about privacy were "merely speculative" and lacked "factual underpinning"); Evancho v. Pine-Richland School District, 237 F. Supp.3d 267, 292 (W.D. Pa. 2017) ("there is no record evidence of an actual or threatened outbreak of other students falsely or deceptively declaring themselves to be 'transgender' for the purpose of engaging in untoward and maliciously improper activities in the High School restrooms").

51. Just as the stark racial pattern of permit denials gave rise to an inference of animus against Chinese laundry owners, so too the mismatch between the Colorado amendment's actual effect and the state's asserted goals implies a political desire to harm sexual minorities.

52. The Supreme Court has found a right to make certain life choices such as procreation, Griswold v. Connecticut, 381 U.S. 479 (1965); Roe v. Wade, 410 U.S. 113 (1973), and to engage in consensual sexual intercourse, Lawrence v. Texas, 539 U.S. 558 (2003), but it has remained silent about many other bodily needs.

53. G.G. ex rel. Grimm v. Gloucester County School Board, 822 F.3d 709, 723 (4th Cir. 2016) (expressing doubt that allowing transgender student to use common bathrooms would necessarily violate rights of other students).

54. Aaron Belkin, PhD, "Caring for Our Transgender Troops—The Negligible Cost of Transition-Related Care," *New England Journal of Medicine*, Sept. 17, 2015.

55. Julie Hirschfeld Davis and Helene Cooper, "Trump Says Transgender People Will Not Be Allowed in the Military," *New York Times*, July 26, 2017; Presidential Memorandum for the Secretary of Defense and the Secretary of Homeland Security Re: Military Service by Transgender Individuals, Aug. 25, 2017. A federal trial judge blocked President Trump's ban on transgender service members in October 2017. Doe 1 et al. v. Trump, 2017 WL 4873042 (D.D.C. Oct. 30, 2017). The president then reaffirmed the ban after the Secretary of Defense made findings that allowing some transgender individuals to serve in the military could "undermine readiness, disrupt unit cohesion, and impose and unreasonable burden on the military that is not conducive to military effectiveness and lethality." Helene Cooper and Thomas Gibbons-Neff, "Trump Announces New Limits on Transgender Troops in the Military," *New York Times*, Mar. 24, 2018.

56. U.S. Constitution, art. I, § 8, cl. 12–14.

57. Nan Hunter has described the concept of an interregnum, when LGBT controversies fall into a "political discomfort zone." Nan D. Hunter, "Twenty-First Century Equal Protection: Making Law in an Interregnum," *Georgetown Journal of Gender and the Law* 7 (2006): 141–69.

Chapter 4: No Cruelty

1. Weems v. United States, 217 U.S. 349, 373 (1910).
2. Denis Kearney and H. L. Knight, "Appeal from California: The Chinese Invasion: Workingmen's Address," *Indianapolis Times*, Feb. 28, 1878.
3. Ho Ah Kow v. Nunan, 5 Sawy. 552 (D. Cal. 1879). Justice Field presided over the local federal court as part of his duties riding the circuit.
4. Rev. O. Gibson, *The Chinese in America* (1877), 28.
5. Immanuel Kant, *Groundwork of the Metaphysics of Morals* (1785), 4:429. Robert Audi, *Means, Ends, and Persons: The Meaning and Psychological Dimensions of Kant's Humanity Formula* (2016).
6. The English Bill of Rights (1689) provides that "excessive bail ought not to be required, nor excessive fines imposed, nor cruel and unusual punishments inflicted." Maryland's 1776 constitution barred "cruel and unusual punishments and penalties." Twenty states, like Maryland and Virginia, employ the "cruel and unusual" formulation, while twenty-one states, including Massachusetts and New Hampshire, prohibit "cruel or unusual" punishments. Six other states—Delaware, Kentucky, Pennsylvania, Rhode Island, South Dakota, and Washington—simply ban "cruel" punishments. The differences in word choices didn't seem to mark a difference of opinion about the principle itself, which revolved around proportionality and nonbarbarity. Weems, 217 U.S. at 373. The United States signed and ratified the Convention Against Torture and Other Cruel, Inhuman or Degrading Treatment or Punishment, June 26, 1987.
7. Dawson v. State, 274 Ga. 327 (2001). By the time of this ruling, only three states were still executing inmates in the electric chair. Some 4,372 inmates were executed in this fashion in the United States from 1900 to 2001. Sue Anne Pressley, "Georgia Supreme Court Outlaws Electric Chair," *Washington Post*, Oct. 6, 2001.
8. Trop v. Dulles, 356 U.S. 86 (1958); Weems, 217 U.S. at 379.
9. California and Florida require that repeat sex offenders undergo chemical castration before they are released into society. These states are joined by Georgia, Louisiana, Oregon, Montana, Texas, and Wisconsin in requiring chemical castration as a condition of release. Texas allows repeat offenders to elect surgical castration.
10. The Supreme Court has occasionally drawn on international law and the practices of other countries in deciding some Eighth Amendment questions. It has generally done so to confirm a conclusion already reached about a consensus within the United States rather than using foreign law to supplant American law. See, e.g., Roper v. Simmons, 543 U.S. 551 (2005); Atkins v. Virginia, 536 U.S. 304 (2002).

11. Trop, 356 U.S. at 99. See Thompson v. Oklahoma, 487 U.S. 815 (1988); Hudson v. McMillian, 503 U.S. 1 (1992).

12. Bowers v. Hardwick, 478 U.S. 186 (1986) (Powell, J., concurring). Since the charge against the gay man was dropped, however, Justice Powell concluded that he wasn't currently exposed to the threat of punishment.

13. John Stinneford, "Rethinking Proportionality Under the Cruel and Unusual Punishment Clause," *Virginia Law Review* 97 (2011): 899–978.

14. Trop, 356 U.S. at 599.

15. Rebecca C. Hetey and Jennifer L. Eberhardt, "Racial Disparities in Incarceration Increase Acceptance of Punitive Policies," *Psychological Science* 25(10) (2014): 1949–54

16. Harris v. McRae, 448 U.S. 297, 323 (1980) ("Poverty, standing alone, is not a suspect classification").

17. Weems, 217 U.S. at 373.

18. Congressional Globe, 39th Congress, 1st Session, 2542, quoted in Furman v. Georgia, 408 U.S. 238, 241 (1972) (Douglas, J., concurring); Michael Kent Curtis, "John Bingham and the Story of American Liberty: The Lost Cause Meets the 'Lost Clause'" (paper on file with author), https://papers.ssrn.com/sol3/papers.cfm?abstract_id=343460. See also Michael Kent Curtis, *No State Shall Abridge: The Fourteenth Amendment and the Bill of Rights* (1990); Garrett Epps, *Democracy Reborn: The Fourteenth Amendment and the Fight for Equal Rights in Post–Civil War America* (2006).

19. Oregon Constitution (1857), art. I, § 35; Indiana Constitution (1851), art. 13.

20. Curtis, *No State Shall Abridge*, 59–61; Martha S. Jones, *Birthright Citizens: A History of Race and Rights in Antebellum America* (2018), 24–27.

21. Furman, 408 U.S. at 255–56.

22. Trop, 356 U.S. at 100; Pope Paul VI, Declaration on Religious Freedom *Dignitatis Humanae* on the Right of the Person and of Communities to Social and Civil Freedom in Matters Religious, Dec. 7, 1965; Universal Declaration of Human Rights, Dec. 10, 1948, art. I.

23. There is so much overlap between dignity and equality that some have taken to calling for a single concept of "equal dignity." Laurence H. Tribe, "Equal Dignity: Speaking Its Name," *Harvard Law Review Forum* 129 (2015): 16–32. Some are wary that "[d]ignity does its work by shifting stigma from one group to another," such as unmarried mothers or people in relationships that don't conform to respectable forms. Katherine Franke, "'Dignity' Could Be Dangerous at the Supreme Court," *Slate*, June 25, 2015; Franke, *Wedlocked: The Perils of Marriage Equality* (2015).

24. Roper, 543 U.S. 551; Kenji Yoshino, "A New Birth of Freedom? *Obergefell v. Hodges*," *Harvard Law Review* 129 (2015): 147–79.

25. Oral argument transcript, Roper v. Simmons, No. 03–633, Oct. 13, 2004.

26. Brief for Respondents, Roper v. Simmons, No. 03–633, 2004 WL 1947812 (July 19, 2004), *34–35.

27. John J. DiIulio, Jr., "The Coming of the Super-Predators," *Weekly Standard*, Nov. 27, 1995; Robert F. Worth, "A Crime Revisited: Wilding; A Word That Seared a City's Imagination," *New York Times*, Dec. 6, 2002; Clyde Haberman, "When Youth Violence Spurred 'Superpredator' Fear," *New York Times*, Apr. 6, 2014. Jonathan Simon, *Governing Through Crime: How the War on Crime Transformed American Democracy and Created a Culture of Fear* (2007).

28. Six states that wanted to continue executing juveniles filed a joint friend-of-the-court brief. Instead of engaging the arguments about social consensus over punishment practices, they simply recounted the gruesome facts of six murders committed by individuals on death row when they were under eighteen. Brief of the States of Alabama, Delaware, Oklahoma, Texas, Utah, and Virginia as Amicus Curiae in Support of Petitioner, Roper v. Simmons, No. 03–633, 2004 WL 865268 (Apr. 20, 2004). At oral argument, Justice Kennedy called this brief "a chilling read"—yet another data point of how truly powerful images of uncontrollable young people can be.

29. Hillary Clinton, speech, Keene, New Hampshire, Jan. 25, 1996.

30. Brief of the NAACP Legal Defense and Educational Fund et al., Roper v. Simmons, No. 03–633, WL 1636450 (July 19, 2004), *10–11; Office of Juvenile Justice and Delinquency Prevention, Office of Justice Programs, U.S. Department of Justice, *Juveniles in Corrections* (June 2004), 12; Office of Juvenile Justice and Delinquency Prevention, Office of Justice Programs, U.S. Department of Justice, *Minorities in the Juvenile Justice System 2* (Dec. 1999), 2; Samuel R. Gross et al., *Exonerations in the United States 1989 Through 2003* (Apr. 19, 2004), 24 tbl.6.

31. Atkins, 536 U.S. at 320–21. The judicial bans on the execution of the "mentally retarded" and the execution of juveniles both are categorical in nature. An operative difference is that it's easier to discern when a particular person falls on the wrong side of the age line than it is to gauge intellectual disability, which relies on a host of scientific evidence including IQ, which is subjective, as well as an assessment of a person's adaptive functioning. The anti-cruelty approach can help cut through these debates, which are fraught with scientific uncertainty and erratic moral line-drawing.

32. Raymond Bonner and Sara Rimer, "Executing the Mentally Retarded as Law Begin to Shift," *New York Times*, Aug. 7, 2000.

33. In 2011, the Supreme Court ruled that mandatory life in prison for juveniles violated the Eighth Amendment. Miller v. Alabama, 567 U.S. 460 (2012). Drawing on cases like *Roper* and *Atkins*, Justice Kagan stated that an adoles-

cent's impetuosity, immaturity, and recklessness should be considered as part of an appropriate prison term. It's not entirely clear whether this outcome will enhance equality or create new inequities. On the one hand, more discretion for a sentencing body may mean that some juvenile sentences for murder will be reduced. After all, some 85 percent of life-in-prison sentences for juveniles come from jurisdictions with mandatory schemes. On the other hand, if past experience is a guide, increased discretion could worsen racial disparities.

34. Sandin v. Conner, 515 U.S. 472 (1995).

35. Sandin, 515 U.S. at 486.

36. Brief of Respondents, Hudson v. McMillian, No. 90–6531, 1991 WL 536892, Aug. 12, 1991; Oral Argument Transcript, Hudson v. McMillian, No. 90–6531.

37. Hudson, 503 U.S. at 13–17 (Blackmun, J., concurring). Justice Stevens also joined the outcome and key aspects of O'Connor's ruling, but wrote separately to express his disagreement with the gloss added about the "sadistic" use of force, which sounds like a higher standard.

38. Adam Nossiter, "Judge Rules Against Alabama's Prison 'Hitching Posts,'" *New York Times*, Jan. 31, 1997.

39. Brief Amicus Curiae of American Civil Liberties Union et al., Hope v. Pelzer, No. 01–309, 2002 WL 257537 (Feb. 21, 2002); Austin v. Hopper, 15 F. Supp.2d 1210 (M.D. Ala. 1998).

40. Hope v. Pelzer, 536 U.S. 730, 745–46 (2002).

41. Brief for the United States as Amicus Curiae Supporting Petitioner, Hope v. Pelzer, No. 01–309, 2002 WL 257538 (Feb. 19, 2002). Technically, the dispute involved whether a prison guard who used the hitching post was entitled to qualified immunity. That question turns on whether the law gave guards fair warning that the practice could violate the Eighth Amendment.

42. Lynn M. Burley, "History Repeats Itself in the Resurrection of Prisoner Chain Gangs," *Law and Social Inquiry* 15 (1997): 127–55; Benno Schmidt, "Principle and Prejudice: The Supreme Court and Race in the Progressive Era, Part 2: The Peonage Cases," *Columbia Law Review* 82 (1982): 646–718, 651. Penal labor is explicitly permitted by the Thirteenth Amendment, which abolished slavery and involuntary servitude, "except as a punishment for a crime whereof the party shall have been duly convicted." U.S. Constitution (1789), amend. 13.

43. Erinn J. Herberman and Thomas P. Bonczar, "Probation and Parole in the United States" (2013); Jesse Jannetta et al., "Examining Racial and Ethnic Disparities in Probation Revocation: Summary Findings and Implications from a Multisite Study," Urban Institute, Apr. 2014.

44. Commission on Reducing Racial Disparities in the Wisconsin Justice System Final Report, Wisconsin Office of Justice Assistance (2008).

45. The Supreme Court has deemed sex-offender registries nonpunitive for purposes of the Ex Post Facto Clause. Smith v. Doe, 538 U.S. 84 (2003). That would strongly suggest a similar outcome under the Eighth Amendment.

46. Editorial, "Court Decision on Minnesota's Sex Offender Program Shouldn't End Reform Efforts," *Star Tribune*, Oct. 8, 2017; Noah Feldman, "Appeals Court Got it Wrong in Upholding Indefinite Commitment of Sex Offenders," *Bloomberg*, Jan. 5, 2017.

47. Scott Michels, "Thirteen and Locked Up for Life?," *Salon*, Oct. 2, 2012.

48. Ibid.

49. Jeremiah McWilliams, "Atlanta City Council Passes New Anti-Panhandling Law," *Atlanta Journal-Constitution*, Oct. 2, 2012; News Release, Mayor Kasim Reed Announces Support of Substitute Panhandling Ordinance, Sept. 25, 2012.

50. Robinson v. California, 370 U.S. 660 (1962).

51. Writing separately, Justice Harlan called it an "arbitrary" use of criminal law.

52. Compare Papachristou v. City of Jacksonville, 405 U.S. 156 (1972) with Powell v. Texas, 392 U.S. 514 (1968) (arrest for public drunkenness not cruel and unusual because it doesn't criminalize "chronic alcoholism").

53. Jones v. City of Los Angeles, 444 F.3d 1118 (9th Cir. 2006).

54. Articles of Confederation (1781), art. IV.

55. Congressional Globe (1859), 35(2), 985 c. 1.

56. Mohamedou Ould Slahi, *Guantanamo Bay Diary*, ed. Larry Siems (2017).

57. Almerindo Ojeda, interview, "Confessions of a Guantanamo Guard," *Independent*, Feb. 18, 2009.

58. Mary Dudziak, *War Time: An Idea, Its History, Its Consequences* (2012); Stephen M. Griffin, *Long Wars and the Constitution* (2013).

59. Jane Mayer, *The Dark Side: The Inside Story of How the War on Terror Turned Into a War on American Ideals* (2008); Jack Goldsmith, *The Terror Presidency: Law and Judgment Inside the Bush Administration* (2007).

60. Memorandum for Daniel J. Bryant, Assistant Attorney General, Office of Legislative Affairs, from John C. Yoo, Deputy Assistant Attorney General, June 27, 2002; Memorandum to the Attorney General from Jay S. Bybee, Assistant Attorney General, Office of Legal Counsel, Re: Determination of Enemy Belligerency and Military Detention, June 8, 2002.

61. Hamdi v. Rumsfeld, 542 U.S. 507 (2004).

62. Detention tactics should be seen as part of a broader antiterror strategy that has focused largely on Muslims and noncitizens. Stephen Legomsky, "The Ethnic and Religious Profiling of Noncitizens: National Security and International Human Rights," *Boston College Third World Law Journal* 25 (2005): 161–96.

63. Memorandum for John Rizzo, Acting General Counsel of the Central Intelligence Agency, from Steven G. Bradbury, Principal Deputy Assistant Attorney General, Aug. 1, 2002; Memorandum for John A. Rizzo, Senior Deputy General Counsel, from Steven G. Bradbury, Principal Deputy Assistant Attorney General, Re: Application of 18 U.S.C. §§ 2340–2340A to the Combined Use of Certain Techniques in the Interrogation of High Value al Qaeda Detainees, May 10, 2005; Memorandum for Alberto R. Gonzalez from Jay S. Bybee, Assistant Attorney General, Re: Standards of Conduct for Interrogation under 18 U.S.C. §§ 2340–234A, Aug. 1, 2002, 13.

64. Department of Justice Office of Responsibility Report, Investigation into the Office of Legal Counsel's Memoranda Concerning Issues Relating to the Central Intelligence Agency's Use of "Enhanced Interrogation Techniques" on Suspected Terrorists, July 29, 2009, 63–64; Eric Lichtblau and Scott Shane, "Report Faults 2 Authors of Bush Terror Memos," *New York Times*, Feb. 19, 2010.

65. Carol Rosenberg, "U.S. Troops Detail Skirmish with Guantanamo Captives," *Miami Herald*, Sept. 30, 2014.

66. Memorandum for William J. Haynes II, General Counsel of the Department of Defense, from John C. Yoo, Deputy Assistant Attorney General, Mar. 14, 2003; Memorandum for David S. Kris, Associate Deputy Attorney General, from John C. Yoo, Deputy Assistant Attorney General, Re: Constitutionality of Amending Foreign Intelligence Surveillance Act to Change the "Purpose" Standard for Searches, Sept. 25, 2001; Memo to Gonzalez from Bybee, 2.

67. Isaiah Berlin, "A Message to the 21st Century," *New York Review of Books*, Oct. 23, 2014.

68. Justice O'Connor's opinion for the Court sidestepped the administration's most brazen claim about inherent presidential authority through a generous reading of the law that authorized military force against those who perpetrated the 9/11 attacks. Hamdi, 542 U.S. at 507. The Army Field Manual follows the Convention Against Torture and principles established under the Fifth, Eighth, and Fourteenth Amendments to the U.S. Constitution. It explicitly bans waterboarding, hooding, sexually demeaning tactics, and forms of physical pain. Army Field Manual 2–22.3 (2006), § 5–75. Congress codified President Obama's ban on torture in the National Defense Authorization Act (NDAA) (2016), § 1045.

69. Salahi v. Obama, No. 05-CV-0569 (D.D.C. Apr. 9, 2010), 30–31.

70. Director of National Intelligence, Summary of the Reengagement of Detainees Formerly Held at Guantanamo Bay, Cuba. Intelligence officials estimate

that about 13.5 percent of those released have reengaged in terrorist or insurgent activities.

71. Unclassified Senate Select Committee on Intelligence, Committee Study of the Central Intelligence Agency's Detention and Interrogation Program, Findings and Conclusions: Executive Summary, Declassification Revisions Dec. 3, 2014, 2–3.

72. Jenna Johnson, "Donald Trump on Waterboarding: 'Torture Works,'" *Washington Post*, Feb. 17, 2016.

73. Some courts have so found. Aamer v. Obama, 742 F.3d 1023 (D.D.C. 2004) (Guantanamo detainees on hunger strike could challenge constitutionality of DOD's force-feeding policy); United States v. DeLeon, 444 F.3d 41 (1st Cir. 2006) ("If the conditions of incarceration raise Eighth Amendment concerns, habeas corpus is available"); Kahane v. Carlson, 427 F.2d 492, 498 (2d Cir. 1975) (Friendly, J., concurring) (saying that § 2241 would furnish "wholly adequate remedy" for federal prisoner seeking to vindicate religious exercise claim); Woodall v. Federal Bureau of Prisons, 432 F.3d 235 (3d Cir. 2005) (habeas proper vehicle for challenging "conditions of confinement"); Adams v. Bradshaw, 644 F.3d 481, (6th Cir. 2011) (Eighth Amendment claim to legal injection could be brought via habeas corpus).

74. United States v. Verdugo-Urquidez, 494 U.S. 259 (1990); Johnson v. Eisentrager, 339 U.S. 763 (1950).

75. Memorandum for Prosecutors Along the Southwest Border, Apr. 6, 2018; Miriam Jordan and Ron Nixon, "Trump Administration Threatens Jail and Separating Children from Parents for Those Who Illegally Cross Southwest Border," *New York Times*, May 7, 2018.

Chapter 5: Free Speech

1. Julie Ray, "Reflections on the 'Trouble in Little Rock', Part II," Gallup, Mar. 4, 2003. For more on the NAACP's history and strategy, see Susan Carle, *Defining the Struggle: National Racial Justice Organizing, 1880–1915* (2013); Mark V. Tushnet, *The NAACP's Legal Strategy Against Segregated Education, 1925–1950* (1987). On the new model of constitutional litigation and the changing ethics involved, see Abram Chayes, "The Role of the Judge in Public Law Litigation," *Harvard Law Review* 89 (1976): 1281–1316; Susan D. Carle, "From *Buchanan* to *Button*: Legal Ethics and the NAACP (Part II)," *University of Chicago Law School Roundtable* 8 (2001): 281–307.

2. During the subsequent lawsuit over these provisions, sheriffs testified that integration in their counties would lead to bloodshed. The superintendent of the state police wanted lists of persons "active in racial matters," which would have numbered in the thousands. NAACP v. Patty, 159 F. Supp. 503 (E.D.Va. 1958).

3. Brief of Petitioner, NAACP v. Gray, No. 5, 1961 WL 101714 (Sept. 25, 1961), *20–21; Del Dickson, *The Supreme Court in Conference (1940–1985): The Private Discussions Behind Nearly 300 Supreme Court Decisions* (2001), 316–20.

4. Seth Stern and Stephen Wermeil, *Justice Brennan: Liberal Champion* (2010).

5. Harry Kalven, Jr., *The Negro and the First Amendment* (1965), 85.

6. Brennan's original draft opinion was grounded in due process of law, but expanded the discussion of the NAACP's expressive rights after incorporating Douglas's suggestions. Douglas still chose to write separately to say he was persuaded by the equality argument while concurring with the result. Goldberg joined Brennan's lead opinion. White concurred in the free-speech approach, but wrote separately saying that a narrower statute might survive a First Amendment challenge.

7. In DeJonge v. Oregon, 299 U.S. 353 (1937), a meeting of the Communist Party in Oregon was raided by police and speakers were charged with criminal syndicalism. On facts even closer to the NAACP's situation, Texas police arrested a union leader for unlawful solicitation when he tried to organize workers. See Thomas v. Collins, 323 U.S. 516 (1945).

8. Hurley v. Irish-American Gay Group of Boston, 515 U.S. 577 (1995); Roberts v. United States Jaycees, 468 U.S. 609 (1984); Boy Scouts v. Dale, 530 U.S. 640 (2000).

9. Robert L. Tsai, *Eloquence and Reason: Creating a First Amendment Culture* (2008).

10. Robert P. Ludlum, "The Antislavery 'Gag Rule': History and Argument," *Journal of Negro History* 26(2) (1941): 203–43; Daniel Wirls, "The Only Mode of Avoiding Everlasting Debate': The Overlooked Senate Gag Rule for Antislavery Petitions," *Journal of the Early Republic* 27(1) (2007): 115–38.

11. Michael Kent Curtis, *No State Shall Abridge: The Fourteenth Amendment and the Bill of Rights* (1990), 32–33 (quoting Bingham); Michael Kent Curtis, "The Curious History of Attempts to Suppress Antislavery Speech, Press, and Petition in 1835–37," *Northwestern University Law Review* 89 (1995): 785–870, 803–5.

12. Curtis, *No State Shall Abridge*, 132–39; Select Committee Report on the New Orleans Riots, Feb. 11, 1867; Eric Foner, *Reconstruction: America's Unfinished Revolution, 1863–1877* (1988), 262–63.

13. Salman Rushdie, "Excerpts from Rushdie's Address: 1,000 Days 'Trapped Inside a Metaphor,'" *New York Times*, Dec. 12, 1991.

14. Palko v. Connecticut, 302 U.S. 319, 327 (1937) (Cardozo, J.); Hugo L. Black, "The Bill of Rights," *New York University Law Review* 35 (1960): 865–81; Whitney v. California, 274 U.S. 357, 376 (Brandeis, J., concurring).

15. Steven J. Heyman, *Free Speech and Human Dignity* (2008); C. Edwin Baker,

Human Liberty and Freedom of Speech (1989). But Mike Seidman warns that the use of free speech won't necessarily lead to progressive outcomes. Louis M. Seidman, "Can Free Speech Be Progressive?" (paper on file with author), https://papers.ssrn.com/sol3/papers.cfm?abstract_id=3133367.

16. NAACP v. Claiborne Hardware Co., 458 U.S. 886 (1982).

17. Toward the end of *Button*, Justice Brennan adds this disclaimer: "That the petitioner happens to be engaged in activities of expression and association on behalf of the rights of Negro children to equal opportunity is constitutionally irrelevant to the ground of our decision. The course of our decisions in the First Amendment area makes plain that its protections would apply as fully to those who would arouse our society against the objectives of the petitioner."

18. Cohen v. California, 403 U.S. 15 (1971).

19. James E. Fleming and Linda McClain, *Ordered Liberty: Rights, Responsibilities, and Virtues* (2013); Lawrence G. Sager, *Justice in Plainclothes: A Theory of Constitutional Practice* (2004); Michael J. Sandel, *Democracy's Discontent: America in Search of a Public Philosophy* (1996).

20. Citizens United v. Federal Election Commission, 558 U.S. 310, 340–41 (2010).

21. Lamb's Chapel v. Center Moriches Union Free School District, 508 U.S. 384 (1993); RAV v. City of St. Paul, 505 U.S. 377 (1992); Matal v. Tam, 137 S. Ct. 1744 (2017).

22. The principle of evenhanded management of government resources set aside for expressive purposes applies not just to physical spaces, but also government funds. Rosenberger v. Rector and Visitors of the University of Virginia, 515 U.S. 819 (1995).

23. Leslie Kendrick, "Speech, Intent, and the Chilling Effect," *William and Mary Law Review* 1633 (2013): 1633–91; Frederick Schauer, "Fear, Risk and the First Amendment: Unraveling the 'Chilling Effect,'" *Boston University Law Review* 58 (1978): 685–732; Note, "The Chilling Effect in Constitutional Law," *Columbia Law Review* 69 (1969): 808–42.

24. ACLU v. Reno, 521 U.S. 844 (1997); Ashcroft v. Free Speech Coalition, 535 U.S. 234 (2002); NAACP v. Alabama, 357 U.S. 449 (1958); Board of Airport Commissioners of the City of Los Angeles v. Jews for Jesus, Inc., 482 U.S. 569 (1987).

25. Shelton v. Tucker, 364 U.S. 479 (1960).

26. Harsh laws of all sorts can deter individuals from exercising other kinds of rights. Speech isn't special in that regard. Brandice Canes-Wrone and Michael C. Dorf, "Measuring the Chilling Effect," *New York University Law Review* 90 (2015): 1095–114.

27. N.C. Gen. Stat. §§ 14–208.6A, 14–208.7, 14–208.21.

28. Oral Argument Transcript, Packingham v. North Carolina, No. 15–1194, 2017 WL 749021 (Feb. 27, 2017).

29. Packingham v. North Carolina, 137 S. Ct. 1730 (2017).

30. Chicago v. Morales, 527 U.S. 41, 54 (1999); Risa Goluboff, *Vagrant Nation: Police Power, Constitutional Change, and the Making of the 1960s* (2016).

31. Coates v. City of Cincinnati, 402 U.S. 611 (1971).

32. 8 U.S.C. § 1324(a)(iv).

33. "[T]he constitutional guarantees of free speech and free press do not permit a State to forbid or proscribe advocacy of the use of force or of law violation except where such advocacy is directed to inciting or producing imminent lawless action and is likely to incite or produce such action." Brandenburg v. Ohio, 395 U.S. 444, 447 (1969).

34. Laws of the Territory of Kansas, ch. 151, §§ 3–7, 11–12 (Sept. 15, 1855).

35. Congressional Globe, 34th Congress, 1st Session, Mar. 6, 1856, 124 (Rep. Bingham, OH).

36. Ibid., Mar. 5, 1856, 146 (Rep. G.A. Grow, PA).

37. Ibid., Mar. 12, 1856, 150 (Rep. Mark Trafton, MA).

38. Angela Behrens et al., "Ballot Manipulation and the 'Menace of Negro Domination': Racial Threat and Felon Disenfranchisement in the United States, 1850–2002," *American Journal of Sociology* 109 (2003): 559–605.

39. Christopher Uggen, Ryan Larson, and Sarah Shannon, "6 Million Lost Voters: State-Level Estimates of Felony Disenfranchisement, 2016," The Sentencing Project, Oct. 2016.

40. Harper v. Virginia State Board of Elections, 383 U.S. 663, 667 (1966); Yick Wo v. Hopkins, 118 U.S. 356, 370 (1886); Robert A. Caro, *The Years of Lyndon Johnson: The Passage of Power* (2012), 569; President Lyndon B. Johnson, Remarks in the Capitol Rotunda at the Signing of the Voting Rights Act, Aug. 6, 1965.

41. Matt Ford, "The Racist Roots of Virginia's Felon Disenfranchisement," *Atlantic*, Apr. 27, 2016; J. H. Lindsay (ed.), *Report of the Proceedings and Debates of the Constitutional Convention, State of Virginia* (1906), vol. 2, 3073–76 (Remarks of Sen. Glass, Apr. 4, 1902).

42. U.S. Constitution (1789), amend. 9. The relevant language in Section 2 of the Fourteenth Amendment reads: "But when the right to vote at any election for the choice of electors for President and Vice-President, Representatives in Congress, the Executive and Judicial officers of a State, or the members of the Legislature thereof, is denied to any of the male inhabitants of such State, . . . or in any way abridged, except for participation in rebellion, or other crime, the basis of representation therein shall be reduced in the proportion. . . .";

Akhil Reed Amar, *America's Unwritten Constitution: The Precedents and Principles We Live By* (2012).

43. Jeff Manza and Christopher Uggen, *Locked Out: Felon Disenfranchisement and Democracy* (2006), 57; Behrens et al., at 598; Garrett Epps, "The 'Slave Power' Behind Florida's Felon Disenfranchisement," *Atlantic*, Feb. 4, 2016; Pema Levy, "How Jeb Bush Enlisted in Florida's War on Black Voters," *Mother Jones*, Oct. 27, 2015.

44. Hand v. Scott, No. 4:17-cv-00128-MW-CAS (N.D. Fla. Feb. 1, 2018), *30.

45. Ibid., 41.

46. Williams v. Taylor, 677 F.2d 510 (5th Cir. 1982).

47. West Virginia State Board of Education v. Barnette, 319 U.S. 624 (1943).

48. A Bill for Establishing Religious Freedom, June 18, 1779; Shawn Francis Peters, *Judging Jehovah's Witnesses: Religious Persecution and the Dawn of the Rights Revolution* (2000). Meetinghouses from Rockville, Maryland, to Kennebunk, Maine, were destroyed by angry and fearful citizens. In actuality, Justice Jackson's original draft of the opinion also recounted private acts of violence against Jehovah's Witnesses, but he was encouraged by Chief Justice Harlan Fiske Stone to tone down those concerns. See Robert L. Tsai, "Reconsidering *Gobitis*: An Exercise of Presidential Leadership," *Washington University Law Review* 86 (2008): 363–443.

49. Niraj Chokshi, "2 Texas Students Sue Schools to Freely Protest the Pledge," *New York Times*, Oct. 30, 2017; Jason Jordon, "At High Schools, It's 'Real Life'; Players Take Action Against Injustice, Get Mixed Reaction," *USA Today*, Nov. 7, 2017; Christine Hauser, "High Schools Threaten to Punish Students Who Kneel During Anthem," *New York Times*, Sept. 29, 2017; Lindsey Bever, "11-Year-Old Sat for Pledge So His Teacher Violently Snatched Him From His Chair, Boy Says," *Washington Post*, Sept. 16, 2017.

50. In this sense, the *Barnette* case is on the same footing as religious freedom rulings that prevent state-sponsored prayer or mandatory recitation of the Ten Commandments. 319 U.S. 624; Engel v. Vitale, 370 U.S. 421 (1962); Stone v. Graham, 449 U.S. 9 (1980).

51. Street v. New York, 394 U.S. 576 (1969).

52. Robert L. Tsai, *America's Forgotten Constitutions: Defiant Visions of Power and Community* (2014).

53. Mari Matsuda et al., *Words That Wound* (1993); Richard Delgado and Jean Stefanic, *Must We Defend Nazis? Why the First Amendment Should Not Protect Hate Speech and White Supremacy* (2018); Alexander Tsesis, *Destructive Speech: How Hate Speech Paves the Way for Harmful Social Movements* (2002).

54. Mark Bray, *Antifa: The Anti-Fascist Handbook* (2017), 149–54.

55. Terminiello v. Chicago, 337 U.S. 1 (1949) (Jackson, J., dissenting).

56. Frederick Schauer, *Free Speech: A Philosophical Enquiry* (1982).

57. David M. Rabban, *Free Speech in Its Forgotten Years* (1997); Mark A. Graber, *Transforming Free Speech: The Ambiguous Legacy of Civil Libertarianism* (1991); Harry Kalven, Jr., *A Worthy Tradition: Freedom of Speech in America* (1988); Thomas I. Emerson, *The System of Freedom of Expression* (1970).

58. Time, place, or manner restrictions on speech can be required so long as they are done in a way that doesn't turn on the content of a speaker's message. Clark v. Community for Creative Non-Violence, 468 U.S. 288 (1984); Timothy Zick, *Speech Out of Doors: Preserving First Amendment Liberties in Public Spaces* (2008). And even reasonable restrictions can be placed on the right to bear arms, especially when other, fundamental rights are at stake. District of Columbia v. Heller, 554 U.S. 570 (2008).

59. Corey Brettschneider, *When the State Speaks, What Should It Say? How Democracies Can Protect Expression and Promote Equality* (2012); Amy Gutmann, *Identity in Democracy* (2003).

Conclusion

1. LBJ, Radio and Television Remarks, July 2, 1964; President Lyndon B. Johnson, Remarks in the Capitol Rotunda at the Signing of the Voting Rights Act, Aug. 6, 1965.

2. E. W. Kenworthy, "Civil Rights Passed, 73–27; Johnson Urges All to Comply; Dirksen Berates Goldwater," *New York Times*, June 19, 1964. LBJ made this statement in defending voting rights legislation. Robert A. Caro, *The Years of Lyndon Johnson: The Passage of Power* (2012), 80.

3. Langston Hughes, "Call to Creation," *New Masses*, Feb. 1931, in Arnold Rampersad and David Roessel (eds.), *The Collected Poems of Langston Hughes* (1995), 135.

4. Frederick Douglass, "The Mission of the War," *New-York Daily Tribune*, Jan. 14, 1864, reprinted in John Stauffer and Henry Louis Gates, Jr. (eds.), *The Portable Frederick Douglass* (2016), 326–44.

INDEX